Trend setter: the MG Midget J2 of 1932 with its double humped scuttle, cutaway doors and flat backed body with external petrol tank set the pace for MG styling right up until the TF ceased production in 1955. Power was provided by a 847 cc four cylinder single overhead camshaft engine. 2083 examples were built between August 1932 and early 1934

The Restoration and Preservation of

Vintage and Classic Cars

Jonathan Wood

New Edition

ISBN 0 85429 391 4

First published October 1977
Second edition published 1984

British Library Cataloguing in Publication Data

Wood, Jonathan
   The restoration and preservation of vintage
   and classic cars.—2nd ed.
   1. Automobiles—Conservation and
   restoration—Amateurs' manuals
   I. Title
   629.28'722   TL152.2
   ISBN 0–85429–391–4

   Library of Congress Catalog Card Number
   84–48794

Published by
HAYNES PUBLISHING GROUP
Sparkford, Yeovil, Somerset BA22 7JJ. England

HAYNES PUBLICATIONS INC.
861 Lawrence Drive, Newbury Park, California 91329, USA

a FOULIS motoring book

Printed in England by the Haynes Publishing Group
Editor Tim Parker
Jacket design Rowland Smith

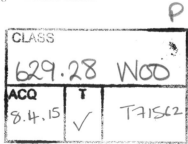

Pictorial acknowledgement

Associated Engineering Ltd.; 94, 100, 101 (top), 106, 114 (middle)

Autocar; frontispiece, 53 (left), 81 (top), 91 (bottom), 29 (top), 132 (top), 135 (top)

Automotive Products Ltd.; 72, 75, 76, 77, 79, 80, 123

Black and Decker Ltd.; 29 (bottom), 242 (second from bottom)

Citroen Cars Ltd.; 32 (middle), 246 (bottom)

David Cooksey Esq.; 34/35, 37 (top), 202/203, 208 (bottom), 244

DeVilbiss Co.; 208 (top and middle)

L. T. Duff Esq.; 98 (bottom)

Maurice Evans Esq.; 18

Ford Motor Co.; 26 (bottom), 27 (bottom), 29 (middle), 134 (middle)

Girling Ltd.; 67 (bottom), 69, 70, 72 (left top)

Paul Grist Esq.; 17 (middle)

Jarrot Engine Co.; 17 (bottom), 36, 37 (bottom), 51 (top, right), 199 (top and middle), 227 (top)

David Kennard Esq.; 170, 266

Leyland Cars; 38, 49, 51 (bottom), 52, 53 (right), 66 (top, left), 108, 126, 156 (top, left), 164, 175 (bottom), 179 (bottom, left), 183, 234 (bottom)

Joseph Lucas Ltd.; 172, 175 (top), 179 (top), 180, 184 (top), 185 (middle and bottom)

Marston Radiator Services; 121

Tudor Rees Esq.; 236 (top)

Smiths Industries Ltd.; 234 (left, top)

SU Carburetters Ltd.; 151, 152, 161

G. Thompson Esq.; 36 (bottom)

Thoroughbred and Classic Cars; 17 (top), 19, 20 (middle and bottom), 21 (top), 39, 40, 71, 82, 90 (bottom), 91 (top), 93, 95, 96, 97, 98 (top), 105, 107 (top and middle), 111, 118 (bottom), 119, 121 (bottom), 122, 129 (bottom), 132 (bottom), 135 (bottom), 150, 199 (bottom), 201 (top), 205, 206, 210, 212, 227, 229 (middle), 230, 234 (top, right), 236 (middle and bottom), 242 (top)

Zenith Carburetter Co Ltd., 154, 156

† *Denotes service relates specifically to pre-1940 vehicles*
* *Denotes service relates specifically to post 1945 vehicles*

Contents

Introduction

I suppose that most people can look back and isolate the time when they were first bitten by the old car bug. In my own case it was a book that first fired my interest in pre-war cars. For when a friend lent me a copy of Ken Purdy's *The Kings of the Road*, I devoured the distinctive trans-Atlantic prose with undisguised enthusiasm. Of course, I had set my heart on a type 35 Bugatti, but when I heard of a non-running Austin 16/6 sitting in the corner of a local farmyard and available for £15, I jumped at the chance. Although the Austin was in sound bodily condition, the engine was in a sorry state, suffering from a cracked block and bearing failure. Despite these fairly major shortcomings, I nevertheless decided that the car was a good buy and I became the proud owner of RX 1809, although a slightly elaborate method of paying for it was agreed on, as recounted in Chapter One!

When I finally got the Austin home, I was faced with the problem of restoring it. My enthusiasm knew no bounds, but my knowledge, as far as the restoration process was concerned, was minimal. Fortunately my local old car organisation was the Bean Car Club (makes other than Beans were fortunately eligible) and I quickly benefitted from the collective knowledge available from other club members. Consequently the restoration of the Austin was soon under way and its successful completion would not have been possible without the help I received from my friends in the BCC. Therefore, I cannot stress too strongly the importance of joining a car club and talking to people with cars which have already gone through the restoration process.

In this book, covering such a broad canvas, from 1920 to the 1960s, it is obviously only possible, in many instances, to talk in generalities, but there are exceptions to practically every rule, so do not hesitate to consult 'those who know'.

Each chapter is divided into three sections, the main portion being devoted to the practicalities of restoring the components under review. The second section, which I have entitled 'Notes on development', contains, in a British context, a brief historical account of the evolution of the aforementioned parts. I have included this information for two reasons. Firstly, I think it will help the reader to put his particular car into some sort of historical perspective. Secondly, I have endeavoured to pinpoint just *why* certain techniques and components were introduced or rendered obsolete which should help to give the parts an additional sense of relevance. But the reader should be reminded that these are nothing more than 'Notes'; this is, after all, a practical book.

Many people have been of great assistance to me in compiling this book and first and foremost my thanks must go to Robin Townsend of Jarrot Engines of London SW19 for the help he gave with the chapters relating to engine and chassis restoration. Similarly, Bob Krafft of Auto Services of London SE27 put his considerable knowledge of car electrics at my disposal, the results of which are reflected in Chapter Six. David Cooksey not only told me how to build a car body, but was also responsible for some of the excellent drawings in this book, the 'exploded' bodywork in Chapter Seven being a notable example. I am also indebted to Eric Longworth, not only for his help in compiling the chapter on tools, but for his advice on all aspects of car restoration over the years.

In every instance they endeavoured to steer me in the proper direction as far as their own subjects were concerned, but any shortcomings in the appropriate chapters are my responsibility; not theirs'.

My grateful thanks must also go to Peter Graham, MA, LL.B (Cantab) for updating the excellent notes on old car legislation he first set down for the Vintage Sports-Car Club, which can be found in Appendix One.

Thanks are also due to my colleague Paul Skilleter for photographic assistance.

In addition, I would like to acknowledge the assistance of the following companies and individuals for their co-operation and in many instances for their permission to reproduce illustrations: A.C. Delco Division of General Motors Ltd; Angell and Williams (Peckham) Ltd, (L. T. Duff); Associated Engineering Ltd, (Michael Hurn); Automotive Products Ltd, (Colin Baker); Black and Decker Ltd; Connolly Brothers (Curriers) Ltd, (Anthony Hussey); The DeVilbiss Company Ltd; Ferodo Ltd; Girling Ltd, (Bryan Jones); Guysons International Ltd; Holt Products Ltd, (Nick Hewer); ICI Paints Division, (Paul Kent); IPC Business Press Ltd; Leyland Cars Ltd; Marston Radiator Services Restoration Unit; Silentbloc Ltd; Smiths Industries Ltd, (Patrick A. M. A. Fitz-Gibbon); SU Carburetter Company; Vandervell Products Ltd, (D. F. Green); Vintage Racing Cars (Northampton) Ltd, (Mrs Diana Russell); James Walker Ltd, (K. K. Gibbs); Zenith Carburetter Company (Malcolm Smith).

My thanks also to Tim Parker, Group Managing Editor, Haynes Publishing Group, for his patience and forebearance in coping with a somewhat 'elastic' deadline, as far as the delivery of this manuscript was concerned.

I trust that this book will encourage plenty of potential restorers to 'take the plunge', as I have tried throughout to retain the image of myself, back in 1962, wanting to restore a car, but not knowing where to begin. Good luck!

Jonathan Wood,
Farnham, Surrey.
April 1977

Introduction to Second Edition

Since this book was first published seven years ago, in 1977, there has been a transformation and impressive expansion of the classic car movement. I have therefore dramatically expanded the first chapter of this book to broaden the scope and number of the cars included, which, I trust, will be of assistance to prospective purchasers.

I have added a section in Chapter Seven on the basics of welding and a guide to the sort of work that can be undertaken by the enthusiast. This is of particular relevance to those with later cars who must overcome the problems associated with repairing unitary construction bodies. For illustrations in this section I am grateful to Lindsay Porter for providing photographs from his highly acclaimed *Guide to Purchase and DIY Restoration of the MGB* (Haynes, 1982). I have also extended the scope of the chapter on interior renovation to include some advice on the renovation of woodwork.

A feature of the first edition of this book was a listing of firms which undertook restoration work but, inevitably, in time this has become outdated and, thus, the entry has been deleted. I would, therefore, commend readers to the *Thoroughbred and Classic Cars Directory of Specialist Firms and Services* which is published at regular intervals and is being continually updated. I have, however, retained a list of one make car clubs which can offer a wide range of advice and facilities.

The restoration of a car of *any* age is a fascinating but demanding exercise. I trust that this book will be of some help whether you've never attempted the task before or are a well seasoned expert.

Jonathan Wood
Farnham, Surrey
April 1984

Chapter One

The right car for you

Few undertakings require more care and caution than the choice of a motor car . . . The difficulty in choice is increased by the fact that almost every enthusiast recommends the particular kind of carriage he himself possesses . . . **Alfred Harmsworth (later Lord Northcliffe)**

Alfred Harmsworth, that journalistic maestro, founder of the *Daily Mail* and dedicated motoring enthusiast, wrote these words in the early days of this century when the motor car was still in its infancy. Yet his advice has a cogency and relevance today, though one might add that the older the vehicle under consideration, the greater is the *care and caution* required. For the purchase and consequential restoration of the *right* elderly motor car can provide a tremendous source of enjoyment and satisfaction, the process of rejuvenation being a particularly demonstrative one, as many 'before' and 'after' photographs will testify.

But it is absolutely essential that you recognise your limitations, particularly when you are buying your first old car. Get the wrong one, and what should be a pleasure becomes a penance, and what you initially envisaged as a pride and joy can often end up relegated beneath an unsightly tarpaulin, condemned to a corner of the back garden. And when you are eventually forced to sell it, you find that half the parts are missing! No, if you get bitten by the old car bug, and I warn you it can bite pretty hard, do not let your enthusiasm get the better of you, so that you snap up the first old wreck you happen to stumble across.

I would first like to define exactly what I mean by the term 'old car', as to many people this can mean last year's Cortina. We start off with Veterans. These are vehicles built before 1905, and are therefore eligible to compete in the Royal Automobile Club's London to Brighton Commemoration Run, which provides such a splendid spectacle on the first chilly Sunday of November. Then, between 1905 and 1918, comes the Edwardian class and after that, from 1919 to 1930 we move into the Vintage era. The term 'Vintage', in relation to motor cars, seems to have been coined in 1934 at the time of the formation of the Vintage Sports-Car Club. In fact the original rendering was Veteran Sports-Car Club, but, not surprisingly, the then recently formed Veteran Car Club fortunately took exception, and the name was soon changed. It was not until 1936 that the definition of a Vintage car was ratified by the club; thus no vehicle manufactured after December 31 1930 was eligible. At the same time, a section was established, which formed the basis of the aforementioned Edwardian class, although the name itself did not come into use until a later date. It was in 1945 that the VSCC extended its entry to include Post Vintage Thoroughbreds, which allowed in owners of certain approved makes, or models, built on, or before, December 31 1940. The definition embraces such marques as AC, Aston Martin, Bentley, Lagonda, Riley, Rolls-Royce and the pre-Rootes Talbots, in fact those firms who continued to uphold the traditions of craftsmanship or individuality into the nineteen thirties. Incidentally, the VSCC's office (121 Russell Road, Newbury, Berkshire) will be able to tell you exactly which

The first view I ever had of my own vintage car, my 1928 Austin 16, pictured in the Autumn of 1962 sitting in the corner of a farm yard in Earley, Berkshire. Clearly it deserved closer inspection!

The Austin, following restoration. As can be seen by the injudicously placed L plate, I still had to pass my driving test!

'thirties cars are eligible, particularly as the definitions have recently been revised. Although the list tends to favour the more expensive end of the market, Austin owners, for example, may be pleased to note that the Nippy, Speedy and Ulster variants of the Seven are included. This leaves us with those cars built in the 'thirties which are not on the PVT list, and those post-war cars that are beginning to become 'collectable'. Unfortunately, no one has yet come up with a really satisfactory title for these two groups, though latterly the more desirable cars of the 'forties and 'fifties have been dubbed 'classic cars', though this title has American origins, and relates, in that country, to notable vehicles manufactured *before* the Second World War. In truth, I do not think that titles matter very much. The main question you have got to ask yourself about a car is: "Do I like it?". Do not be lulled into the position of assuming that because a car was made before 1930, it must be right for *you*, and do not buy it for this reason, turning your back on a perfectly worthy vehicle of the 'thirties that in size, running costs and spares availability, is much more your cup of tea.

As I said earlier, when deciding on the purchase of an old car, you have first got to consider your limitations; these can be roughly divided into four. The principle one is financial. For there is no point in stretching your resources to the limit buying an expensive and exotic car, only to find that you have shackled yourself to a novel and delectable ball and chain. Apart from the initial purchase price, the cost and availability of spare parts, the type of repair work required and finally the running costs when the vehicle is complete, all have to be taken into consideration. Just how much cash you have available will probably dictate the age of car you buy. There are, of course, exceptions. For you will certainly pay more for a high performance sports car of the post-war era, than, say a 'thirties charming, though pedestrian, saloon. And, of course Vintage car prices have accelerated dramatically in recent years. It seems incredible now, but back in 1962 I bought my Vintage car (a 1928 Austin 16) for £15. Not that I actually had any money on me at the time, so a hire purchase scheme of £3 a week for five weeks was agreed on! Today, my car is probably worth around the £2000 mark, not that I have the slightest intention of ever parting with it, but it is, nevertheless, a relevant reflection of the rise in old car prices. Unfortunately those days of the early 'sixties now seem remote as the pre-war years when you could pick up a Grand Prix Bugatti for £150. However, I am digressing, for the point is that unless you have plenty of spare cash, you can rule out a Vintage car as your first old car and concentrate your resources on a 'thirties or interesting post-war vehicle.

The second consideration is really an extension of the first, for this is a matter of facilities. Having bought your car, you have then to find somewhere to put it. If you have the use of a garage, that is all well and good, but if you have not, what then? It may mean renting suitable premises and if this is the case, try to arrange this before you have the car, not afterwards, when you may be forced to take on an unsuitable, cramped and expensive garage, because it is the middle of winter and you cannot stand the sight of your potential pride and joy exposed to the elements. A warm, well lit and comprehensively equipped workshop is a great incentive to tackle the business of restoring a non-runner. But if you are having to rent a garage that is cold, in a way that only concrete structures can be, has no electricity and not enough room to swing the preverbial cat, you will be a lot better off with a car that is already mobile and can respond to a running restoration.

The next, and most difficult factor to assess, is that of your own mechanical capabilities. If you have been hailed a budding Royce, obviously you will have no problems, and are probably just the person to take on a re-build from the chassis up. But if the household shelves you put up fell down within minutes, or the washing machine you repaired has never been the same since, then you would be far better off enjoying the driving of an old car than the restoring of one.

Your final consideration is that of time. I have never heard of a restoration which was finished in the prescribed time, so when you estimate how long the renovation is going to take you, it is not a bad idea to double it, and work on that basis. And if your spare time is at a premium, think in terms of years, not months. Incidentally, I am not suggesting that you stick rigidly to these guidelines when contemplating your purchase, as this can, to some degree, take out some of the fun of buying an old car as enthusiasm is always the vital spark. None the less you should do *some* thinking before signing the cheque, or handing over the pound notes.

15

Having assessed these various factors, you can start looking around for a suitable vehicle. A perusal of the classified advertising columns of *Thoroughbred and Classic Cars, Motor Sport, Veteran and Vintage, Exchange and Mart* or even your local newspaper, will give you a good idea of the prices being asked, or the popularity, or otherwise, of the make or model in which you are interested. If you favour a pre-war car, it is a good idea to join the Vintage Sports-Car Club as an associate member, and get along to one of their monthly pub meetings. You will find that people are usually only too pleased to talk about their cars and you can collect a lot of valuable information as a result, though always bearing in mind Alfred Harmsworth's advice that "almost every enthusiast recommends the particular kind of carriage he himself possesses . . ." There are, of course, plenty of one-make clubs and registers for pre-war cars, and having defined your preferences you can then move on to one of their 'Noggin and Natters', even if this sounds like an excuse for a pub crawl! As far as post-war cars are concerned, again seek out the particular make in which you are interested, though as there is not an overall club for cars of this era, you can probably establish the pros and cons of a particular model from the specialist motoring press. The importance of talking to someone who is running the type of car in which you are interested cannot be over-emphasised. He will be able to pinpoint the pitfalls, the prices and availability of spare parts and the areas for scrutiny when you, a gullible newcomer, are faced with weighing up a second-hand car. Even better, if you can take said chap along with you when you come to make your purchase, you may be saved from wasting your money on a heap of rubbish, for a restraining influence can be of help on such occasions . . . When you do go to look at a car, try to do so in broad daylight, as the most tatty wreck can take on the most pleasing air of respectability in twilight, or worse still, by the light of a torch. The same goes for a car that has just been rained on. The body then tends to look better than it really is, and there is the added discouragement of getting down on your hands and knees to make an all-important check of the chassis.

This is probably an appropriate moment to reflect on the position of spares availability in relation to old motor cars; firstly, the pre-war situation. Obviously vehicles that were in production for a long period of time, like the Austin Seven (1922 to 1939) and of which some 290,000 were made, are going to be well served as far as spare parts are concerned. And at the other extreme, the Vintage Bentley fraternity put their own house in order many years ago when original stocks dwindled. Similarly, the Bentleys produced by Rolls-Royce Ltd., from 1931 onwards, are well provided for when it comes to mechanical parts, and the same of course, goes for owners of 'The Best Car in the World'. Also owners of the more popular pre-war MGs are well served with original or replica parts. Most one-make clubs have the spares situation well in hand and can usually be relied on to know the sources (or supply themselves), such items as cylinder head gaskets, valves, pistons, clutch and brakes parts, which are the sort of spares which are in constant demand. These remarks apply, in the main, to mechanical parts. Again, vehicles made in large numbers, such as Austin Sevens, Morris Eights and MGs are reasonably well served when it comes to the supply of replica metal body parts. Things are not quite so straightforward at the higher end of the market, because manufacturers like Rolls-Royce, Alvis and Bentley only built their cars in chassis form, and these were then packed off to the coachbuilder to have the distinctive coachwork, associated with that particular establishment, fitted. Therefore, every body repair job on these particular cars has, in the main, to be considered individually. Fortunately, there are a number of restoration establishments who keep the old coachbuilding traditions alive, and will tackle this sort of problem. It's fair to say that the older the body the easier it is to imitate. Simplicity, both in mechanical and coachbuilding terms, was the keynote of motor cars built in the 'twenties.

Mechanical spares for post-war cars are, naturally enough, rather easier to come by. Obviously engines which have been in production over a number of years, such as the XK Jaguar engine (1948) and the A series power unit, which originally appeared in the Austin A30 of 1952 and are still going strong, have a great appeal. Fortunately new clubs are cropping up all the time to cater for post-war vehicles, though again there is a great shortage of body spares at the cheaper end of the market. The body situation is far healthier on the sporting front, replica metal body parts being available for MG, Jaguar and Austin Healey owners. Also glass fibre parts are available, but they should only be regarded as a short term expedient. It is certainly tempting to

You really can discover them like this. This is a pre-First World War White and Poppe engined Bullnose Morris

Quite a find! This 5.3 litre straight eight supercharged Stutz, pictured on discovery on an Essex farm in 1973. It later emerged that this car had been raced at Le Mans in 1929, driven by George Eyston and Gordon Watney

This Austin Seven engine was fished out of the River Thames at Richmond. The camshaft was salvaged and is now doing sterling service in another engine

A 1920 11.9 hp Bean ripe
for restoration

The Bean's 1795 cc two
bearing crankshaft fixed
head engine of decidedly
Edwardian design, being
based on the 1914 11.9
Perry. Note the original
armoured cable wiring

go for a cheaper material, but if originality is your watchword (and it should be), then save up and buy the genuine article.

Check points on a pre-war car

Whatever the age of car you have decided on, the condition of the vehicle's bodywork should be your overwhelming consideration. Consequently, you should reserve your closest scrutiny for the examination of the chassis and bodywork. (Only a few cars made before the war favoured chassis-less construction, so I will be dealing with the particular problem associated with this type of structure in the post-war section.)

Apart from those vehicles produced at the very end of the 'twenties, most car bodywork during the Vintage era was constructed using the traditional method of cladding an ash framework with steel or aluminium panels, the wings, sills and running boards being *bolted* on to the chassis. However, the dominance of the pressed steel body on mass produced cars from about 1929 onwards, largely eliminated the use of wood in the structural sense, which meant that many more components could be *welded* together. So, whereas, usually you can take a car of the 'twenties apart with a set of spanners, the same cannot always be said for its counterpart of the late 'thirties. So bear these factors in mind when considering the condition of a car's bodywork.

David Cooksey of Wokingham, Berkshire built this replica 'Double Twelve' MG Midget

A rear view of the same car which has the advantage of looking absolutely 'right'

As I mentioned, many Vintage cars were fitted with aluminium bodies, so corrosion is usually the least of your worries. Your main concern is the condition of the ash framework, and as this is usually concealed by the trim, its state can often be difficult to evaluate. One give-away, however, is the state of the door hinges and how well the doors fit. They should close without undue effort; gently move them up and down and check that any movement present is in the hinge itself, or if it is the door pillar that is moving! You can reckon that a saloon is usually going to be in better condition than a tourer, particularly as the former's interior will not have been exposed to the rigours of our climate. If, as a result of these probings, you are of the opinion that the ash frame has seen better days, then brace yourself for a body re-build; a fairly tricky job unless you have a flair for carpentry and have a next door neighbour who is a panel beater. Incidentally, these remarks also apply to those cars fitted with bodywork by specialist coachbuilders and, for example, those open two seaters built by MG up until 1955, and Morgan to the present day. And if you are fortunate enough to expose part of the ash frame, be very wary of its condition if you can dig your fingernails into the wood, as the material is usually renowned for its hardness! Take into account the condition of the wings (probably they will be aluminium, rather than steel, on a more expensive car) but bear in mind that many can be unbolted and taken to a specialist panel beater if their condition demands it.

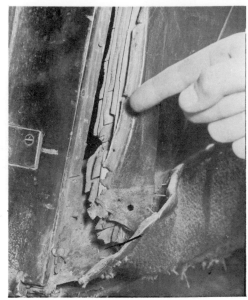

When you're checking your potential purchase of a pre-war car, always bear in mind that it may have an ash frame, though the woodwork may not always be as obvious as it is here

The sort of problem you can expect at the bottom of doors, usually caused by the plywood delaminating

Also keep a weather eye open for trouble where wings join body work. Sometimes bi-metallic corrosion can be the culprit. This is an important checking area on the MGA coupe

Here is clear evidence that all is not well. Keep a watch out for signs of bubbling paint and bodged repairs

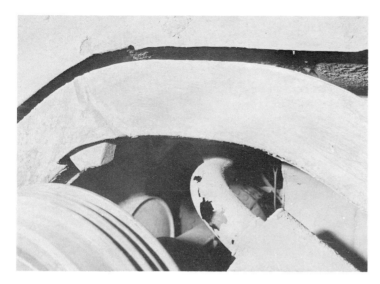

While you're under the car look out for a corroded exhaust system as replacements can be expensive

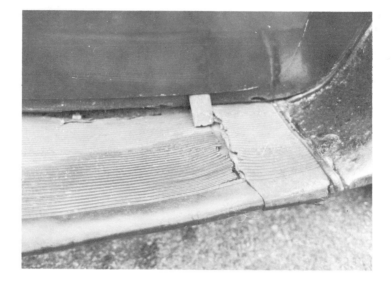

Damaged running boards are by no means uncommon and are often caused by rusted chassis outriggers

This rear wing has obviously seen better days; another vital check area

21

Passing on to pressed steel bodies, you can usually reckon that the products of the 'Big Six' (Austin, Morris, Ford, Rootes, Standard and Vauxhall) in the 'thirties were produced in this way, the last named also being a pioneer of chassisless construction. Exceptions would be small production touring bodies and, as we have seen, the products of specialist coachbuilders.

When you are first contemplating a car, if it is at all possible stand well back from it and examine it from as many angles as you can. Any bodged or recent repair will show up better from a distance. Do not be put off by faded or dull paintwork, your main concern should be the soundness of the bodywork. Again, check the doors, for evidence of corrosion along the bottoms, a possible reminder of blocked-up drain holes. Metal running boards are also vulnerable and do not forget to have a look at the roof, particularly if it is a fabric one. Also sliding roofs, if neglected, can let the weather in, to the detriment of the interior.

Now, arming yourself with a torch and sturdy screwdriver, have a good look underneath the car. Most Vintage cars have a simple channel section chassis, so its condition will be readily apparent. However, in the early 'thirties, chassis were stiffened up considerably, and your prodding with the vital screwdriver can reveal the horrors of a Pandora's Box section. As water and mud can get trapped inside these box section chassis they are far more vulnerable to rusting. You will probably find that the area of the chassis around the engine, gearbox and rear axle are in good condition, due to the respective component's inability to remain completely oil tight. Danger points on the chassis are naturally enough, stress areas such as spring hangers, pedal and steering box mountings. Also keep an eye open for flitch plates, indicating a past repair, possibly the result of some long forgotten accident. Another reminder of some unpleasant past encounter with another vehicle, resulting in a bent chassis frame, is the angle of the spring hangers. Obviously only the rear spring can be checked if independent front suspension is fitted, but if not, examine all round. Each shackle should be at approximately the same angle as its opposite number. Make a mental note and wait for the test drive, if the angles do vary to any degree. And while you are examining the rear shackles, check for evidence of any oil which may be present around the bottom of the back plates. This is by no means uncommon and indicates worn rear axle oil seals; the brakes will not take too kindly to this unwelcome lubrication. A favourite area for corrosion is the point where the chassis cross members join the side member. Also do not forget to examine the area of bodywork immediately surrounding the battery (if it is not fitted under the bonnet), as this is, again, a vulnerable area for rust. Take a final look at the state of the wiring, if its visible, and emerge from your sortie solemn faced and frowning!

Having given the exterior a thorough going over, you can turn your attention to the interior. The state of the seats is obviously a fairly good guide to the amount of use that the car has received. If the leather (for even the cheapest pre-war models used this material) is badly torn, or beyond repair, then you should think hard about your intending purchase, unless you can get the car at a knock down price, for professional re-upholstery is an expensive business. Do not be afraid to lift the carpets, it is surprising the horrors that can lurk beneath! The condition of the metal floor of a car with a chassis is not as critical as that in a car without one, though wooden boards are often to be found with the former type. The state of the headlining will probably indicate how watertight the roof is.

All the aforementioned remarks could apply to a car whether it is running, or not. But we now come to the business of weighing up the state of the engine. If the car is a non-runner then you are very much at the vendor's mercy, but one assumes that the asking price reflects this major shortcoming. "Fraid she's just blown a head gasket" is one of the more common excuses, which can mean anything from a broken crankshaft to a worn big end, to yes, even a blown head gasket. So let us concern ourselves for the moment with the state of the engine of a car that runs readily enough, and that you can drive. Remember, it does not always follow that a grubby engine means that all is not well within, although a thick covering of oil and grease *can* conceal a bodged repair. Ask for the location of the breather and see how mucky the immediate area appears, most engines are bad liars in this respect. Also check the dipstick to see if the oil is revoltingly dirty, and *after* the engine has been running, the state of the water, though allow plenty of time for the motor to cool down. Obviously, there should just be water in the radiator, not a mixture of coolant and lubricant, which could indicate our old friend the blown head gasket, or at worst a crack in the block or cylinder head. On a car built up to the early 'thirties pay particular attention to the state of the radiator, as the core probably is not hidden behind a grill, or false honeycombe, checking for unsightly repairs or leaks. Radiator repairs, apart from the very simplest ones, are difficult to do in your own workshop, and are expensive to farm out. With later cars, the radiator was usually out of sight. It is therefore far cheaper to repair, as its appearance is nothing like as critical.

While you are at the front of the car, it is the time to check the front suspension and steering. The vast majority of pre-war cars are fitted with a simple cart-sprung front axle, and although it is important to scrutinise the state of the king pins and steering joints, it is an even more relevant port of call if the car is fitted with independent front suspension. I deal with the peculiarities of that check in the next section, but if you want to find out the state of the king pins, bushes and steering on a car with a straightforward beam front axle, jack up the car in the middle of the axle, and then ask an accomplice to get into the car and depress the foot brake (this is so you do not mistake any slack in the wheel bearings for king pin wear). Then, placing your hands at the 12 and 6 o'clock positions, try and rock the wheel. If you do feel any wear, then the chances are the king pins and bushes have seen better days. To check for slackness in the steering system, carry out the same test, but with your hands at the 9 and 3 o'clock positions. You should be able to see (and hear) any wear in the joints.

Right. The moment has now come to ask the owner to fire the car up, but beware the vendor who requests a push start. A dodgy starter motor can be easy enough to rectify, but badly worn teeth on the starter ring is a different proposition altogether. Make a note of how easily the engine starts, and once the choke has been returned to its customary position, examine the exhaust smoke. Ideally, it should be barely noticeable, but while *black* smoke will simply indicate an over rich mixture, *blue* tends to spell out worn bores and you know you have an oil burner. And do not forget to keep an eye on that breather pipe. Listen to the engine running with the bonnet open. A deep seated knock may be a worn big end, but this will become all too apparent when the engine is under load. Once the oil is warm the oil pressure gauge will spell out bearing trouble by a low pressure reading. It is worth pausing for a moment to consider just what the gauge will tell you, because readings can vary tremendously, depending on the age and type of car. For example, an Austin Seven, with its splash lubrication will settle down to around 5 psi when hot, while a Morris Eight of the mid 'thirties can give a reading of about 20 psi, which really is not very high by modern standards. Remember the oil pressure on most cars can drop very low on tickover. The really important thing is that when you go for your test drive, try to make it as long as possible. A quick trip round the block will *not* do as hot oil and water are your best allies for showing up an engine's deficiencies.

Now for the drive itself. If the vendor drives initially, as he probably will, watch if he changes up earlier in some gears than others. Also if he keeps his hand on the gear lever. This usually spells out worn synchromesh, or selectors, for if the revs are taken up too high, the lever will jump out of gear. On three speed boxes second gear is the most likely culprit, while third is usually the guilty party on a four speed box. Keep an ear open for any transmission noise, particularly from the gearbox and rear axle. This particularly applies if you are testing a car with a pre-selector gearbox. Be particularly suspicious of a high noise level and make sure that all gears engage. See that your test route includes a hill (sorry, East Anglian readers), and, if possible, try to include this as one of the last parts of your drive, as it will reveal whether the clutch is slipping. This can be caused by worn linings, or through oil leaking through from the engine or the gearbox. And beware a clutch which has to be depressed all the way to be engaged. Feel the steering wheel for play. One of the delights of a Vintage car is the light and high geared steering. But in the 'thirties, engines were moved farther forward to allow more space for the passengers in the lower horsepower cars, the steering becoming lower geared to deal with the adverse effects of the extra weight. Therefore, there should be no play on the steering, of a Vintage car, though later on anything up to an inch can be tolerated. Steering shake can indicate that the wheels need balancing (which is probably what the owner will tell you), though it is more likely to be caused by worn king pins or spring shackles. Vintage brakes work with varying degrees of efficiency. There is a tremendous variation of retardation between, for examples, an Austin Seven's brakes (uncoupled until 1930) or a Bean's, which used the French Perrot system, produced by the Dudley car

23

company under licence. The rod and cable varieties were pretty ghastly (there will always be people who will say they have made them work), though Girling rod brakes, from the mid-thirties onwards, were a great improvement on most earlier arrangements. However, if you opt for a post vintage Morris or associates, then the excellent Lockheed hydraulics brakes are a big plus. Note when you apply the brakes whether the car pulls to one side, and if they are hydraulic whether you have to pump the pedal to obtain the best results. Afterwards, feel the drums. If one is hotter than the others, obviously some re-adjustment is called for.

After the drive, you are obviously getting to the point of making a decision on whether you want to buy the car, or cannot get away from it quickly enough. But assuming that you decide positively, now the bartering can begin! Do not be afraid to point out any faults, the owner is probably only too aware of them himself. Worn tyres are a good bargaining point, mainly because their state cannot be disguised. On a pre-war car, when you could be paying anything from £20 per cover, this is a good area for negotiation. Do not forget to ask to see the spare wheel as the tyre may well have seen better days. I once bought a car that had just that, a spare wheel, nothing more. Inquire when the car's DOE test certificate is due to expire. If the test date is imminent, be particularly suspicious, as the owner may be wanting to get rid of the beast as quickly as possible, as he knows that it does not have a chance of passing. Ask to have a look at the log book. This may tell you how many owners the car has had. If there are a lot, be especially suspicious, the fewer owners the better. Should you decide to take the plunge ask the seller if he has any old log books, as looking up previous owners can be a beneficial occupation. I have heard of such items as clocks, handbooks, tools and mascots being retrieved from former owners who are often delighted to see these items re-united with their old car. In my own case, I was given the original list of Austin agents for 1928 which came with my car, together with that most useful of items: a Zenith carburettor jet key.

However, to revert to your intending purchase. Remember that cash is an important bargaining point, and can often sway a deal in a way that a cheque never can. A cheque will, of course, have to be cleared before you can take the car away. A dangerous hiatus this, when a cash bearing opponent could step in.

To sum up, then. On the plus side, and here I am mainly concerned with the cheaper, and consequently more numerous, pre-war cars, you have a relatively simple, sound chassis construction, reasonable mechanical spares availability and tremendous charm. On the debit side there is sluggish performance, may be poor brakes, indifferent road holding and expensive replacement tyres. If the disadvantages outway the advantages, then you are probably a candidate for a post-war car, which is the next category I will deal with.

Check points on a post-war car

Obviously, many of the areas covered in the pre-war section also apply to more modern cars, but there are some areas that require amplification.

Again, the bodywork is your first port of call, but your checks are all the more crucial. If the car has a chassis, so much the better, but with a few exceptions, from around the late 'forties and early 'fifties, monocoque construction had taken over; the state of the load bearing panels is even more important, and they are more difficult to repair. So when you are contemplating the bodywork of a post-war car, scrutinise such familiar rust points as the areas of the front wings which adjoin the doors, the part of the wing surrounding the built-in head lamps (if fitted), the bottoms of the doors, the front of the rear wings adjoining the doors and the floor of the boot. On a monocoque car, pay particular attention to those high stress areas such as the spring hangers, seat and pedal mountings, steering mountings, shock absorber and anti-roll bar securing points. You will also come across under body sealing compound on these post-war vehicles, which can be something of a mixed blessing, because it can be used to disguise some horrific corrosion. The state of the sills is another crucial area for scrutiny, as they can play an important role. Also be on the look out for bi-metallic corrosion, that is to say where steel and aluminium meet; always an uneasy union. The condition of the interior is not quite so critical on a post-war car as you do have a better chance of coming across complete seats and other trim parts from scrap cars, unless you are going for the more exclusive end of the market. And do not forget to lift those carpets or rubber mats to check the state of the floor. While you are scouting around underneath, make a note of the state of the jacking points as they are notorious rusters; another bargaining point.

Check the condition of the independent front suspension, carrying out exactly the same procedure as with the beam axle layout, but with one important exception. Do not jack up the car in the middle of the cross member, but do each side individually, placing the jack immediately beneath the suspension unit. If you do not, the unit will simply expand, taking up any wear that may be present. If you are contemplating a car with MacPherson strut independent front suspension, keep an eye open for rusting on the mountings you will find prominently positioned under the bonnet. They *are* prone to wheel imbalance, incidentally. When looking around a car fitted with disc brakes, make a point of checking the condition of the discs. If they are incised and furrowed, this might indicate a score of lazy owners, and is something that cannot be disguised. Shock absorbers played a far more important role on post-war cars than pre-war ones, so to check their condition; press down hard on the front wing, and let go. The car should not rebound more than once. If it does, then you are going to have to foot the bill for a new set of shock absorbers. Items of brightwork should be in good condition, for radiator grills and badges can be expensive to replace.

When you go for your test drive, beware the owner who turns on the car radio to let you know how nice it sounds, and leaves it on; you are not in the car to test that and it could conceal some unpleasant noises. Oil pressure (if a gauge is fitted) will also be higher, the reading should be at least 40 psi when the engine is hot. If the car is fitted with automatic transmission be on the look-out for slipping brake bands or a sluggish change up. Power steering is another post-war complication, so be suspicious of any system which feels unnaturally heavy or unbelievably light. Both these extremes indicate that trouble is not far away.

The advantages of a post-war car are numerous; relatively good spares availability, adequate performance, reasonable fuel economy and low purchase price, while on the minus side, their main drawback is difficult and expensive body restoration which may have to be farmed out to an expert.

There is another variant, which I briefly touched on earlier, and that is the pre- or post-war car that is a non-runner. This is something of an unknown quantity and should be approached with considerable caution. Obviously your priority is to find out just why the car is not going, but if you are embarking on your first restoration, you may have some difficulty in tracking the reason down. I would definitely advise against taking on a car which does not go unless you can satisfy yourself beyond any reasonable doubt as to the cause of the trouble. However, if you are well versed in the business, then this type of purchase does have appeal because (in theory) your initial outlay is that much less. There is another type of restoration that is one stage further than taking on a non-runner, and this is the car that is completely dismantled, the enthusiastic owner running out of time, patience and/or money. Again, it is a cheap way of buying a car, but unless you are particularly well acquainted with the model in question, putting a vehicle together that someone has taken apart can turn into a bit of an automotive nightmare!

After all these dark warnings, probably you have the impression that anyone who sells an old car simply is not to be trusted and every statement that the vendor makes should be treated with the utmost suspicion. This certainly is not the case and the vast majority of people selling elderly motor cars are enthusiasts like yourself who are disposing of them for perfectly legitimate reasons. But there are always a few rotten eggs in any cross section of society, and there is no harm in being on your guard.

Now, having got your car, you can decide on the type of restoration that is going to be required, but do resist the temptation of tearing everything apart, the moment you get the car home. There will be plenty of problems ahead and not being able to find vital parts is a quite unnecessary one. I remember an extremely skilled restorer telling me once, "When it comes to re-building old cars, I'm an eternal pessimist, and I've never yet been disappointed".

Alvis's good looking 3 litre, the Graber styled TD 21 of 1958 with coachwork by Park Ward. The style had been introduced on the TC 108G of 1956 and output of the succeeding TE and TF 21 continued until Alvis ceased car production in 1967. Be on the lookout for rust on these handsome cars, particularly around the headlamps, the sills can be real shockers and the same goes for around the rear wheel arch. Mechanically the cars don't present many problems though the independent front suspension can be expensive to overhaul and wears if neglected. Petrol consumption is around 18 mpg and mechanical spares availability is good. The Alvis Owner Club caters for these cars. Number built: TC 108G 30; TD 21 1060; TE 21 350; TF 21 105

Armstrong Siddeley's Sapphire was introduced for 1953 and remained in production until 1960. The $3\frac{1}{2}$ litre six cylinder engine was available with either pre-selector, manual all synchromesh or, from 1955, automatic transmission. Rust is a major problem with these cars. Look for it around the wings, door pillars and sills though there is a substantial chassis which is a plus. The engine is reliable but noisy when worn. Trouble with the pre-selector gearbox may be caused by blown fuses. Petrol consumption is in the 18 mpg region and spares are in good supply through the good offices of the Armstrong Siddeley Owners' Club. Number built: 7697

The 3.6 litre Aston Martin DB4 was introduced in 1958, a superbly styled GT by Touring of Milan. The DB5 with 4 litre engine followed in 1963 and in 1966 came the DB6 with longer wheelbase and spoiler tail which lasted until 1970. Body problems are mainly confined to the platform chassis rusting adjacent to the scuttle and can be expensive to rectify. The DB4 can suffer from gearbox and clutch bothers but the aluminium twin overhead camshaft engine is reliable enough providing it's regularly maintained. But it is expensive to overhaul; not a car to be run on a shoestring. Fuel consumption around 17 mpg and mechanical parts are in good supply. Club is Aston Martin Owners. Number built: DB4, 1110; DB5, 1025; DB6, 1330

Austin A40 Devon saloon, introduced in 1947 and remaining available until 1952, was Longbridge's best selling model of the early post war years. Body problems are mostly confined to the inner front wings, sills and rear wings. These cars retain a chassis frame which is certainly robust but might deteriorate alongside the footwells. The 1200 cc engine is a reliable, long lived unit but is prone to the cylinder head gasket blowing between number two and three pots. Fuel consumption is around 28 mpg with spares confined to mechanical ones and body parts practically non-existent. The Austin Counties Car Club caters for these cars. Number built: 273,958

Austin's answer to the Morris Minor was the Austin A30 of 1952 which was upgraded to the A35 for 1957 with an increase in engine capacity from 803 to 948 cc. Output ceased in 1962. It is mostly body problems with these cars with the inner front wings and sills the worst offenders. The independent front suspension wears badly if unattended and the A30's gearbox is weaker than its A35 successor. Fuel consumption is around 35 mpg and only mechanical spares are available. Club is A30/A35 Owners'

Austin's A40 of 1958 was adventurously styled by the Italian Pininfarina company and because there is no apparent boot still looks relatively modern. In 1961 came the Mark II version with a 1098 cc engine in place of the 948 cc unit. Rust points are the rear end of the sills and the apron just below the rear bumper. The Mark II cars suffer from rust around the bottoms of the wings. Engines are reliable enough but the gearbox wears badly, though post 1963 units are very much better than the earlier ones. Petrol consumption is about 33 mpg and mechanical spares are available. The A40 Farina Club caters for these cars. Number built: approximately 340,000

The BMC Farina saloons were introduced in 1958 and remained in production until 1971. Initially fitted with four cylinder 1489 cc and 2912 cc six cylinder engines, the former's capacity was increased to 1622 cc for 1962. Rust is a major problem with these cars with all the usual areas, front and rear wings, sills and front floor vulnerable. The independent front suspension can wear though the engines are reliable enough. While the Austin and Morris versions have vinyl upholstery the upmarket MG, Riley and Wolseley variants have leather wearing surfaces and walnut facias. The fours have a 24 to 32 mpg consumption range while the sixes return about 17 mpg. Spares are mostly confined to mechanical ones. Clubs are Austin Cambridge/Westminster, Cambridge-Oxford Owners, Riley Motor, MG Car and MG Owners' and Wolseley Register

The Mini Cooper first appeared in 1961 in 997 cc form, capacity being upped to 998 cc in 1964 and available in Austin and Morris forms. An S version of 1071 cc was introduced in 1963, reduced to 970 cc in 1964 and discontinued the following year. The final version of the Cooper of 1275 cc arrived in 1964 and continued to be available until 1971. Notable departures from standard Minis are twin carburettors and front disc brakes. Rust points are the rear sub frame, around the headlamps and the tops of the wings. Fuel consumption is around 26 mpg (997 cc). Spares both body and mechanical are in good supply and the club is the Mini Cooper Owners'. Number built: 96,513

The Austin Healey Sprite was introduced in 1958 with cheeky 'Frog eye' bonnet and 948 cc engine. A conventional front end appeared for the Mark II version of 1961 and an MG Midget version was introduced simultaneously. Engine capacity was upped to 1098 cc for 1962 and the Mark III version arrived in 1964 when the original quarter elliptic rear springs were dispensed with. A Mark IV version appeared in 1967 with 1275 cc engine and the model was discontinued at the end of 1970 though some *Austin* Sprites were built in 1971. Body problems can be expected at the lower forward edge of the bonnet on the Mark 1 while the inner wings and extremities of the sills are vulnerable on all models. On the pre-Mark III cars the rear box section housings for the quarter elliptic springs are well worth inspecting as they can rust badly. Mechanically the cars are reliable enough though you might expect gearbox problems on the Mark 1 cars. Mechanical spares are in good supply though body parts are difficult. Availability is generally better on the post Frog Eye models. The Austin Healey Club caters for these cars. Number built: Mark 1 48,999; Mark II 31,665; Mark III 25,905; Mark IV 22,963

Two for the price of one. The Austin Healey 3000 Mark I (left) was introduced in 1959 and continued until 1961. On the Mark II of 1961/2 triple SU carburettors replaced the twin units of the earlier models while the Mark III of 1963/68 was the fastest of the big Healeys. Check for bubbling paint between the steel and the aluminium bonnet surround; also, the floor rusts around the front end. The engines are long lived, reliable units but the gearbox suffers from a weak first gear. Petrol consumption is around 17 mpg. Spares, both body and mechanical, are in good supply. The Austin Healey Club caters for these cars. Number built: Mark I 13,650; Mark II 12,953; Mark III 16,321

The Riley One-Point-Five, along with the Wolseley 1500, was introduced in 1957. A Mark II version with a slightly more powerful engine appeared in 1960 while the Mark III for 1962 had re-styled side grille trims. A 1489 cc engine was fitted throughout. Production ceased in 1965. Check points are the front wings, sills and floor. Mechanics are well mannered and mechanical spares are available but not body ones. Fuel consumption is around the 24 mpg mark. The Riley Motor Club welcomes the model and the Wolseley Register the 1500. Number built: Mark I 18,021; Mark II 9777; Mark III 12,084; Wolseley 1500 Mark I & II 68,954; Mark III 31,790

The SP 250, a glass fibre bodied sports car, represented Daimler's belated attempt to cash in on the American car market. Introduced in 1959 it survived the Jaguar take over of 1960 and output continued until 1964. Body problems are limited to the occasional over-flexible bonnet while the sills on the later cars have a habit of rusting away. The V8 3 litre engine is reliable enough but be prepared for worn valve guides, attendant high oil consumption and the main bearings are rather prone to wear. Fuel consumption is around 22 mpg. Parts are in reasonable supply and the Daimler and Lanchester Owners' Club caters for these cars. Number built: 2645

Ford's best selling 100E, introduced in 1953, was available in two door Anglia and four door Prefect form and continued in production until 1959. The four door 107E of 1959-61, was powered by the new 105E engine with overhead valves and replaced the 1172 cc side-valve unit employed hitherto. The rear end of these models is particularly vulnerable to rust as are the sills and the bottoms of the front wings. Also check the front suspension mounts and the forward end of the rear spring hangers. The engine is almost unburstable but the cylinder head can crack. Fuel consumption is around the 28 mpg figure. Mechanical spares are in good supply and the Ford Side Valve Owners' Club looks after these cars. Number built: Anglia 348,841; Prefect 100,544; Escort estate 33,131; Squire 17,812; 107E 38,154

The Ford Classic appeared in 1961 in 1340 cc form and capacity was increased to 1498 cc in 1962, production ceasing in 1963. There was also a sporty two door Capri variant of 1961/64 vintage. Be on the lookout for rusty sills, bottoms of front wings and MacPherson strut mountings. Mechanical spares are in good supply and there are a few body parts available. Fuel consumption is around 27 mpg (1340 cc) and the club is the Ford Classic 315 Owners'. Number built: Classic/Capri 128,208

Ford's Lotus Cortina appeared in 1963 and remained in production until 1966. Available in two door form only the model is instantly identifiable by its white bodywork and distinctive green side stripe and Lotus badges on the radiator grille and rear wings. Aluminium doors, bonnet and boot lid were departures from standard. This 100 mph plus Q car is powered by the Ford based twin overhead engine of 1588 cc as fitted to the Lotus Elan. Body problems are usually associated with the bottoms of the front wings and the outrigger/jacking points can rust while the A bracket rear suspension on the pre-1965 cars can collapse though it will have probably been converted to conventional leaf springs. Be prepared for around 200 miles per pint oil consumption, and the timing chain may require regular attention. Petrol consumption is around the 20 mpg mark. Spares, both body and mechanical, are in good supply. Club Lotus caters for the model. Number built: 2894

The Ford Cortina 1600E, the 'executive' version of the Cortina MKII, was introduced in September 1967. Though only in production for three years its success was enormous, reflecting the fact that it provided luxury and performance at an affordable price. Rust in the body can be a problem, though it does vary considerably from car to car. Look particularly at the lower rear wings and rear wheel arches and the wheel arch joints, the sills and, most importantly, the MacPherson strut towers for the front suspension. The engine and gearbox are both fundamentally high-mileage units although early wear of pistons and valve gear can cause high oil consumption.

The 1600E illustrates nicely the advantages and disadvantages of the later production 'classic' car: very many replacement parts are available, especially for mechanical components, but refurbishment of the interior and trim can be difficult unless genuine factory items can be had. A fuel consumption of about 25 mpg can be expected. The marque is served by the Ford Cortina 1600E Owners' Club and the Ford Cortina 1600E Enthusiast's Club. Number built: four door 55,833; two door 2749

Rootes was one of the last manufacturers to offer convertible versions of their models. This is the open version of the Hillman Super Minx, introduced for 1962 and listed until 1964. Rust is, inevitably, a problem, around all the wheel arches and on the front wings adjacent to the doors: sills likewise. The engine is robust and long lived while petrol consumption is about 22 mpg. Parts are confined to mechanical replacements. The Hillman Owners' Club is the one to join

The XK range of Jaguar sports car appeared in 1948 with the 120 model, shown above. It was replaced in 1954 by the XK 140 with bigger bumpers and rack and pinion steering. In 1957 came the XK 150 with higher wing and door line and wider radiator grille. A 3.8 litre engine in addition to the 3.4 litre engine arrived in 1959. Production ceased in 1961. Crucial check points are the sills, that effectively hold the body together, along with the bottoms of the wings and around the side ventilator. The robust chassis is an undoubted plus. Expect long life and reliability from the twin overhead camshaft six cylinder XK engine and around 18 mpg. Spares, both body and mechanical, are in good supply. The Jaguar Drivers' Club caters for these cars. Number built: XK 120 12,055; XK 140 9051; XK 150 9395

The Jaguar E-type was introduced in coupe and roadster form in 1961. It had a 3.8 litre engine until 1964 when the capacity was increased to 4.2 litres and a new all-synchromesh gearbox replaced the Moss unit, with output continuing until 1971. As the E-type employs a monocoque hull be on the lookout for rust in the important sill structures and around the rear wheel arches. The massive front bonnet section may harbour corrosion within its air intake; also check how well it fits. Poor alignment may reveal evidence of a past accident. Mechanically you shouldn't have many problems with the long lived, reliable engine but the all independent rear suspension system may produce some expensive surprises. Parts, both body and mechanical, are in good supply. Expect around 18 mpg (3.8). Club is Jaguar Drivers'. Number built: 3.8 15,496; 4.2 22,916

Jaguar S-type is effectively a combination of the Mark II saloon and Mark X rear end and E-type-like independent rear suspension. Available in 2.4 and 3.8 litre forms, the S, introduced in 1963, remained available until 1968. Check for rust around the bottoms of the front wings, sills and rear wheel arches. You shouldn't suffer any major mechanical shortcomings but beware that sophisticated independent rear suspension system which, although relatively easy to remove, is expensive to overhaul. Expect around 18 mpg (3.8). Club is Jaguar Drivers'. Number built: 3.4 10,036; 3.8 15,135

The most revolutionary British car of its day, the Jowett Javelin was introduced in 1947 and remained in production until 1953. The engine was a forward mounted $1\frac{1}{2}$ litre flat four and there were torsion bars all around. Rust problems are mostly confined to the rear end and the independent front suspension can wear badly. Although the Javelin's engine did have a reputation for unreliability, nowadays most cars will have been converted to the more reliable Series Three unit. Also up to the spring of 1951 a Meadows built gearbox was fitted; thereafter a Jowett built one featured which can give trouble. Petrol consumption is around 28 mpg and mechanical spares are in good supply. The Jowett Car Club caters for these cars. Number built: 22,799

Morris Minor 1948-1971. Probably Britain's best loved post-war car, the Minor was 918 cc side-valve engined until 1952 when the Austin A30's 803 cc overhead valve engine was fitted. The original split windscreen was discontinued in 1956. The Minor saloons and tourer were joined in 1954 by the Traveller with distinctive composite wood and steel body. Engine capacity was upped to 948 cc in 1957 and again to 1098 cc for 1963. The tourer was discontinued in 1968, the saloon in 1970 and Traveller in 1971. Check the front wings, particularly the area adjoining the doors. Underneath the car check the condition of the cross member that runs beneath the front seats which acts as the front torsion bar anchor and a jacking point. Raise the carpets and check the state of the floor edges. The rear spring hangers, both front and rear, have a habit of deteriorating. Spare parts, both body and mechanical, are in good supply, particularly for the later cars. Petrol consumption is around 30 mpg (1098 cc). The Morris Minor Owners' Club looks after Minors of all ages. Number built: 1.3 million

MG's first model to be offered with independent front suspension was the Y type saloon, introduced in 1947. It remained in production until 1951 when it was replaced by the YB with deeper valancing on the rear wings and 15 inch rather than 16 inch wheels. Output ceased in 1953. Danger points are bad rusting of the rear body mounts while the underslung box section chassis can deteriorate where it passes beneath the rear axle. The front suspension will wear if neglected and the Y's gearbox is a weak point as are the rear axle's half shafts. As many points are shared with the TD two seater they are in good supply though body spares are not. Fuel consumption is around 26 mpg and clubs are the MG Car and MG Owners' and this applies to all the MGs depicted here.

Number built: YA 6158; YB 1301

The MG TC was basically a carry-over from the pre-war TB. Introduced in 1945 the 1250 cc-engined TC continued until 1949 when it was replaced by the TD with a new box section chassis and independent front suspension. Last of the T Series MGs was the TF of 1953-55 vintage which, from 1954, was 1500 cc engined. The problem with these stylish two seaters is that the ash frame, to which the body panels are attached, can rot and rectification is a skilled job. Feel under the running boards and you should be able to feel the chassis rail, and you shouldn't be able to pull the rotten wood away in handfuls! Weak mechanical parts are the TD/TF box section chassis and the TD's gearbox. Engines are reliable enough except for a tendency for the valves to drop. Parts, both body and mechanical, are in a good state of supply. Petrol consumption is around 28 mpg (TD). Number built: TC 10,000; TD 29,664; TF 9600

The pre-war Magnette name was revived for the ZA saloon of 1954 which was derived from the contemporary Wolseley Four/Fourty Four. It was the first Abingdon product to be fitted with the 1498 cc Austin-designed BMC B Series engine and remained available until 1956 when the ZB was introduced with detail engine changes and externally identifiable by straight, rather than curved trim, around the front wheel arch. Rust is a major problem with this model that is of monocoque construction. Check around the headlamps, bottom of the sills and the floor around the brake pedals. Mechanics are fairly sound though expect a weak synchromesh on second gear. Mechanical parts are in reasonable supply, body parts are not. Number built: ZA 12,754; ZB 23,846

The first modern MG sports car of the post war era, the MGA, introduced in open two seater 1498 cc form in 1955, was produced until 1959. A 1588 cc engine and front disc brakes followed, along with a coupe and a Mark II version, 1622 cc powered, continued until 1962. The A had a robust box section chassis but it can rust along its inside edges adjoining the wooden floor boards. Other body rust points are the bottoms of the front wings, forward end of the rear ones and sills. Doors, bonnet and boot lid are aluminium, however, and mechanics are generally sound though the independent front suspension wears badly if neglected. Parts, both body and mechanical, are in good supply. Fuel consumption is about 28 mpg. Number built: 1500, 58,750; 1600 Mark I 31,501; Mark II 8719

A 1588 cc twin overhead camshaft version of the MGA was introduced in 1958, instantly identifiable by its handsome Dunlop knock off wheels. It did not prove to be a success, however, and output ceased in 1960. Shortcomings are similar to those applied to the pushrod cars. Problems are mostly confined to the engine and can include bore and tappet wear while the pistons can burn out if the mixture is weakened, so don't attempt to improve the mpg figures that way! Later rear axles were unique to the Twin Cam and replacement could cause headaches. Spares, both body and mechanical, are in reasonably good supply, and expect around 22 mpg. Number built: 2111

The MG version of the Austin Healey Sprite, which saw a revival of the Midget name, appeared in 1961 and the 948 cc engine was replaced by a 1098 cc engine for 1963. A Mark II version of 1964 saw the introduction of wind up windows and half elliptic rear springs replacing the original quarter elliptics. A Mark III version with 1275 cc engine followed for 1967 and this remained in production until 1975 when the Midget was fitted with the 1500 cc engine from the in-house Triumph Spitfire. Output continued until 1979. Inner wings, sill and rear wheel arches are check points as are the rear springs boxes on the Mark I cars. The pre-1975 A Series engine has a better reputation for reliability than the Triumph one. Expect around 29 mpg (1098 cc). Number built: Mark I 25,981; Mark II 26,601; Mark III 100,372; Mark III (1500) 73,899

MG's long running MGB was introduced in 1962 and remained in production until 1980. The model's basic specification of an 1800 cc four cylinder engine remained constant throughout its life while the roadster was joined by a GT version in 1965. The principal modifications to the model's appearance came in the 1975 model year when rubber bumpers were introduced front and rear and the model's ride height was also increased to permit sales to continue on the all important American market. Check for rust around the headlamps, sills and rear wheel arches. Mechanical spares are readily available for the post 1964 Bs when the engine's crankshaft bearings were upped from three to five. Body panels for the later cars are also in excellent supply. B return around 27 mpg. Number built: Roadster 387,259; GT 125,621

Porsche's evergreen 911; introduced in 1965 and still going strong. When announced this model was powered by a rear mounted 2 litre air cooled flat six engine which was increased to 2.3 litres in 1971/3, to 2.7 litres in 1973/7 and 3 litres from 1977. These power units are robust enough but they do suffer from valve guide wear which will probably be the reason for a high oil consumption figure demonstrated by a smoky exhaust. An engine rattle will probably indicate a worn timing chain tensioner. Rust is a problem, even on the post-1976 cars which were rust protected, with the front wings and rear valance particularly bad offenders. Spares both mechanical and, significantly, of body parts are available. The Porsche Club Britain caters for these cars

Riley's first post-war model, introduced in 1945, was the 1½ litre (RMA) powered by the traditional Riley high twin camshaft/short pushrod hemispherical cylinder head engine. In 1953 the styling was mildly modified with a higher roof line and larger rear window. There was a re-designation to RME which remained in production until 1955. The 2½ litre version (RMB) was introduced in 1946 and output ceased in 1953. These RM Rileys have a robust chassis but check the body and its vulnerable fabric roof, particularly around its rear, and for signs of water penetration inside the car. The 1½ litre engine is prone to bottom end wear unless regular oil changes are undertaken. Fuel consumption is around 23 mpg (1½ litre) and mechanical spares are in good supply. Clubs are the Riley Motor and Riley RM. Number built: 1½ litre 13,950; 2½ litre 8960

Rolls-Royce's version of the Pressed-Steel-bodied Bentley Mark VI, the Silver Dawn, was introduced in 1949. Engine capacity was upped from $4\frac{1}{4}$ to $4\frac{1}{2}$ litres in 1951, the big booted R type Bentley followed in 1952 and remained in production until 1955. You should be on the lookout for body problems and if the rear mounting points have rusted away then this is really serious. Check the bottoms of the doors, sills and spare wheel locker. The later $4\frac{1}{2}$ litre engine, with a full flow oil filter, is rather more reliable than the smaller capacity unit. Petrol consumption is around 15 mpg. Mechanical spares are in good supply and clubs are Bentley Drivers' and Rolls-Royce Enthusiasts'. Number built: Silver Dawn 760; Bentley Mark VI 4946; R type 2320

Introduced in 1955 the 4.9 litre Rolls-Royce Silver Cloud was the last Crewe car to feature the overhead inlet/side exhaust six cylinder engine introduced in 1946. Production continued until 1959. Bodywork checks are crucially important, particularly around the rear body mountings. Doors, bonnet and boot lid are aluminium, so you won't have to worry about these but rust can break out around the front wheel arches, sills and lower portions of the rear wings. The substantial box section chassis also has a weak point directly above the rear axle. The engine is good for around 300,000 miles and the automatic gearbox is also well mannered. Clubs are Bentley Drivers' and Rolls-Royce Enthusiasts' and mechanical spares are in good supply. Number built: Silver Cloud 2359; Bentley S1 3431

Rover's P4 range began with the six cylinder 2.1 litre 75 and was joined by a 2.6 litre 90 (illustrated) for 1954. There was also the more powerful 105S and R, the latter with semi automatic transmission of 1957/9. A four cylinder model, the 2 litre 60, was produced between 1954 and 1959. The range was simplified in 1959 when all previous models were dropped to be replaced by the 2.6 litre 100 and the 80 with the 2.2 litre Land-Rover engine and an overhead valve unit while all other P4's have an overhead inlet/side exhaust valve configuration. Both models were replaced from 1963 by the 90 and 110 which were discontinued in 1964. With the exception of most 110s, the P4 range has aluminium doors, bonnet and boot lid. Body problems are confined to around the front wing flashers, if fitted, the base of the door pillars and the bottom of the front wheel arch. The chassis can rust directly above the rear axle. Engines are reliable but gulp down the oil when worn. Mechanical spares, particularly post 1959, are in good supply as are some body panels. Petrol consumption is around 19 mpg (100). Clubs are Rover P4 Drivers Guild and Rover Sports Register. Number built: 60 9261; 75 43677; 80 5900; 90 35,891; 95 3680; 100 16,621; 105R 3499; 105S 7201; 110 4612

Rover's stylish 2000 was introduced in 1963 and remained in production until 1977, being 2.2 litre-engined from 1973. A twin carburettored version of the overhead camshaft four, the TC, was produced between 1966 and 1973. The model, designated P6 in Rover nomenclature, employs a base frame construction so the body panels are bolted rather than welded in position, which is a plus for the home enthusiast. Early cars suffered from gearbox and de Dion rear axle problems though the model does rust so aim for as late a one as possible. Spares, both body and mechanical, are in reasonable supply though better for the later cars. Fuel consumption is around 24 mpg. Club is the Rover Sports Register. Number built: 248,959

Standard's Vanguard models was introduced in 1948 and the Series II version (illustrated) which followed in 1953 used similar mechanics but featured a re-designed rear end. This remained available until it was replaced by the Series III Vanguard with unitary body construction. Although these models rust in the usual places – front wings, sills, lower portion of the rear wings – there is a robust chassis and mechanical problems are confined to worn front suspension, the engine being a reliable and economic unit. Mechanical spares are available; fuel consumption is around 25 mpg. Club is the Standard Motor

Introduced in 1494 cc form in 1959, the Sunbeam Alpine's capacity was upped to 1592 cc for 1961 (Series II) and a more powerful Series III version followed in 1963 while the 1964 Series IV had cut down rear wings (illustrated). The final Series V, in 1725 cc form, came in 1965 and remained in production until 1968. Rust is the principal problem with this car so check around the front headlamps, sills, bottoms of the doors and rear wings. There is also an all important front cruciform below the front floor which isn't prone to rusting but if it has succumbed then avoid that example. Mechanical spares are in good supply as are some body panels. Fuel consumption is around 21 mpg (Series II) and Club is the Sunbeam Alpine Owners'. Number built: Series I 11,904; Series II 19,956; Series III 5863; Series IV 12,406; Series V 19,122

43

Outwardly similar to the Series IV Alpine is the Sunbeam Tiger, 4.2 litre Ford V8 powered, while the 1966 Mark II version had a 4.7 litre unit, production ceasing later the same year. The same checks apply to the Tiger as for the Alpine and it is important that the V8's engine oil is changed regularly at 4000 mile intervals, otherwise you might expect big end problems. Mechanical spares are in good supply though the steering rack was peculiar to the model and may present problems. Some body parts are available. Petrol consumption is around 20 mpg. The Sunbeam Tiger Owners Club caters for these cars. Number built: Mark I 6495; Mark II 572

Triumph's Renown was introduced in 1949 starting life as the 1946 Town and Country saloon and was named Renown with the fitment of the 2088 cc Vanguard engine, replacing an 1800 cc Standard power unit. The wheelbase was lengthened in 1952 and production ceased in 1954. The coachbuilt razor-edged body is a problem with these cars and you're in real trouble if the ash frame has rotted. Look for tell tale bubbles on the paintwork and rust around the door shuts. Mechanical problems are few but the steering idler can wear badly. Expect around 22 mpg. The Triumph Razor Edge Club caters for these cars. Number built: 6501; Limousine 190; Long wheelbase 2800

44

Triumph's best selling model of the post-war years was the Herald produced between 1959 and 1971. It was available in saloon, coupe and convertible form with the 948 cc engine. This was upped to 1147 cc from 1961 when an estate car version was introduced, again, to 1296 cc from 1967 to 1971 when the model was designated 13/60. The backbone chassis rusts at its rear extremities as do the outriggers. Be prepared for trouble with the swing axle rear suspension, usually the radius arm bushes. Parts, both body and mechanical, are available for the later cars. You can expect around 31 mpg (1200) for the Herald. The Triumph Sports Six Club caters for these cars. Number built: 948 cc 100,275; 1200 298,575

Based on the Herald chassis, the 1147 cc Spitfire was introduced in 1962 and output continued until 1965 with the advent of a more powerful-engined Mark 2 model. The Mark 3 of 1967 featured a revised front end with raised front bumper and 1296 cc engine. There was a sharpening of the model's profile and a revised tail with the 1970 Mark 4. A further increase in capacity came in 1975 with the arrival of the Spitfire 1500 with enlarged 1493 cc engine, built until 1980. The problems associated with the Herald chassis also apply to the Spitfire. Body problems usually apply to the bonnet's lower edges, wings, inner wings and forward end of the sills. Spares, both body and mechanical, are available for the later cars and the Triumph Sports Six Club caters for the Spitfire. Fuel consumption is about 30 mpg (Mark I). Number built: Mark I 45,753; Mark II 37,409; Mark III 65,320; Mark IV 70,021

Triumph TRs are rugged, stylish sports cars and prior to the 1961 TR4 shown here, came the TR2 of 1953/55, to be followed by the TR3 of 1955 to 1957, both versions being powered by a 1991 cc version of the Standard Vanguard engine. The TR3A from 1959 was available with an optional 2138 cc power unit, perpetuated exclusively for the TR4. All were variations of the original Canley-styled TR2 but the TR4 was a Michelotti full width design as was the all independent suspension TR4A of 1965/67 and the six cylinder TR5 made between 1967 and 1968. The cars are, in the main, hard wearing and reliable though beware problems with the TR4A independent rear suspension and fuel injection snags with the TR5. Mechanical parts for both four and six cylinder models are in good supply though not, alas, body ones. The TR Register and TR Drivers' Club cater for these models. Number built: TR2 8628; TR3 12,377; TR3A 58,236; TR4 40,253; TR4A 28,465; TR5 2947

The 3 litre V8-engined Triumph Stag was introduced in 1970 and remained available until 1977. Later Stags are more reliable than earlier ones. There were overheating problems with the engine and gasket failure along with timing chain shortcomings. Although many of these difficulties were rectified, regular maintenance is essential if you want to get the best from a Stag. Expect around 19 mpg. Body and mechanical spares are available. The Triumph Stag Owners' Club looks after these cars. Number built: 25,877

The Volkswagen Beetle entered series production in 1945 and is still being manufactured in Mexico and Brazil. It was 985 cc engined until 1953 and then with a 1200 unit to date. There was an additional 1300 model of 1965-75 along with a 1500 of 1966-70 vintage. Versions with MacPherson strut front suspension were produced between 1970 and 1975 in 1300 and 1600 form. Engines are normally reliable with the 1600 cc version probably being the unit most likely to present problems. Bodywork, therefore, will be your main concern and the earlier the example the better will be the quality. The split rear window, shown above, was discontinued in 1953, incidentally. As a rough guide you can reckon that pre-1965 Beetles are likely to be in better condition than later examples. The 1200 version is probably the most reliable but also the most pedestrian! Clubs are Volkswagen Owners', Historic Volkswagen and VW Split Screen. Fuel consumption is in the region of 30 mpg. Number built: over 20 million

Volvo's stylish P 1800 coupe was introduced in 1961 and remained available until 1969. There was also the fuel injected 1800E of 1969-72 and a 1800ES estate version of 1971-73. The 1.8 litre four cylinder engine possesses a passing resemblance to the BMC B Series unit. Initially built in Britain by Jensen, production was transformed to Sweden in 1963. The sills are particularly vulnerable, around the headlamps and the base of the rear wheel arches are further suspect areas. Petrol consumption is around 25 mpg and mechanical spares are in reasonable supply. The Volvo Owners' Club has a P1800 Register. Number built: P1800 30,093; 1800E 9414; 1800ES 8078

Wolseley 14, 1818 cc 1945-48. The 14 was a well built, nicely finished car for its day, being an unashamed updated version of a pre-war design. It shared a similar body style to the 12, but the same wheelbase as the 18. A distinctive note was the illuminated radiator badge, a feature of the marque since 1933. Rust danger points are the bottom of the doors and running boards. A 1948 example is shown here

The Wolseley Fifteen-Fifty evolved from the 1953 Wolseley Four-Forty four which was powered by a 1.2 litre Morris engine. The 1956 Fifteen-Fifty, however, was 1489 cc BMC B Series-powered and is identifiable by the body side flash being extended to meet the rear wing moulding. Output continued until 1958. Mechanically these cars are reliable enough but beware rust along the bottoms of the doors, sills and headlamp surrounds. Mechanical but not body parts are available for this model. Petrol consumption is around the 26 mpg mark and the Wolseley Register caters for Wolseleys of all ages. Number built: 15,552

Chapter Two

Restoring the chassis, suspension and steering

The frame of the motor car, which carries each part in its proper place . . . has received much attention by designers. The ordinary owner and chauffeur pay but small attention to it. **Rankin Kennedy (The Book of the Motor Car), 1914**

Once you have your car home, now is the time to consider your plan of campaign. You may be lucky. Your vehicle could have led a sheltered life, or had very few owners who regularly serviced and maintained it. If this is the case, you will probably get away with some routine tidying up and leave it at that. You will have a totally original car, and providing you continue to lavish the care and attention that it has been used to, it will probably continue to do sterling service for many years. There is no point in restoring a car just for the sake of it, for the gentle gleam of well cared for cellulose and the delights of a totally original interior which retains the distinctive smell of horse hair, well maintained leather, with a dash of old oil thrown in for good measure, should be preserved, not destroyed.

Unfortunately, such cars are few and far between. Most owners were not careful and a fair proportion ran their vehicles until they stopped. So when you commence the sort of restoration I am talking about, I am thinking of a runner that is somewhat down at heel, having spent much of its time in the open air and is thus in need of a re-build. Obviously the 'chassis' section of this chapter deals only with those cars fitted with a detachable body.

As I said earlier there is, I am afraid, a tremendous temptation to pull everything apart as soon as you get the car under cover. This, in my experience, is when enthusiasm is at its height, but it is also when you need most restraint! Before starting the dismantling it is an excellent idea to take a cross-section of photographs of the car. This will serve two purposes. The first, and most important reason, is that they will give you an accurate record of the layout and positioning of components, while secondly, it is pleasant to be able to reflect on the car's original state when the restoration is complete. And if there are particular areas that are difficult to photograph, then drawings will suffice. Before starting the dismantling procedure, make a list of any parts that may be missing, not when the vehicle is in pieces!

The order in which you proceed with the restoration depends very much on the state of the car's body. If you are not going to remove it from the chassis, and are intending to tidy it up, or give it a re-spray, then tackle the mechanics first, following with coachwork renovation. But if you are intending to take the body off the chassis and re-build it, then tackle this part of the restoration first. I will explain why. It is certainly by no means unusual for a body (and this certainly applies to tourers) to fall apart when it is taken off the chassis, and the chances of re-building it exactly as it was, may be one or two years hence, are pretty remote. So the first thing to do is to get to grips with the body, using the best work bench of the lot, the car's chassis. Then, when you come to spill glue, paint and the like on the chassis, it will not matter, though it would certainly do so if the

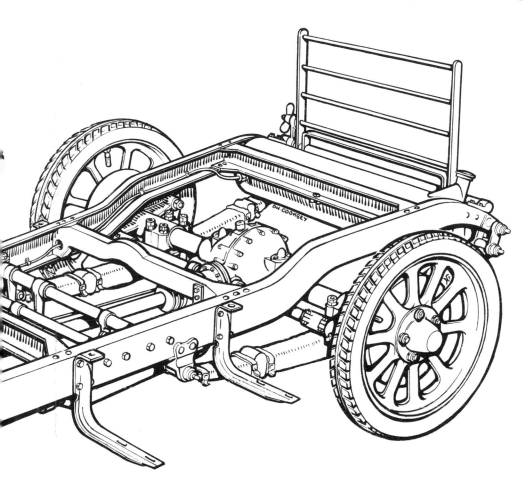

BEAN "FOURTEEN" (1923 model)
BEAN CARS, LTD., DUDLEY, WORCS.
4 cylinders, 75mm. by 135mm. 2385cc.

A typical chassis of the vintage era. The sturdy 14 hp Bean was built by A. Harper Sons and Bean Ltd (later Bean Cars Ltd) between 1923 and (in short chassis form) 1928. The 75×135 mm four cylinder engine was of 2385 cc. The Perrot front wheel brakes were a £25 optional extra on this 1923 example

51

Off comes the body

You will probably find that the body is secured to the chassis, or sub frame with coachbolts, and invariably these will be badly rusted. Any stubborn bolts can either be hacksawed off, and the nuts split with a chisel or with a nut cracker, and I do not mean the sort that usually lives on the side-board! Disconnect any stray electrical connections between the body and the chassis, and with the help of a few friends, loosen the body from the chassis. Its restoration can now proceed, as detailed in Chapter Seven. When this is complete you can continue with your restoration of the chassis, which by then should be devoid of its petrol tank, engine and gearbox. You should leave the springs and axles until last because, at least you will be able to move the frame around if the wheels are fitted. When dismantling the front suspension, make sure you check the positions of any castor wedges that may be fitted between the springs and the front axle, ie whether the thick end is at the front or the rear. If the former arrangement is favoured, the castor angles of the front wheels is reduced, while it will be increased if the latter course is adopted.

One of the golden rules about taking a car to pieces is not to take everything down to the last nut and bolt, but leave the components as complete as possible, in this way you avoid loosing pieces. And if you remove a nut and bolt from a hole, then replace them as soon as the separation is effected. At this stage, do not throw *anything* away; place the parts in marked boxes. If you have any doubts about the positioning of a component, or whether it could be inadvertently re-fitted back to front (like the front axle), clearly mark it 'front' or any similarly appropriate legend.

By this stage you should be left with a bare chassis frame, and this should be cleaned with paraffin and checked for alignment, details of which you will see in the adjoining diagram. If the chassis is out of true, then it will have to be straightened though this requires fairly heavy equipment, and is outside the scope of most individuals. Rubery Owen Ltd., of Wednesbury, Staffordshire (who probably made the frame in the first place) offer an excellent reconditioning service. But whoever you take your chassis to (it could be your local engineering works), check it *after* it has been straightened out. At the same time get the company to make any structural repairs, while any unnecessary holes can be filled in with weld. You can laboriously wire brush and prime the chassis, but a time-saving alternative is to have it shot blasted. Thornton Heath Shot Blasting of Thornton Heath, Surrey is just one firm who will take this sort of operation on. Finish is often a matter of personal preference, though the same company will spray on a red oxide undercoat (never leave a shot blasted surface bear for long), which makes an ideal base for paint. A completely stove enamelled chassis looks very acceptable, though the finish does tend to chip rather easily. Black Valspar is therefore a cheaper, and popular, alternative. Incidentally, make sure that the shackle pin and shock absorber mounting points are masked over, whatever type of finish you decided upon.

Historic restoration: the chassis frame of one of the famous side valve Austin Seven racers of the nineteen thirties in the course of restoration at the Donington Collection's workshops. The rear axle, with distinctive offset drive, can be seen in the background

This is the box section chassis frame of a 1956 MGA, owned by MG Car Club member, Bill Clark

A head-on view of the same chassis

A 1929 Austin Seven Chummy, with body in the background. The forward section of the rear portion of the body has been renewed

55

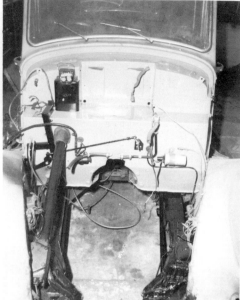

The bulkhead of a 1951 Mark V Jaguar, before and after restoration

Overhauling the springs and shackle pins

The areas which are likely to have suffered most wear are spring shackles and pins. As far as these are concerned, you will find that they are probably more worn at the front than at the rear, where they are exposed to steering stresses. If you cannot obtain new spares, the interior of the shackle yokes will have to be built up with weld, while new shackle pins of case hardened steel will have to be made, together with phosphor bronze bushes.

The **leaf springs** have a fairly hard working existence, so either try to obtain new ones, or have the old ones re-tempered. Gwynne Townsend, of London SE19 will do this for you. You will find probably, that the phosphor bronze bushes in the spring eyes can be tapped out with a drift of a slightly smaller diameter than the bush itself. If it still stubbornly refuses to budge, then make a simple extractor, consisting of a bolt fitted with a washer of a smaller diameter than the bush. Place the bolt, with its attendant washer in the bush, and at the other end position a distance tube, which is large enough to allow the bush to pass through it. The puller is completed by fitting a bolt and washer at the other end. Place a spanner on the nut and turn away! This should effectively remove the bush, and the process is particularly useful for extracting Silentbloc bushes. You may find, however, that this type of bush is located by peaning over the edge of the spring eye at a number of points. These must obviously be cleaned up, prior to removing the bush. It is worth noting that Silentbloc bushes are still available from the manufacturers, Silentbloc Ltd., of Crawley, Sussex, who report that as far as the really old bushes are concerned (Silentblocs first appeared in 1926), "we only have blueprints and no printed list, but parts are available on request".

Leaf springs should be carefully cleaned after dismantling

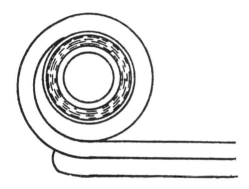

The correct spring eye for Silentbloc bushes. The replacement shackle bolt should be coated with a zinc based or graphited grease

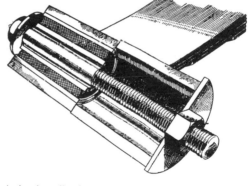

A simple puller for removing Silentbloc bushes from spring eyes

Close up of a 1930 Morris Oxford spring shackle which has been nicely renovated

New spring gaiters, by Wefco, fitted to the front axle of the same Morris Oxford

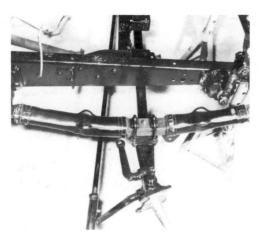

An overhead shot of a properly restored front axle assembly. Note the chassis support

The radiator assembly installed into the chassis. Note the gaitered leaf springs and hydraulic brake pipe

If you suspect, or can see, that one of the springs is fractured, then it is advisable to dismantle the one in question. It is also likely that those immediately below and above the damaged one are also suffering in some way, in view of the extra load thrust upon them. Prior to dismantling the leaves, mark the end of each leaf with a centre punch to make sure that you re-assemble them correctly. Then mount the springs in a vice, on their side, undo the central nut and unbend the securing clips. Gradually open the vice and the springs will gently separate, and can then be individually examined. Now you can clean each one thoroughly with a wire brush and paraffin, for a hitherto unnoticed crack may reveal itself once the leaf has dried. If leaves are cracked, then new ones can be made by Gwynne Townsend. If you are faced with the unenviable task of re-assembling the springs after they have been re-tempered, mount them on a section of rod, the same diameter as the central bolt. Place the whole lot in a vice, compressing all the leaves until you can remove the slave rod and fit a new centre bolt. Also fit new clips. Remember to lubricate the leaves with a heavy oil, ideally containing colloidal graphite, rather than grease.

As far as fitting new bushes is concerned, these are pressed into the spring eye with a vice, though you should make up a small distance piece to prevent damage to the bush's flange. When you come to fit the new shackle pins, you may find that they are unexpectedly tight, which is usually the result of the bush being mildly compressed during the fitting operation. If this is the case, a reamer, of the same diameter as the pin, should be sufficient to clean up the hole. Another alternative way of fitting bushes to springs is to reverse the process of the bolt and spacer routine. You may also like to fit a set of spring gaiters. These keep the springs clean and look very presentable. They are available from Wilcot (Parent) Co. Ltd., of Bristol.

When refitting the springs to the chassis, fit the rear end of the spring to its appropriate shackle, but do not tighten the nut until the other end is secured. Thrust washers are usually positioned between the bush and the shackles, and the clearance should be between 0.003 and 0.005 in. Anything greater than this can affect the car's handling. If you are replacing springs which are fitted with Silentbloc bushes, make sure that you do not finally tighten the nut on the shackle pin until the car is completely re-assembled, so that its full weight is taken on the springs. If this is not done, and you tighten the shackle pin nuts early on, you will subject the Silentbloc bushes to unnecessary stress which will considerably shorten their working life. Only completely tighten the nuts after the car has been bounced up and down a few times. Having dealt with those hard working springs, it is now time to consider the overhaul of the axles. I will begin with the front.

Overhauling a beam front axle

Start off by mounting the axle in a vice. If you have not marked the appropriate side 'front' by this time, do it now. Take off the brake drums, which are usually held in position by set screws. However, in some instances the drum and wheel hubs are integral and therefore cannot be removed until the wheel spindle nuts are undone. Be prepared for the nut on the near side to have a left handed thread. Next, off can come the bearings and hubs, but you will need a puller if ball races (there are two of them) are fitted. The other alternative, taper rollers, allow you to remove the hub manually. You then should be able to remove the brake anchor plates, complete with shoes, but they will require separate dismantling. Note their correct positioning. Brake overhaul is dealt with in Chapter Three.

Now comes the potentially tricky business of removing the king pins. They are usually held in place by a cotter pin, and this must first be loosened off. The king pin can come out of either the top or the bottom (designs vary). If the pin comes out of the top, it is often drilled and tapped to take an extractor, as in the case of the Austin Seven. Otherwise you can use a hammer and drift. The most likely parts to be worn are the pins themselves, the bushes and thrust washers, also the pins can be loose in the axle eye. You should now be left with the axle itself, and you can get down to the business of checking its geometry. The first thing to do is to check that the spring saddles are in the same plane. You can do this by using an engineering protractor, which contains a miniature spirit level. Both readings in line with the axle and at right angles to it should be identical. If they are not, there is no point in continuing the test for correct alignment, as the axle will probably require correcting professionally, or you may find it easier and cheaper to use a substitute unit. Incidentally, do not be tempted to apply heat to the axle yourself to correct a deficiency, as most axles are made from alloy steels, and applying localised heat is likely to lower their strength. However, if the first test reveals that all is well with the spring saddles, the next stage is to ascertain whether the castor angle or king pin inclination is correct. It is, however, an appropriate moment to consider what these two terms mean.

Castor angle   A feature of a car's steering is that the front wheels are self-centring, an effect produced by castor trail angle. This is achieved by the king pin being inclined to the vertical in fore and aft directions, being backward at the top and forward at the bottom. As a result, the wheels are trailed, and tend to return to the straight when the vehicle is in motion. You have probably noticed that the castors on a tea trolley work in a similar way.

King pin inclination   In addition to castor angle, the king pins are given an inward rake towards the top. The reason for this state of affairs is to enable the axis of the pin to nearly intersect the vertical centre line of the wheel where the tyre touches the ground. The tyre, of course spreads, so only an approximation of this ideal can be achieved. In addition to this, the wheels are also cambered to enable the load of the wheel bearings to be evenly distributed. As can be seen, steering is very much a matter of compensating for the fact that the tyre tread is only running in true harmony at one point. To counteract these forces, the wheels at the hub centres are closer at the front than at the rear, the measurement between the wheel rims being about $1/8$ in. shorter forward of the axle.

After that brief excursion, perhaps we can continue our overhaul! Position the king pin partially in the eye of the axle beam, checking with the protractor in the same plane as the axle and at right angles to it. Both sides should produce the same reading; half a degree variance is the maximum allowable. For the final test, partially position the other king pin and then place a straight edge along the length of the beam, on top of the spring eyes, using the pins for location. Using a small set square, measure the distance between the spring tables and the straight edge. They should be identical. If the axle survives all these rigorous tests, you can now turn your attention to the king pins, so beloved of the DOE tester!

You will, of course, have removed the old pins in the course of dismantling the axle. You will probably need new pins and bushes. If you cannot get replacements, then new ones will have to be made of case hardened steel and phosphor bronze respectively. The Jarrot Engine Company, of London SW19 will be able to do this for you. Make sure that any lubricating holes are drilled in the bushes, and that they line up with the greasers on the stub axles. If, by chance, the bushes have not been drilled, then remove the nipples, and with the bushes in situ,

This stub axle required no more work other than cleaning and painting

1930 Morris Oxford steering mechanism showing restored king pin and steering arm

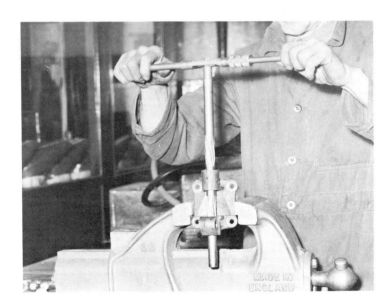

Reaming out swivel pins ready for new king pins

drill the holes. Of course, it is quite likely that the new bushes may have closed up slightly, and that they will have to be opened up with a reamer that will suit the king pin. You may have to farm this part of the job out to a specialist. The whole point of the operation is to assure the correct alignment of *both* holes. If, on the other hand, split type bushes are used, it is only necessary to remove a small amount of metal, and then honing is better than reaming.

Once this is done, offer up the stub axles to the beam end with a new thrust washer in between the two thrust faces, which are between the bottom of the eye and the lower face of the stub axle. If there is still a clearance between the non-thrust faces, then fit a felt washer to prevent dirt, or water getting in. Make sure that you get the stub axles the right way round, as the offside does differ from the near . . .   Once the pin is well and truly pressed home, lock up the retaining cotter. The stub axles should swivel freely without binding. Grease or oil until lubricant oozes from the thrust-washer faces. You are now in a position to replace the brake anchor back plates and shoe assemblies, and fit new wheel bearings, if they are required.

A good turn

As we have seen, the wheel bearings are likely to be a pair of taper rollers, or two ball races, so it is probably a suitable moment to consider these components in general terms. Ball and roller bearings consist of four basic parts: Initially, you have the outer race which provides the track on which the balls or rollers roll, and is usually fitted into a suitably shaped housing. Then there is the inner race which rolls on either the balls or rollers and is usually fitted to a shaft, spindle or spigot. Then, positioned between the inner and outer races, come the balls or rollers themselves. Some bearings also have a cage to position them, but this is not always the case.

As a rule, either the outer race remains stationary and the inner race revolves, or vice versa. Remember, the revolving race is always a press fit in its housing or shaft, while the stationary race is a push fit in the housing or shaft. This simple rule should be remembered when it comes to dismantling or fitting these types of bearings. The rule is this: when applying force, or blows, confine your activities to the *tight* member. If the opposite is carried out, it can cause strain or damage to the race.

Taper roller bearings can be removed by hand

Normally bearings should be removed with the aid of a special extractor, but on occasions it is possible to get round the need for this tool. When you are faced with the problem of a bearing fitted on a shaft tight against a shoulder, then it is possible to jerk it off by striking the shaft on the end grain of a piece of wood. A similar process can be adopted to a bearing fitted into a blind housing. If you are faced with a reluctant bearing in an alloy housing, it can be removed by slightly heating the housing. The differential expansion of the alloy should allow the race to be removed without much difficulty.

Once the bearing has been removed, it should be thoroughly washed and spun in clean paraffin. Examine the balls, rollers or races for chips or scratching. This can usually be confirmed by spinning the bearing. Any uneveness will audibly make its presence felt. Also check the condition of the shaft to which the bearing has been attached. For if either of the races has been moving on its shaft, or in its housing, wear may take place, making the fitting of a replacement, pointless. Welding, or metal spraying, followed by machining of the shaft can be a way round the problem.

When you come to reposition the bearing, cleanliness is absolutely essential. Where possible, the tight portion should be taped, or drifted, into place, without tilting, or binding the whole unit. Remember that dual purpose bearings should always be assembled so that any thrust is applied to the face of the outer race marked 'thrust'.

By contrast, adjustable taper roller wheel bearings should be done up tight, and the securing nut then slackened by one castellation. Hubs fitted with ball races should be secured by a nut and tab washer, or split pin in the normal way. A high melting point grease (HMP) should be used to lubricate wheel bearings.

Overhauling independent front suspension

Make a point of checking the condition of the front suspension, *before* you dismantle the car. This is because wear is far more likely to manifest itself when the full weight of the vehicle is making its presence felt. These days, the DOE yearly test ensures that cars with badly worn independent front suspension units are winkled out in the testing station. The ease with which the suspension can be reconditioned obviously varies from model to model. There are, in the main, three types of suspension: the parallelogram type, the swinging arm variety and finally the strut and link layout.

It will no doubt be of some help to briefly describe these variations. First, the **parallelogram type.** This layout can use a coil spring placed between two wishbones, by a single transverse spring which replaces the lower wishbone, or a double transverse spring which also replaces the upper one. In many cases the lower wishbone is made longer than the upper, which results in the wheel tilting as it rises, so avoiding tyre scrub. Although a swivel pin is very popular these days, an older alternative is a king pin and stub axle layout, which is a hang over from the beam axle. Another variation in the design occurs when the coil spring is replaced by a torsion bar.

Secondly, there is the **swinging arm** variety. The hub, wheels and bearings are carried at the end of an arm and this carries the steering swivel pin, the whole assembly pivoting on this pin, as on the Dubonnet system.

Thirdly, and finally, comes the **strut and link** type, which is exemplified by the MacPherson strut. Here, the conventional top link is replaced by a flexible mounting and the telescopic damper acts as a king pin.

Many of the suspension units built during the era under consideration, bristled with grease nipples, and these should be regularly attended to, particularly when the car is in regular use. If this is not done, wear will take place and this can be rather difficult to track down, particularly as there may be a dozen or so bushes either side. You will need an accomplice for this checking operation, getting him (or her) to lever the wheel vertically up and down, with the car jacked up, but without using sufficient force to lever the suspension against the spring. It is surprising just how much force is necessary to show up wear on the inner bushes. While all this activity is raging on, put your hands on the steering joints and feel for any movement. Remember to pay special attention to where the weight of the car rests on the swivel. For example, if you have ball joints top and bottom, then the bottom ball will be doing all the hard work. But should your car retain the traditional king pin layout, then the weight will be taken on the thrust bearing. With other layouts, both ends (or just the bottom) of the king pin is threaded into bushes; these are notorious wear points.

Some suspension units are bushed with rubber, but do not be completely satisfied, even if you cannot feel any movement present. If you noticed, on your test drive, that the car did not feel quite right at the front end, be on the lookout for rubber bushes squashing out at the ends. Slight squashing is not too critical, but if the end has belled out and feels wobbly and soggy, then obviously all is not well. These bushes should *not* be lubricated as they tend to deteriorate quickly if they come in contact with oil or grease. If they do require replacement and are of the one-piece pressed in type, you may well experience difficulty in getting the new bush into the eye of the suspension member. Should this be the case, it may be well worthwhile seeking out an agent for the car you own (if the marque is still current) as special tools may be required. This is not as unlikely as it sounds, for suspension systems tend to soldier on for years, even though your particular model may be obsolete. And while on the subject of rubber bushes and their fitting, remember not to fully tighten the securing nuts until the car is well and truly on the ground and is under normal load. If you do not take this precaution, the bush's life will be considerably shortened.

To revert to the suspension checks. If all appears well so far, then use a smaller lever (a tyre lever is ideal), and try levering each joint apart. When carrying out all these checks, jack up each suspension unit in turn, *do not* raise the car, by positioning the jack in the centre of the cross member.

If you come to dismantle a suspension system that employs a **coil spring** (most do), then get a friend (preferably a heavy one) to sit on the front of the car with the wheels firmly on the ground, and then fit a spring compressor. The spring can then be removed with safety and will not go through the workshop roof, taking you with it! While you are doing the dismantling, watch out that you do not loose any shims which may be fitted to control the castor and camber angles. Post-war Jaguars, for example, veritably bristle with the things.

Torsion bars   These suspension bars are often splined into short arms, and then are anchored to the body by a form of adjustable attachment. A set screw can be used, or the fixed end of the arm can be attached to a vernier plate. This plate contains a number of holes which allows the bolt which is used to attach the arm to the plate, to be moved to varying heights, so altering the degree of 'twist' in the bar.

It is possible to check that each bar retains the same amount of 'twist' by placing the vehicle on a level surface and measuring the distance from the bottom wishbone to the ground. However, the bar should only be adjusted with the wheels off the ground, so that they are unaffected by the weight of the car. If it is not possible to restore the correct height by the aforementioned adjustment, it may be easier to adjust it at the wishbone end, as this is usually splined. If you do fit a new bar, then a small difference in height must be allowed for, which will disappear once the new bar has settled. In truth, torsion bars give remarkably little trouble through their very simplicity, though the mountings at the 'chassis end' should be checked for corrosion.

Steering wear and tear

I have dealt with how to check for steering wear on page 23. Nevertheless, it is worth going through the motions again. Should you discover any wear, it is most likely to occur in the adjustable ball joints which are fitted to many of the vehicles under discussion. One of the drawbacks of this particular system is that the ball tends to wear oval because the steering is moving in a limited arc. This wear results in the steering being at its loosest when it is in the 'straight ahead' position, and tightens up when cornering. Unfortunately, if these joints are worn, there is no alternative to having new balls and cups made, unless you are lucky enough to come across some new replacements. More recently, a form of adjustable ball joint is to be found connecting the tie rods to the outer ends of the rack and pinion steering layout. Here adjustment is achieved by increasing, or removing, shims which are sandwiched between the two halves of the ball housing.

Unfortunately, steering can be subjected to a number of shortcomings, which you may well have noticed during your test drive. The following are reckoned to be the worst culprits.

Wander   This is often caused by tightness, or excessive play, in the steering box itself, the knuckle joints or wheel bearings. Also check the king pins and bushes for excessive wear.

Incorrect castor angle   This has the effect of reducing the steering's self-centring effect. For should the castor angles of the wheels differ, the car will pull to the side with least castor. This could be the result of a twisted axle. Similarly, if the front and rear axles are out of alignment, this could produce the same trouble.

Tramp   Excessive wear in the steering box is the first port of call for this condition, together with similar shortcomings in the knuckle joints or wheel bearings.

Shimmy   Gross play in the steering connections can produce an effect best described as 'see-sawing' transversely, with the centre of the front axle as the pivot. Distorted brake drums can also cause the brakes to bind, which can also result in shimmy.

Wheel wobble   Any of the earlier causes can result in this condition. Cars fitted with MacPherson strut front suspension are particularly vulnerable. Examine the axles and springs to check that

63

there is not undue side play between the springs and shackles. Check the pressure, condition and treads of the front tyres, also the condition and play in the wheel bearings.

If it appears that the front tyres are wearing badly, then the car's track may be incorrectly set up. To check this, jack up the front of the car and spin each wheel in turn against a stationary object to check the run out. If this exceeds $^1/_{16}$ to $^1/_8$ in. then try a wheel from the back of the car, or the spare. Now set the wheels in the straight ahead position. You can be sure of this by measuring the distance from the inside of the rim to the respective spring shackle or chassis member. If the wheels are straight ahead, the measurement should be identical on both sides. Now mark a point on the rim of each wheel at the centre height, in *front* of the axle. Measure the distance between the two points and then push the car forward until these same two points are at the same height *behind* the axle and then measure again. If the car is designed for toe-in (as most cars are), then this second measurement should be greater than the first one, or if toe-out should be specified, then the reverse will be true. If you do have occasion to fit new track rod ends, then count *exactly* the number of turns on the thread of the old ball, so that you can fit the new unit in exactly the same position. Otherwise, you may upset the track.

I will deal now with the dismantling and adjustment of a number of popular steering boxes, the worm and wheel, rack and pinion, Burman and Bishop. These instructions can only be regarded as guidelines, as there are many variations on these themes.

Worm and wheel/sector   End play of the worm wheel is removed in a number of ways, as designs vary somewhat. A milled adjusting ring fitted to the top of the box may be used, or an adjustable screwed end plug may be favoured. On the other hand, shims may be fitted between the bottom cover plate and the box. There are a similar variety of methods to eliminate end float (if a worm and sector design is used) on the sector by varying the number of shims between the side cover and the casing, or an adjusting screw. Methods of compensating for wear in the mesh are equally varied. The sector may be carried in an eccentrically mounted boss; turning the boss moves the sector into, or out of, mesh with the worm. On occasions, the bolt holes on one side of the flange are marked + or −, showing that rotating the sector housing in the relevant direction will increase or decrease the degree of mesh. If your box is fitted with a complete wheel, it can be turned, and a new portion brought into use. This is carried out by removing the drop arm, and then turning the steering wheel to rotate the drop arm shaft half a turn. Then re-connect the arm.

Rack and pinion   The pinion is usually integral with the inner steering column and is mounted on two adjustable taper roller bearings. End float on the column must be removed to prevent backlash between the gears and the teeth. A plunger is usually used to keep the end of the rack, on which the gear teeth are cut, in contact with the pinion. If excessive backlash is present, then this plunger should first be checked, as a weakened spring may be the likely cause. On the post-war Morris, if wear is present, undo the plunger and take the shims and spring out. Then replace the plunger and then screw in so that the pinion shaft can only just be turned when the rack is pulled through its casing. Clearance between the hexagon of the cap and the seating on the rack housing should be measured and to this figure should be added the specified tooth clearance of 0.002 – 0.005 in. The correct thickness of the shims is thus indicated and these must be fitted between the damper cap and the housing.

Remember that the oil seals play a particularly important role, as the rack often operates in oil. The condition of the rubber gaiters at both ends of the shaft is, therefore, critical. If split or torn, water or grit can enter, often with disastrous results.

Burman steering gear   Wear which develops between the nut and screw in this layout cannot be corrected, and the only answer is to fit a new nut; more of this anon! The ball race at the top of the steering column is the principle area of adjustment. End float in the column is taken up by loosening a locking nut and then tightening the adjusting nut underneath. Do not overdo it though, or the steering will stiffen up. The accessibility of the nut varies. Sometimes it is easy to get at, and a pair of thin spanners are sufficient to loosen off the flats. Rather more often, the nuts are hidden by the steering wheel boss, and this must first be lifted. On some other Burman boxes, a secondary adjustment is available, which compensates for end float on the rocker shaft. This is a set screw which is locked by a nut which passes through the box's side cover plate and bearing on the end of the rocker shaft.

To overhaul the box, the splined drop arm must be removed; then the side cover plate. The rocker shaft can then be withdrawn. This is followed by the end cover plate and the lock nut at the top of the inner column is loosened and the adjusting nut undone. Once this has been achieved, the inner column can be carefully knocked downwards and the loose ball bearings removed. The column can then be pushed downwards and taken out of the box, with the bronze nut still in position. Before dismantling, mark the position of the nut in relation to the thread, to aid reassembly, if you find that new components are not needed. The lower cone of the thrust bearing may be left in situ unless it is pitted or damaged. Also examine the ball bearings and cone for the same sort of flaws. Other replaceable parts are the rocker arm bushes and these are a push fit and can be tapped out once the oil seal has been taken out. If wear has taken place in the thread of the bronze nut, it is possible to obtain the nut separately, in some cases, from Motolympia of Welshpool, Wales, although the thread is undersized when supplied and must be lapped on to the thread.

Bishop cam steering Wear which has taken place can be compensated for in this box by moving the roller closer into mesh. This can be done by the familiar method of withdrawing shims between the side cover plate and the casing. Removing the side cover will reveal three thicknesses of shim, the thinnest being brass and 0.0025 in., while the steel shims are of 0.005 in. and 0.010 in. thick. Before checking the adjustment, the roller must be in its correct position, in relation to the cam. To ascertain this, disconnect the drag link. Then the amount of backlash between the roller and cam can be ascertained by pushing the base of the drop arm to and fro. The backlash

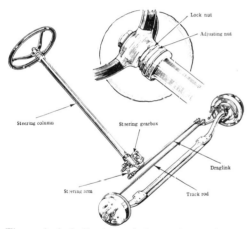

The method of adjusting end play on the steering column of a 1929 Morris Minor

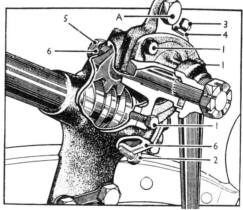

A worm and sector steering gear of the 'thirties, as used on the Austin 10. *Key* 1, side plate set screws; 2, end cover screw; 3, mesh adjusting screw; 4, locknut; 5, cross shaft locking nut; 6, shims; A, oil plug

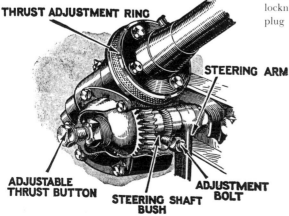

Austin 12 steering gear, showing the provisions for adjustment

increases when the roller reaches its maximum travel and will be less apparent in the centre of the cam track. This is quite deliberate as the layout allows for plenty of adjustment on and near the centre where maximum use is expected.

Adjustment must be carried out at this high spot with shims being removed until there is no back-lash. Adjustment will then be correct for the entire steering arc. You are able also to adjust the box without removing the drop arm, if the box is still mounted in the car. By this method, the front wheels are jacked up and one shim removed at a time, the plate being replaced on each occasion. A tight spot will then be detected by turning the steering wheel, when all sufficient shims have been removed. When this has been achieved, one brass shim (0.0025 in.) should be replaced to give the correct clearance.

On cars fitted with Bishop high efficiency gear, adjustment is made by a setscrew fitted in the cover plate. The setscrew is slackened off, after the lock nut has been undone and the high spot ascertained. Turning the screw in a clockwise direction moves the pin further into mesh with the cam, backlash being eliminated at this point.

The bearing fitted to the upper end of the steering column varies in design. On occasions it is simply a felt bush, or a plain journal ball bearing. An adjustable ball bearing is sometimes fitted in the top of the column and it is usually necessary to raise the steering wheel to gain access to the bearing adjustment nut and lock nut. The upper of the two nuts is the lock nut and this is first loosened, the adjusting nut can then be tightened to take up any slackness there may be present in the bearing.

To overhaul the steering gear, first remove the drop arm. You will probably need a puller for this part of the operation. With the drop arm off and the side cover plate removed, it is time to have a look at the cork gland in the boss of the box. If it requires renewal, it can be cut out of its housing. To fit the new one, cut it at one point and push one end into the slot and gradually work the rest in.

Now have a look at the roller on the rocker arm, for wear, though remember that the layout of this type of box can vary considerably. The most frequent arrangement used a hardened steel peg which was a push fit in the arm. This can easily be pressed out and a replacement fitted. Should, on the other hand, the peg not be too badly worn you can get away with turning it 90 degrees and then re-fitting. With the ball and roller sort of peg, this is simply a press fit in the rocker arm. Yet another variation on the theme, is a peg which turns in a bush pressed into the rocker arm. If this is the case, a replacement peg and bush should be lapped together, following the bush being pressed into the arm by gripping it in a vice and swinging the arm around it. If the lapping is carried out properly, the bush should be just free enough to allow the arm to fall under its own weight. The final type used is that with the peg integral with the arm. In this case there is no alternative, but to renew the entire component. In any event, the shaft should be replaced if the splines are worn.

The vast majority of these boxes are fitted with renewable bushes. These are easily re-moved, though new ones will probably need reaming to make sure that the rocker shaft is a good fit. Unfortunately if no bushes are fitted and wear has taken place, there is no alternative to looking around for another box.

The cam and bearings are the next items to come under scrutiny. To do this, the end cover must be taken off. Usually this is at the bottom of the box, though it can be at the top. The ball race fitted at the top of the steering column should also be dismantled and examined for wear. Once this has been done, the inner column can be tapped into the box carrying the bearing caps with it, so that the cam projects sufficiently so it can be withdrawn. Ideally, the column and cam should be renewed as a complete unit if this is deemed necessary. When you come to reassemble the box, replace the same number of shims that were originally fitted underneath the end covers. Then remove one shim at a time until the column becomes stiff. Then replace the last shim removed and bolt up.

Rear axles

From the front of the car, we now go to the back and consider the rear axle. If you recollect it being quiet in operation, then drain out the old oil and replace it with fresh. However, these components

A hub puller is required to remove many rear axle hubs. Here an Austin Seven rear axle is being dismantled

In the event of rear axle failure, and it is not possible to obtain replacement parts, it may be feasible to have new components made. Here the Jarrot Engine Co., of London SW19 have made a new crown wheel and pinion, fitted new bearings throughout, made new half shafts and re-machined the original casting. The axle is from a 1910 Humber 16

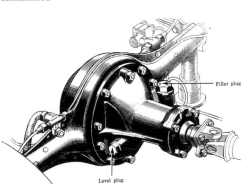

In pre-war days you had a filler *and* oil level plug. Axle is Morris 10/4

do suffer from a number of shortcomings. The most likely are worn oil seals with the result that the lubricant gets on to the brake linings, so rendering them useless. This failure is, in fact, often caused by pressure building up in the casing, through the breather hole being blocked. Another problem can be caused by worn pinion bearings, and their attendant oil seals, but it is something of a specialist job to fit replacements.

Before going any further, it is worth specifying the three types of rear axle you are likely to come across. The **fully floating** type has the hub carried by bearings on the axle casing, the half shaft being splined straight into the hub. With this layout the shaft's only role is to transmit drive to the wheels. However, with the **three-quarter floating axle,** a ball race is again carried on the axle, but there is only one of them. The hub is keyed or integral with the half shaft. Although the shaft does not carry any weight it does provide lateral stability. With the **semi floating** type, the ball race is directly attached to the half shaft, being positioned inside the axle casing. This means that as well as transmitting power, the half shaft also carries the weight of the car and locates the wheel.

Now, felt washers are often used on the rear axles of pre-war cars to prevent oil leaking through on to the brake linings. For example, on the three-quarter floating axle, the washer is positioned behind the ball race. Often a grease nipple is provided to lubricate the bearings, but this should not be overdone as grease can reach the linings.

Renewing some oil seals is carried out by knocking back the tab washer fitted to the nut that secures the race to the casting. Once the nut is removed, the bearing housing and bearing can be drawn off the axle, though a puller may be required. With this done, the bearing can be tapped from the housing and a new washer fitted. Make a point of cutting a new one from industrial felt, if you cannot obtain a standard replacement, and soak it in oil overnight, prior to fitting.

On some axles, there is another oil seal provided by a paper washer which is used to make the joint between the flange of the hub and the bearing housing flange. Should this joint be broken, the washer should also be renewed. Again, with a semi floating axle, it is often positioned behind the bearing. And then there can be an additional seal provided on the outside of the ball race so that the grease from the bearing cannot escape on to the brake linings. Often the seal (particularly the sprung neoprene type) cannot be removed without damage. If this is the case, break it with a sharp chisel.

If it is possible to substitute the old felt type for the neoprene variety do so by all means, but make certain that the inner surface it bears on, is completely smooth, otherwise it will tear the material. And always fit these seals with the concave side facing the source of the oil.

When you are painting the chassis, do not be tempted to paint the inside of the rear axle casing, as the surface will break down and cause trouble. And remember that most aluminium chassis parts were originally painted, not polished.

Shock absorbers

The Hartford friction type shock absorber was one of the most popular units to be found on cars during the 'twenties and early 'thirties. There are two basic types, the S, standing for single type, has a single leaf inner arm, with double outer arm and two friction discs, while the M, or multi type, has twin leaf inner arms and treble outer arms and four friction discs. There are also two sizes, the type 502 (3$\frac{1}{2}$ in. diameter) and 506 (4$\frac{1}{2}$ in. diameter). The arms can vary in length, from 4$\frac{1}{4}$ in. to 10 in. long.

Hartford shock absorbers are usually mounted with the double (or triple) arms attached to the spring with the single (or double) arm bolted to the chassis. The exception to this rule is the telecontrol variation of the M design, where the reverse is true.

In view of their basic simplicity, restoring these shock absorbers is a job that can be easily accomplished in your own workshop. To dismantle the shock absorber, undo the adjusting nut, and then take out the retaining bolt. Now lever the arms apart and extract the two or four discs, taking care not to damage them. If the discs, (the originals were made of maple), are deeply scored they should be replaced, but these are made of beech, so if possible, retain the originals. Spares for the shock absorbers can be obtained from The Complete Automobilist, Baston, Huntingdonshire. You may also find it necessary to rebush with new hardwood bushes (fitted up to 1925); these are a press fit. Now throroughly clean the units, using a rust preventative on the area exposed to the elements. Prior to reassembly, coat the disc and steel housing with a thin layer of grease, as this will improve the action of the shock absorber. On the post 1926 units which are fitted with Silentbloc bushes, one variation has a clamp screw holding the bush in place, while with another type the bush is located at its inner end on two tapered seats, to prevent rotation, with a corresponding chamfer on the securing nut which abuts directly against the bush.

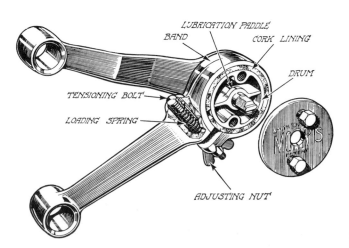

The Smiths friction shock absorber, as fitted to the Morris Minor of 1929

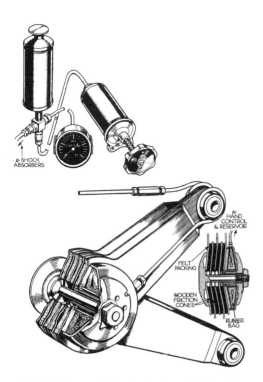

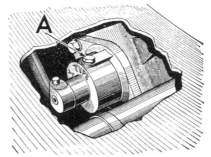

A Luvax hydraulic shock absorber of the mid
'thirties, with filler plug (A) indicated

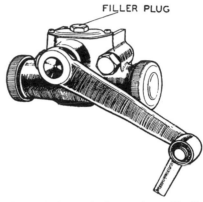

Hartford telecontrol shock absorbers of the 'thirties.
Note that the two bladed arm should be attached to
the axle

Another variation on the Luvax theme. The DoE
test now considers the efficiency of shock absorbers

Prior to attaching the Hartfords to the chassis, clamp one of the arms in a vice and hook a
spring balance to the end of the other, and test the tension. If your car weighs more than 25 cwt,
the balance should register 25lb, and if less, 20 lb. Now the chances are that the figures registered
will be different, so turn the adjusting nut to secure the required tension. To increase the pressure,
turn the nut to the right and to the left to decrease it. When this has been achieved, mark the outer
edge of the shock absorber opposite the pointer, then free off the adjusting nut, so freeing the dial,
taking note of the number of turns necessary to do so. Then turn the dial until the zero (figure one
on the dial) is opposite the mark made previously. Now tighten the nut, turning it to the right, and
counting the number of turns and you should end up with the pointer opposite the figure one. You
should now have the correct setting. Do the same with all the others.

When the time comes to test the car, note the setting. If it is too soft, tighten one graduation, each segment is equivalent to 3 to 4 lb, and if too harsh, slacken off one graduation. You will
probably find that the Hartfords are more effective at higher, than lower speeds, so do not skimp
the test.

Practically all other shock absorbers work on the hydraulic principle. Rotating vanes, or
pistons, force the fluid through small holes, their size controlling the speed at which the fluid
passes through them. The resulting resistance is transferred to an arm which in its turn is
connected to the axle or wheel mounting. These valves control the arm's upward and downward
movement, and, in some cases, are adjustable.

These shock absorbers, like so many other things, can be divided into three types. These are
the vane, rotor and piston varieties. With the first two sorts, a member which can resemble a ship's
paddle wheel, is forced to rotate by the movement of the vehicle's suspension in the hydraulic
fluid. The resistance offered provides the damping effect. With the piston variety, the piston is
forced along a cylinder full of hydraulic fluid which, of course, resents the intrusion, and resists; a
small orifice dictating the rate of flow and so the speed at which the piston can move.

Manufacturers usually recommend that hydraulic shock absorbers be topped every 5000 miles. If the ones on your car are in good condition, make sure that you use the correct fluid. Important this, because the variety suitable for a piston type is rather more 'fluid' than the other sort. Mountings should also be tight, and the shock absorber arm bushes in good order. All too often they are not.

Unfortunately, it is quite common to find that the shock absorbers have been allowed to run dry and air then entered the system. One way of retrieving the situation is to disconnect the arm attaching the shock absorber to the axle and fill up the unit with fluid. Now work the arm up and down until resistance is felt, and this should gradually increase. Now you have to get the two sides equal. One method is to screw all the valves right down and then slacken them off, one and a half to two turns. Then confirm by a test drive and alter the setting accordingly.

Apart from this check, it is very difficult for the amateur to satisfactorily overhaul these units. However, Bar Engineering of York will undertake to overhaul obsolete Armstrong units, while Youngs Motor Stores of London SW17 can offer reconditioned Luvax units, as well as supplying the older Woodhead, Girling and Spax shock absorbers.

Lubrication

The correct type of oil or grease is particularly important in any car, and this equally applies to old ones. As far as the rear axle is concerned, most will run happily with a modern hypoid oil of the correct grade. But if a straight oil is initially recommended, something like Castrol ST or D monograde oils, rated at 80, 90 or 140 should be used. Here is a word of warning though. Never use EP (stands for extreme pressure) oils in gearboxes or rear axles with either bronze gears (a la Morgan Three-wheeler) or phosphor bronze bearings, as it has a somewhat adverse effect on the metal. ST or D would suffice in such cases.

Then there is the business of greasing. All modern high melting point greases are lithium based with a melting temperature of 160 degrees. Prior to that they were sodium based and calcium based, the latter still being available for chassis lubrication. About the only thing to remember about these greases is that they do not mix with old ones, so any traces of the original should be removed before applying fresh. The following greases should be used on the various chassis points:-
Chassis: Medium consistency calcium based grease.
Wheel bearings: High Melting Point lithium based grease.

The right nuts

When you come to restore a car, you are never going to be far away from nuts and bolts. This may sound rather obvious, but the important thing to remember is that there are many different types, so the following observations may be of help in choosing the right sort of spanners. Up until the mid 'fifties two types of thread predominated on cars, the British Standard Fine (BSF) and British Standard Whitworth (BSW). The former was found on engine fittings, where its fine pitch was a good counter to vibration, while the coarse Whitworth, with its quick screwing action, was often used amongst other things, for tapping into aluminium. Not that things were always that straighforward. The Bullnose Morris, for example, used French standard metric threads, but with Whitworth flats, because Hotchkiss's Coventry factory (who built Morris's engines from 1919, and were re-named Morris Motors in 1923), in view of their Gallic roots, were only equipped with metric tool heads. Although Morris later dropped the arrangment, MG, who were, of course, an offshoot, continued to receive their engines from the Coventry factory, and used the old metric dies until the XPEG engine ceased production in 1955! Also Vintage Sunbeams favoured metric sizes, a reflection of the European flavour of the Sunbeam Talbot, Darracq combine.

However, the post Second World War era saw a common thread agreement made between the United Kingdom, the United States and Canada; the outcome was the Unified thread. These threads are divided into two classes; UNF (Unified National Fine) and UNC (Unified National Coarse). You can identify these threads in the following ways; nuts, by a circular groove turned on the end face or by connected circles stamped on a flat of the hexagon; bolts and set screws are marked by a circular depression turned on the head or by the same connected circles stamped end on. Wheel nuts are identified by a notch cut in all the corners of the hexagon.

Although these Unified threads are not interchangeable with Whitworth, BSF or Metric threads, they are with the American National Fine (ANF). And remember that all ANF and Unified threaded nuts and hexagon headed bolts are made to the standard hexagon sizes. Now the trend is to metric, but these ISO Metric threads do not appear on British cars within this survey.

Notes on development

1919 – 1929 A channel section pressed steel chassis, with axles suspended by half elliptic springs front and rear, was the most popular layout featured on cars built at the end of the 'twenties. However, frames were a trifle more complicated early on in the decade because a sub frame was often included to support the gearbox, which was connected to the engine by a short drive shaft. But as unit construction engines and gearboxes attained popularity, the sub frame was dispensed with. In a similar way, manufacturers took a little time to discover that half elliptic leaf springs were the most satisfactory from a manufacturing point of view, though William Morris, for example, persisted with a three quarter elliptic layout on his immortal 'Bullnose' model, which was the best selling British car of the 'twenties. But then, the model's roots went back to 1913 and when it was replaced by the less inspiring 'Flatnose' in 1927, gone were two Edwardian (in the motoring sense) vestigages: the famous, and charming, 'Bullnose' radiator and the archaic spring layout.

There are, of course, exceptions to every rule, and just one case was the transverse half elliptic suspension used on the Model T Ford (1908 – 1927), and which lingered on until 1959 on the Dagenham built Popular! Another exception was provided by the legendary Austin Seven (1922-1939), which favoured a transverse layout at the front, with quarter elliptics (always a firm favourite on cheap cars), at the rear. Although, early on, shock absorbers were regarded as something of a luxury at the cheaper end of the market, the Hartford friction variety gained great popularity and so-called 'Snubbers' were also available, while hydraulic shock absorbers were another variation on the damping theme.

Many of the cars favoured Hotchkiss Drive, whereby the rear springs, attached to the chassis at a fixed point at their front end, and freely shackled at the rear, carried the thrust transmitted from the engine via the road wheels. A pre-war alternative that persisted into the 'twenties was a torque tube which enclosed the propellor shaft and relieved the springs of driving torque reaction as well as the propulsive thrust of the wheels. With this layout the springs were freely shackled at *both* ends. At least two manufacturers persisted with this arrangement into the 'fifties, Riley (until 1952) and Ford (in conjunction with transverse springing) until 1959.

Spiral bevel rear axle crownwheel and pinion gearing from America gradually superceded the noisier, and less efficient, straight cut bevel at the beginning of the 'twenties, and soon gained practically universal acceptance. The decade also witnessed the gradual elimination of the Edwardian practice of building up the rear axle casing in a number of segments, and being replaced by a single banjo unit, at least on all but the more expensive cars.

The main alteration in front axle design came around 1924 with the introduction of front wheel brakes, which meant, in many cases the fork ended Elliott type axle, was replaced by the reversed Elliott variety. Steering was by the universal Ackerman principle (so called because it was patented in this country by Rudolph Ackermann, a fine arts publisher, in 1818, though the inventor was George Lenkensperger of Munich). Although the system was originally used on horse drawn wagons and carts, it was well established before the First World War, each front wheel being mounted on a stub axle which pivoted on the main beam. The arms were linked together with a track rod, and when the vehicle moved to the left hand turn, the left hand wheel moved through a larger angle than the right, and vice versa. This considerably eased steering and tyre scrub, though the latter advantage would hardly have Lenkensperger's mind! Steering boxes changed remarkably little from their pre-war counter parts, worm and sector and worm and nut layouts predominating. During the decade, many manufacturers made their own steering boxes, though the inroads by specialist manufacturers was typified by the appearance of the Marles and Bishop steering boxes.

Although springs were, in the main, shackled by steel pins mounted in phosphor bronze bushes, 1926 saw the introduction of the oil-less Silentbloc rubber bush which was to attain great popularity in the following two decades, not only in spring eyes, but in shock absorber, and independent suspension systems.

Although practically all British cars were pushed along by their rear wheels, at the end of the 'twenties, Alvis produced Britain's first production front wheel drive car, although it only remained in production for two years.

1930 – 1940   One of the drawbacks of the traditional channel section chassis was its flexibility, even though the engine, by being bolted directly to the chassis, did provide some rigidity to the front of the car. However, the trend for rubber mounted engines, designed to eliminate transmission vibration (that appeared on some makes from the mid 'twenties) resulted in stiffer box section chassis in an attempt to compensate for this lack of support. Also, cruciform bracing began to appear half way down the chassis frame. This reinforcement became all the more important when independent front suspension began to appear on British cars. The first car to be so fitted (if one ignores the three-wheel Morgan which had sported sliding pillar IFS from 1910) was the Alvis Crested Eagle of 1933, though the first of the Big Six to go IFS were Vauxhall with a Dubonnet system fitted to their Light Six model of 1935. This allowed Luton to move the engine even further forward in the chassis, unhampered by that obtrusive beam. But by the outbreak of war, the aforementioned makes, together with Rolls-Royce (coils and wishbones since 1936), the larger Rootes cars and later Standards featured independent suspension at the front wheels. At the more exclusive end of the market, W. O. Bentley fitted his V-12 Lagonda of 1938 with Citroen inspired torsion bar indpendent front suspension (though Parry Thomas had used torsion bars on his Leyland Eight of 1920), interestingly all independent suspension was available on the Atalanta sports car from 1937. Apart from these (and other variations), the vast majority of cheap cars remained faithful to the conservative half elliptics all round.

The era saw greater inroads made by specialist component manufacturers, one sector of the market being steering gear, the Burman-Douglas worm and nut layout and the Marles cam and roller being typical of their day. At the other end of the car, rear axles changed remarkably little, though the adoption of the low mounted, quiet and efficient hypoid gearing began to appear on cars at the top end of the market around 1936. The American 'import' had first appeared on that country's Packard and Marmon cars in 1927, the use of the Gleason hypoid bevel permitted a lower floor, as it allowed the bevel centre to be dropped about $2^{1}/_{4}$ in. below the differential centre line.

But the really major departure of the 'thirties, as far as the manufacturer was concerned, came with the introduction of the monocoque body which eliminated the separate chassis. Although this had been a feature of the 11.1 hp Lagonda of 1911 for part of its production life, and had just been one of the outstanding technical features of the Lancia Lambda of 1922, it was when the mighty General Motors took up the idea, that the concept really gained momentum. Their own home built cars were too large to adapt to the process, so the system was first tried out on the corporation's German company, featuring on the Opel Olympia of 1935. It was, perhaps, inevitable that GM's British satellite, Vauxhall, should introduce the system on a large scale to this country, it first appearing on their 10/4 model for the 1938 season. Morris soon followed with his 10 hp the following year. while Rootes also changed to unitary construction with the Hillman Minx of 1940.

Although the more sporting fraternity remained loyal to friction shock absorbers, the system also being sophisticated by a telecontrol arrangement (whereby the driver could adjust his shock absorbers to suit the road conditions), hydraulic shock absorbers gained practically universal acceptance.

The front wheel drive Alvis had quietly faded from the market in 1930, but from 1932 BSA offered a four wheel version of their three wheel front wheel drive car, which appeared at the 1929 Motorcycle Show. The Birmingham company were the only British upholders of FWD during the 'thirties.

1945 – 1960   The use by Vauxhall of a monocoque body in 1938 had pointed the way to the elimination of the separate chassis, for all but the smallest of production runs. Although Ford soldiered on with the separate chassis until the Popular was phased out in 1959 (what an archaic car that was), the new Consul and Zephyr models of 1951 both had monocoque bodies. Even Longbridge finally got round to dispensing with a chassis with the Austin A30 of 1952, though the new Standard Eight which was announced in 1953 was the first departure for this arrangement at Canley. It was in the smaller, sporting market that the separate chassis lasted longest. MG did not abandon it until 1962, the MGA being the last model to leave Abingdon with a separate frame. Jaguar's first series production sports car to have a monocoque hull was the immortal E type of 1961, while Triumph remained faithful to the chassis for longer than most, the TR6, which remained in production until 1974 had a separate chassis frame, while the current Triumph Spitfire still retains one. The chassis frame is also an intrinsic part of glass fibre bodywork of which the Lotus Elite of 1959 was a pioneering example, though such firms as Singer and Jowett had experimented with the material in the early 'fifties.

The adoption by Citroen of front wheel drive and longitudinal torsion bar independent front suspension (and traverse bars at the rear) on their 7CV model of 1934 had a profound effect on the minds of British car designers, which was no doubt strengthened by Ferdinand Porsche's use of transverse torsion bars on his P Wagen Grand Prix Auto Union of the same year. In the early post-war era, Morris, Riley, Jowett and Jaguar all featured this Citroen inspired layout. Austin also got round to adopting IFS (coil spring and wishbone) on their A40 of 1947, Rootes following with the Hillman Minx of the the following year.

The increasing popularity of IFS led more manufacturers to fit the rack and pinion steering (which Citroen had also featured since 1936); namely Riley, Morris and later Jaguar. Nineteen fifty-one saw Ford adopt MacPherson strut IFS on their Zephyr and Consul models, the layout being particularly suitable for integral body construction in view of the load points being so widely spaced.

Although a live rear axle and semi elliptic springs remained (and still are) exceedingly popular, a few manufacturers offered alternatives at the rear. Mercedes-Benz had been responsible for reviving the de Dion axle on their GPW125 of 1937, which although not an independent system, did transfer the heavy and bulky differential unit from the car's unsprung to its sprung weight, thus aiding road holding. Aston Martin featured this popular racing feature on their sports racing DB3 of 1952, and it is no doubt worth noting that Rover adopted the layout on their much lauded 2000 model of 1964.

Nineteen fifty-nine saw all-independent suspension penetrating the cheaper end of the market with the appearance of Alec Issigonis's Mini Minor, probably the most significant British design since the Austin Seven. This front wheel drive car featured a revolutionary suspension system designed by Alex Moulton using rubber both in torsion and compression. Of more questionable advantage was the all independent system fitted to the Triumph Herald of the same year. Although it retained the old Standard Eight's IFS (Standard had acquired Triumph in 1945) it also featured swing axle suspension at the rear, and, as a matter of historical interest, a separate chassis until the model ceased production in 1971.

From 1945 onwards, shock absorbers continued to play an ever important role in the car's suspension system. In addition to the well established lever type shock absorber, the telescopic variety grew increasingly popular.

1960 – 1970 This decade saw no great innovation in chassis/suspension design, merely a development of the new ideas of the early post-war era.

Perhaps the greatest change was a qualitative one in the noticeable improvement in ride and steering accuracy brought about by the refinement of suspension systems and rack and pinion steering. The MacPherson strut IFS of Ford was adopted by many other manufacturers as a means of providing the necessary sophistication but at a reasonable price. Strangely, rear end treatment on many cars was modernized hardly at all, with the continued use of standard axle and 'cart' springs. There was, however, a rejuvenation of the popularity of torsion bar suspension, especially with some of the less expensive models from Continental manufacturers, and BMC dabbled for a short time in the mysteries of their 'hydrolastic' system.

A typical example of the independent front suspension to be found on many post-war British cars. This is an MG Midget

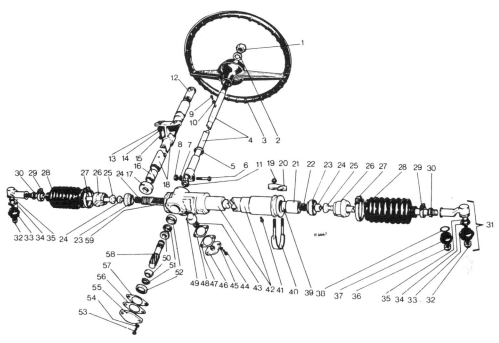

Rack and pinion steering assembly as fitted to a Mini. *Key* 1, Steering wheel nut; 2, Washer; 3, Steering wheel; 4, Column assembly; 5, Washer; 6, Clamp bolt; 7, Washer; 8, Nut; 9, Stud; 10, Locknut; 11, Oil seal; 12, Upper bearing; 13, Washer; 14, Washer; 15, Screw; 16, Lower bearing; 17, Washer; 18, Column tube; 19, Nut; 20, Clamp base; 21, Bush housing; 22, Thrust spring; 23, Locking ring; 24, Ball seat; 25, Tie-rod; 26, Ball bearing; 27, Clip; 28, Gaiter; 29, Clip; 30, Locknut; 31, Balljoint; 32, Nut; 33, Dust cover; 34, Circlip; 35, Washer; 36, Nut; 37, Dust cover; 38, Circlip; 39, Felt bush; 40, U-bolt; 41, Screws; 42, Rack housing; 43, Spring; 44, Bolt; 45, Washer; 46, Damper cover; 47, Shim; 48, Gasket; 49, Damper yoke; 50, Ball cone; 51, Ball cage; 52, Ball cup; 53, Bolt; 54, Washer; 55, End cover; 56, Shim; 57, Gasket; 58, Pinion; 59, Rack

A thoroughly modern set-up. This is the IRS of a Lotus Elan

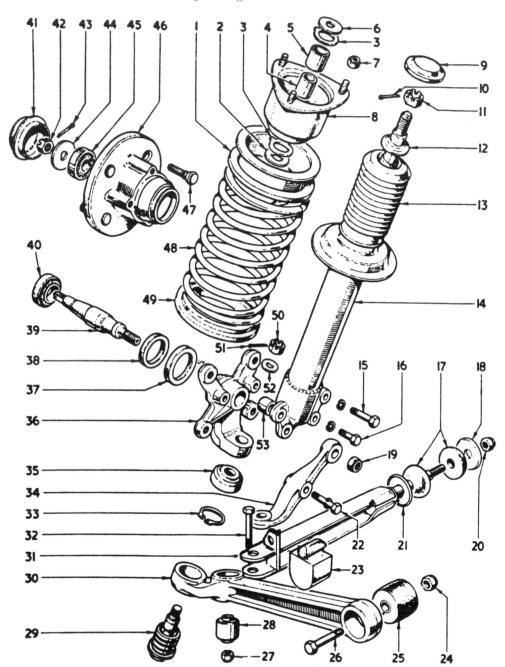

Typical McPherson strut IFS, from a Triumph Stag. *Key* 1, Top rubber insulator, front spring;
2, Washer; 3, Thrust washer; 4, Sleeve; 5, Bearing; 6, Washer; 7, Nyloc nut; 8, Rubber mounting
assembly, strut top; 9, Rubber grommet; 10, Split pin; 11, Slotted nut; 12, Retaining washer,
gaiter; 13, Gaiter; 14, Front damper strut; 15, Bolt; 16, Bolt; 17, Thrust rubber; 18, Thrust washer;
19, Nyloc nut; 20, Nyloc nut; 21, Thrust washer; 22, Bolt; 23, Bump rubber; 24, Nyloc nut;
25, Rubber bush; 26, Bolt; 27, Nyloc nut; 28, Rubber bush; 29, Balljoint assembly; 30, Suspension
arm; 31, Drag strut; 32, Bolt; 33, Circlip; 34, Steering arm; 35, Gaiter; 36, Vertical link; 37, Water
shield for hub seal; 38, Seal, grease; 39, Stub axle; 40, Inner bearing, hub; 41, Grease cap;
42, Slotted nut; 43, Split pin; 44, Washer; 45, Outer bearing, hub; 46, Hub; 47, Wheel stud;
48, Road spring; 49, Bottom rubber insulator, front spring; 50, Slotted nut; 51, Split pin;
52, Washer; 53, Spacer

Chapter Three

Brakes, wheels and tyres

Mountain Ranch,
Dec 3, 1914

Dear Allan,

Received your postal and also the pudding, believe me it was fine . . . We have all of the quail and tree squirrels we could eat, and I will try and send you some if I can only get them when we are going into town, we have to walk about 6 miles so don't get there more than once a week.

We are working on a ledge that runs through our place, that shows some very good prospects in places . . . we are in about 12 feet, and expect to hit the ledge in the next 6 or 8 ft. I found one pocket colour in a little ravine near the cabin, it was about 1 cent in value, but think there are more . . .

I am sending you some sketches of a hydraulic brake system I have figured out, and I believe it would sell easily to one of the companies that are advertising new features, like the Cadillac Co.

It would not only be a big feature to advertise, but would be a big advantage I think. You would not only have the advantage of the brakes on all four wheels, but they would equalise perfectly on acc' of the pressure always being the same on each wheel. . .

It must be about 12 o'clock and is raining hard, so I think I had better get to bed.

As ever,
Malcolm.

It was with these words that 28-year-old Malcolm Loughead, while prospecting for gold in the mountains of Calaveras County, California, informed his brother Allan (with whom he had built the first Lockheed aeroplanes) of his ideas on a hydraulic braking system for cars. (Two of the three Loughead brothers later changed to the phonetic spelling of their name, it first being adopted by the brake company, and then the aircraft one.) His invention was taken up in America after the First World War, Triumph being the first marque to fit hydraulic brakes as standard equipment in Britain, though mechanical actuation remained very popular during the inter-war years. By the 'fifties, however, hydraulics had completely taken over. This chapter, therefore is mainly concerned about the care and maintenance of mechanical brakes which do not 'equalise perfectly'; and hydraulic ones which do.

As far as overhauling a mechanical system goes, the main enemy is to compensate for the wear which will have taken place in its many pivots and joints. Obviously, the pedal is the best place to start, and if this is loose on its fulcrum, then rebush with phosphor bronze. From then on you will find you have got a system actuated by rods or cables, or a combination of the two. Obviously the cables are more vulnerable to wear because they stretch, but new ones can be made by Thomas Richfield and Son Ltd., of London W1. The other main areas for wear are on the fork ends (which apply to both rods and cables), levers and clevis pins. One way round the problem is to drill out the levers and fork ends and fit oversized pins. Often leather washers were used to

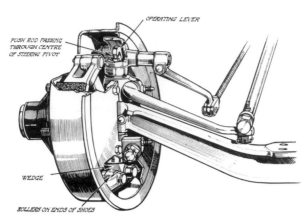

OPERATING LEVER

PUSH ROD PASSING
THROUGH CENTRE
OF STEERING PIVOT

WEDGE

ROLLERS ON ENDS OF SHOES

A typical front brake layout of the 'twenties, fitted to the
Austin 12 and 16

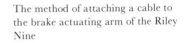

The method of attaching a cable to
the brake actuating arm of the Riley
Nine

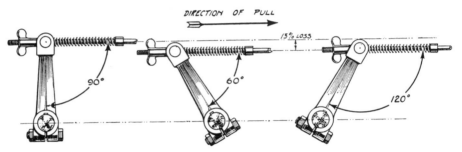

DIRECTION OF PULL

13% LOSS

90°

60°

120°

When actuated, a brake lever should be ideally in the position indicated in the drawing on the *left*,
compared with the position of maximum compromise (*centre*) and maximum permissible travel (*right*)

Three methods of terminating brake cables for attachment

A typical brake pulley shield to protect the cable and
prevent it from jumping out of the pulley groove

stiffen up these joints, and although you may find that the originals have long since rotted away, a local cobbler, or saddler, will be able to make up a fresh set, which really does improve the system. Any missing rods can usually be made up in your own workshop, providing you have got the original ends, though new ones are obtainable from the Complete Automobilist of Baston, Huntingdonshire. One of the main points to remember when setting up the system is to achieve the correct angles for the brake operating mechanism when it is at its 'at rest' position. Remember that all arms and levers must work *towards* their maximum point of leverage. Once they go over centre they loose practically all the leverage effect.

Hydraulic overhaul

If your car is fitted with hydraulic, or hydro-mechanical brakes, I would strongly advise that you give the entire system a thorough overhaul, however well the car appeared to stop on your test drive. Many parts of the system are vulnerable, particularly the pipes themselves which are often made of steel, which does, unfortunately, corrode. Beware if the pipes *look* alright, they can be badly rusted on the side adjacent to the bodywork, or chassis. You can replace this with $^{3}/_{16}$ Kunifer 10, which is made from an alloy of copper, with about 10 per cent nickel and other materials, being developed specifically to combat sea water corrosion! It is available in 25 ft. coils and is guaranteed to last the life of the car but you will need a flaring tool. The important thing to remember when fitting new hydraulic piping is to retain the clips securing the old tubing to the body; do not let it flap around. Also take great care to bend the new pipe over a curved surface when you come to reproduce any sharp turns in the system, it is absolutely vital to ensure that it is not kinked in any way. Hydraulic hoses are also vulnerable to perishing, the areas immediately adjoining the end fittings are the most suspect. These hoses are also very susceptible to exposure to sunlight, so if the car in which you are interested has stood for some years *sans* wings, then change the hoses as a matter of course.

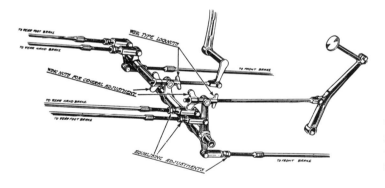

Thank goodness for hydraulics! The rod layout used on the Morris 11.9 and 14/28 hp cars

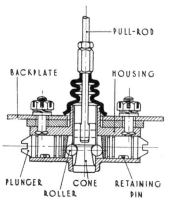

Girling shoe expander

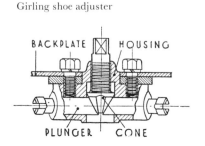

Girling shoe adjuster

Girling mechanical rear brakes. The expander on the left operates the handbrake, while the familiar adjuster is seen on the right

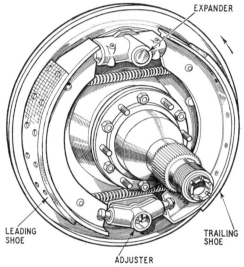

EXPANDER

LEADING SHOE

TRAILING SHOE

ADJUSTER

A pre-war Girling rod brake

Note just how clean this Morris Oxford brake back plate is. When the two streaks of paint are cleaned off all will be perfect

Hydraulic hoses are still readily available for most cars, but if you do have occasion to get new ones, make sure that you do not get them with metric threads, because they are being increasingly standardised. The parts are clearly marked, the steel fittings, such as union nuts, bleed screws and hose ends being coloured black and the parts also stamped M for metric. If you should be in any doubts, then gently try and screw the fitting home with your finger. It should either be impossible, or the joint will feel sloppy. This is particularly important with 10mm and $3/8$ UNF threads, which are very similar. The pipe end flaring also varies. Brake replacement parts generally come with the fitting holes blanked off with coloured plastic plugs, so the following refer specifically to metric sizes:-

Colour	Metric size
White	6
Dark green	8
Orange	10
Purple	12

You will probably require a UNF size, though, and the following plug colours relate specifically the Unified threads

Colour	UNF
Natural	$1/4$
Blue	$3/8$
Green	$7/16$
Pink	$1/2$

Check the wheel cylinder and clutch slave cylinder for any signs of leakage. Then dismantle the cylinders, examining for signs of corrosion or wear. If it is present, you will need a new cylinder, but if they appear intact, then fit new seals. The same applies to brake and clutch master cylinders.

But when working with hydraulic equipment it is absolutely vital that extreme cleanliness is observed. Wash your hands, and spread the parts out on a clean sheet of newspaper, in the kitchen, ideally. The importance of the cleanliness cannot be over-emphasised.

Brake and clutch hydraulic systems are manufactured in this country by Girling Ltd and Automotive Products Ltd., who produce the Lockheed system. As will be discovered in the Notes section at the end of this chapter, Lockheed brakes have been produced by AP in this country since the late 'twenties. Automotive Products hope to provide replacement parts, or recommend alternative replacements, that will give satisfactory performance for cars fitted with Lockheed brakes, particularly when the car is manufactured after 1930. But if you are after replacement Lockheed parts, first try the normal retail outlets. If you draw a blank there, then write to The Field Services Department, Automotive Products Ltd., Parts and Services Division, Southam Road, Banbury, Oxfordshire.

In the case of Girling brakes, try Burchnells (Peterborough) Ltd., of Carr Road Industrial Estate, Royce Road, Peterborough for old parts, or Girling Sales and Service Group, Birmingham Road, West Bromwich, West Midlands. Queries relating to Dunlop brake parts should be sent to this latter address.

A Girling master cylinder unit of the 'fifties

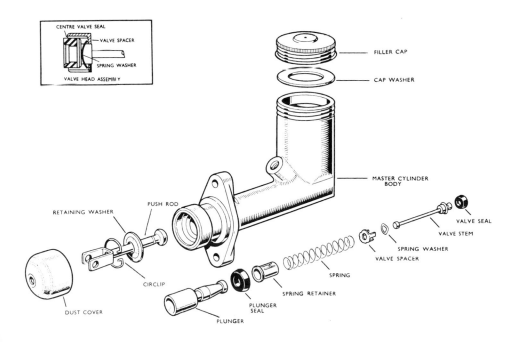

81

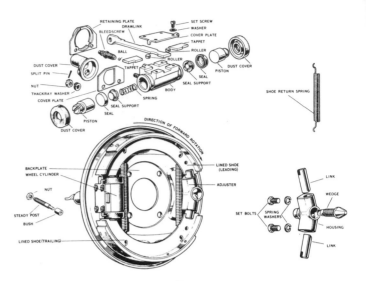

Girling hydraulic wedge
brake, system HW2

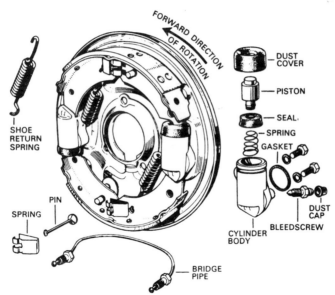

Girling leading shoe brakes,
type HLSS

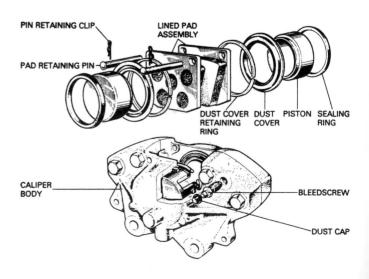

A typical Girling disc brake
layout

Servicing intervals

When you first buy your hydraulic braked old car it is a good idea to flush out immediately the system with new fluid, as you have no idea how long the old has been there. If, on the other hand, the car has been standing, or stored for any length of time, make a brake overhaul your number one priority, as the wheel cylinders are vulnerable to corrosion. But assuming that you are running the car regularly, then the following service intervals must be observed:-

Every 1000 miles: check the fluid level

Every 5000 miles: check the brake linings, or pads, if discs are fitted

Every 10,000 miles or 12 months, the hoses should be inspected for signs of leakage, chafing, or any other deterioration

Every 24,000 miles, or at 18 month intervals, the fluid should be changed

Every 40,000 miles, or the third lining change, all the rubber components, such as seals, gaiters and hoses, should be changed

Wheel cylinder corrosion caused by neglect. The rubber dust cover on this Dunlop disc brake wheel cylinder has been pulled back to reveal the rust and debris present

The business of bleeding

Bleeding is one of those jobs that will require assistance, though it need not be skilled help. Sit said accomplice in the driver's seat and sing out instruction when you are ready. Incidentally, you will need a clean jam jar, a spanner to release the bleed nipple and some new fluid. First pour the new fluid into the jam jar. This is done so no air can be drawn back into the system. Connect the tube up to the nipple, with the other end submerged in the jam jar and slacken the nipple off about half a turn. You usually start at the nipple the furthest away from the master cylinder, that is to say, the near side rear wheel, followed by the offside rear, nearside front and finally offside front. The complete routine will not be necessary if you have only replaced, say the wheel cylinder on one wheel, but should you flush out the entire system, then follow this procedure.

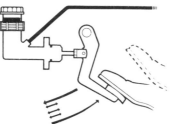

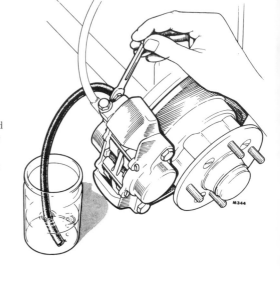

Bleeding Girling hydraulic brakes. The pedal should be pushed down through the full stroke, followed by three short rapid strokes and then the pedal should be allowed to return quickly to its stop with the foot right off. This should be repeated until the air is dispelled at each bleedscrew

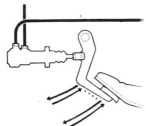

Bleeding a Lockheed disc brake

You are now ready to start. Give your assistant the word to start slowly pumping the appropriate pedal and this should be continued until there are no more bubbles emerging from the hose. (Funnily enough the hydraulic brake manufacturers differ on their pumping instructions. Girling recommend that the pedal should be pushed firmly to the floor, to be followed by three short rapid strokes, then moving the foot quickly away from the pedal, letting it spring back into position. By contrast, Lockheed suggest that the process should follow the more familiar pattern of press, hold and then release, for as long is is deemed necessary.) When carrying out the bleeding, make sure that the master cylinder reservoir does not run dry, or air will get into the system and you will have to start all over again. Then move on to the next nipple.

Now, a few words on the importance of changing the brake fluid at the prescribed intervals. The reason for this is that the fluid is hygroscopic, that is to say, it absorbs water from the atmosphere. If water builds up it means that the boiling temperature of the fluid may be lowered to a dangerous degree and if the fluid should boil when the brakes are applied, a failure could result. This is the main reason why you should not re-use old fluid, as it will already be contaminated. Should you be laying a car up for the winter, flush out the system with new fluid, also painting the brake adjuster and bleed nipples with the stuff, as it is a corrosion inhibitor. Do not let it get near the car's bodywork, for it is a very efficient paint stripper! It is worth pressing the pedal during the lay-up period to prevent corrosion getting a grip in the cylinders, and fill up with new fluid when you put the car back on the road.

Brake drums and shoes

Having dealt with the different types of brake actuation now let us consider what is common to both systems: brake drums and shoes. The chances are that the drums may be badly worn, or scored. If they are particularly worn, and you cannot obtain replacements, they can be built up with metal spray and then skimmed. Alternatively they may just require skimming, and if this is the case, then Brake and Engine Services (Brake Drums) Ltd., of London N15 can do this for you. But if there is evidence that this has been carried out previously, then the drums must be banded as well. If the brake shoe springs are looking tired then Quality Springs Ltd., of Redditch, Worcestershire can provide new ones. Check the condition of the brake shoes. On a Vintage car they will probably be made of aluminium.

When it comes to re-lining the shoes, Ferodo Ltd., of Chapel-en-le-Frith, Derbyshire can still provide new linings. The material they use for many pre-war cars is, in fact, their oldest product BA (Bonded Asbestos). Of course, it is not used just for elderly motor cars, as its main application is as a braking material on colliery winding gear, so you can reckon that as long as we have a coal industry, BA will be in plentiful supply! When ordering your new lining material, send Ferodo the old brake shoes (having first tried all the normal retail outlets). If for some reason this is not possible, then a working drawing will suffice. But remember that the really vital measurement is the thickness of the unworn material. If you do not know it, measure the diameter of the shoes in their 'off' position and then the drum's internal diameter (after skimming, if this has been done). Then halve the distance, and you have your figure. On more modern cars, these problems will not arise to the same extent, and even if the model is obsolete, then a current equivalent lining may suffice. Seek guidance from your club spares registrar. But if your do have occasion to approach Ferodo, specify whether your car is fitted with mechanical or hydraulic brakes, together with its year and model. Ferodo AM linings will probably feature on these later shoes.

Other areas for checking on mechanically operated drum brakes will be the brake cam bushes, which on Vintage cars are usually made from bronze and are therefore fairly straightforward to reproduce. If actuated by shafts, these can be built up with metal spray, or hard chroming. One of the most common mechanical brakes of the 'thirties was the Girling rod system, and I will now consider its maintenance and adjustment.

Disc brake pads should be regularly checked and replaced when the thickness of lining has worn to 0.125 in. (3 mm)

Girling mechanical brakes   One of the advantages of the system was that it transferred much of the adjustment to the brake unit itself, rather than the operating mechanism. This took the form of an adjuster mounted firmly on the back plate. A cone and plunger system was used, the cone having four flats on it which engaged with the inclined edge faces of the plungers. The spindle of the cone was threaded, and could be manipulated when a spanner was attached to the end which projected through the back plate. The shoes themselves were expanded by a loosely mounted expander in the form of a centrally mounted hardened steel cone, which when pulled inwards by the operating rod caused two plungers (which engaged directly on the brake shoe webs), to move the shoes outwards, so expanding the brakes.

To adjust these brakes, you must remember that the aforementioned adjuster should be turned clockwise to bring the linings into closer touch with the drum. To establish the correct setting, the cone should be screwed up until the linings make contact with the drums, and then slackened back two flats. The two clicks will be plainly felt, and heard. Make sure that you have a good spanner to fit the head of the adjuster though, and check that it is well-lubricated. This is the only adjustment necessary to compensate for the normal business of wear and tear, and it is important to remember to carry out this adjustment with the handbrake released. All the drums should be similarly treated, and the brake pedal then applied to centre the shoes on the drums.

Of course, you may be fitting new brake shoes all round. If this is the case, remove the drums and then rest a screwdriver against one of the two small studs (which will be found on the back plate at the expander end of the shoes). It should then be easy enough to prise off one or other of the shoes out of its groove on the expander plunger. The shoes and springs can then be removed. At this stage you can check the plungers in the expander unit by pulling the operating rod. Make certain that the double coil, spring washers are under the brass nuts which hold the expander unit in position, as it is important that this floats freely. Also unscrew the adjuster unit and thoroughly grease it.

When fitting the new shoes, make sure that the springs lie between the webs and the back-plate. You will notice that the shoe webs have half round slots in one end, and these must be fitted first to the adjuster plunger housing. Slip the other end of one shoe into the expander plunger groove. Then refit the drum. Screw up the adjuster nut, and slacken off two clicks as described earlier.

As far as the linkage system is concerned, the rods, which are all in tension, require very little maintenance. The exceptions are the compensators, fitted front and rear, which should be greased. It is also worth remembering that when the brake pedal is at rest, tension is maintained by a push tube and plunger joint. About $1/16$ in. should be left between the plunger and the joint when the brakes are in the 'off' position. This gap must be maintained, otherwise the shoe operating cones will be pulled off their seatings and the rods will rattle.

Girling hydraulic brakes   If you are merely checking the state of the linings, do not allow them to wear down to the rivet heads, or where bonded linings are fitted below $1/16$ in. from the metal shoe. Make a point of checking the position of the shoe return springs. As far as adjusting the front brakes are concerned, the procedure is straightforward. The method is to turn the adjuster head until the shoe or shoes are hard against the drum. Then simply 'click back' until the wheel spins freely. There are two snail cam adjusters, one for each shoe. Turn one adjuster, as mentioned previously, then the other, and the correct clearance will have been achieved. The rear brakes are rather different as there may only be one adjuster for both shoes. Again the same principles apply. It is worth remembering, though, that it is a waste of time tampering with the handbrake cables in an effort to adjust the brakes.

Should you wish to fit new linings, first remove the old ones and clean the backplate, and it is advisable to slip an elastic band over the wheel cylinders to prevent them popping out. Examine the cylinders for any evidence of leaking and for freedom of movement. Also check the adjuster(s) and turn anti-clockwise to the fully retracted position. Remember that new pull-off springs should always be fitted with new shoes. Attach the springs to the shoes, making sure that they are positioned between the shoe webs and the back plate, position one shoe in its correct abutment, then levering the other into place.

Girling disc brakes   Obviously the condition of the discs is a vital factor in the efficient functioning of the brake. It should not run out of true between the pads, the maximum allowed being 0.004 in. If the run-out exceeds this, then pedal flutter will be experienced. Although scratches and light scoring are permissible, any deep furrowing will adversely effect the working of the brake. If it proves impossible to replace a badly worn disc, it is possible to have the original re-ground, but do check with the experts that this can be done in the case of your particular model. A competent engineering company can do the work, the disc being rotary ground with a vertically mounted grinding wheel, traversing the horizontal disc. Both sides should be ground equally, but the thickness of the disc should not, in any circumstances, be reduced to below 0.050 in. of the original thickness.

When fitted, the disc must run equidistant between the caliper cylinders and this should be checked with a feeler gauge between the pad abutment and the disc face. The gap on the opposite sides may differ by 0.101 in., but there should be no difference between the gaps at the two abutments on the same side. New pads should be fitted when the lining has worn to 1/8 in. To do this, first clean the exterior of the caliper, noting the position of any damping shims or anti-rattle springs. Now pull out the clips and remove the pad retaining springs. If the clips are worn, new ones should be fitted on re-assembly. You will probably find that the pads are retained by a plate, so unscrew the bolt and swing the plate round. Now remove the shims and worn pads, using pliers if necessary. Check that the piston dust covers are in good condition and examine the pistons for signs of corrosion. Also examine the disc itself, and if there is evidence of wear on one side only, then one of the pistons has seized. If this is the case, a new disc and caliper unit should be fitted. But if all is well, remove any rust that may have built up on the surface of the disc. An old screwdriver, or scraper, supported in the caliper, with the blade abutting the rotating disc should remove most of the corrosion. Finish off with emery paper.

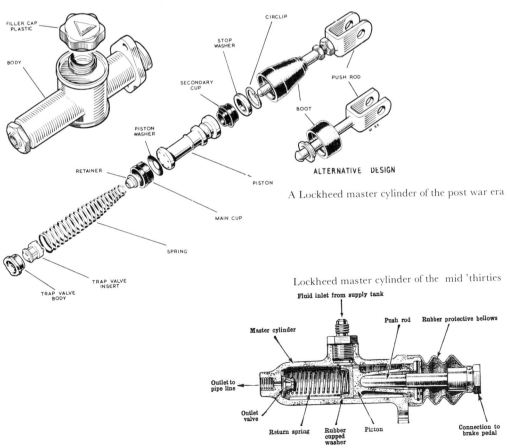

A Lockheed master cylinder of the post war era

Lockheed master cylinder of the mid 'thirties

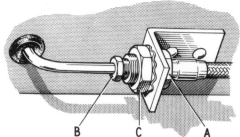

The all-important joint between the brake pipe and flexible hose, a Lockheed system is shown here. To dismantle, unscrew tube nut B. Holding hexagon A, to prevent the hose twisting, unscrew locknut C. Remove the lockwasher and extract the hose from bracket. When re-fitting with replacement hose, use a new copper washer. It is vital that the new hose is not twisted or kinked in any way

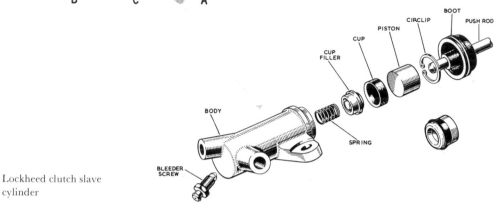

Lockheed clutch slave cylinder

When you come to fit the new pads, open the bleed screw one full turn to prevent fluid pressure building up when the pistons are pushed back. Remember that some calipers have more than one bleed screw, and if this is the case, it should also be opened one turn. Ideally, using a Girling Piston Retracting Tool, slowly and evenly, press each piston back in its cylinder. Then tighten the bleed screws. If damping shims are fitted, these should be replaced and the new shim kit will contain a sachet of Squeal Deterrent Grease. Smear this special grease on both sides of the new shims and on the backplates of the new pads, though ensure that no grease gets on to the pad linings. Now insert the new pads, and if necessary the new shims. Fit the pad retaining pins and secure with hairpin clips. Repeat the procedure with the caliper on the opposite wheel and then pump the brake pedal to move the piston pads up to the discs. Bleeding should not be necessary, but top up the master cylinder.

It is rather more involved if new seals have to be fitted, and to do this you would be best advised to remove the caliper from the car. Drain the fluid, and disconnect the hydraulic hose at the point it joins the bundy tubing, and then undo the bolts securing the caliper to the stub axle. Take out the pads, as described, and check whether the dust covers are retained by rings. Pack a piece of rag between the pistons and eject them, ideally by applying compressed air to the inlet connection. The sealing rings may be removed from the cylinders, but make sure that you do not damage the bore or locating groove. Check the condition of the bores and if they show signs of scoring or corrosion, then a new caliper is the only answer. Clean all parts in brake fluid and fit new pistons or rings, as necessary. Also ensure that the dust covers are correctly fitted and replace pads, retaining pins and clips.

Lockheed pre-war hydraulic brakes Apart from the overhaul procedure described at the opening of this chapter, check that the brake pedal has about $1/2$ in. of free movement before resistance is felt. To adjust the brakes, the two adjusting nuts on the brake backplates should be turned outwards (that is away from the axle) until the shoes make contact with the drum and then backed off until the wheel spins freely. This adjustment is, incidentally, self locking.

Removal of the brake lining on the front wheels is straightforward enough, it only being necessary to remove the split pins and washers from the guide pins passing through the brakeshoe webs. The task is a little more complicated on the rear wheels, as the wheel cylinder assembly has to be disconnected to remove the shoes, or alternatively, the wheel bearing.

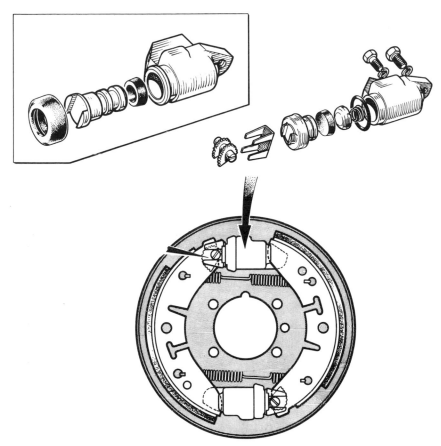

Two leading shoe Lockheed hydraulic brake unit of the post war era

To dismantle this Lockheed wheel cylinder, disengage the rubber boots from the cylinder body. Then pull each piston out of its bore and remove the rubber seal, taking care not to burr the metal, especially the seal groove

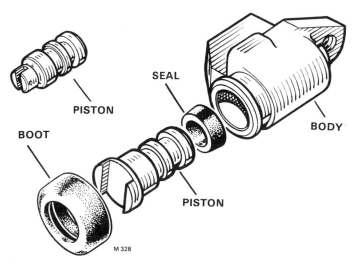

BOOT

PISTON

SEAL

PISTON

BODY

M 328

89

Lockheed post-war hydraulic brakes   This initially refers to twin leading shoe front brakes. After removing the drums, the first priority is to carefully record the correct spring/shoe layout, particularly the position of the top spring which secures the piston to the leading edge of the shoe. They are there to prevent any over retraction of the pistons and consequential risk of any excessive pedal travel. However, this precaution will not be necessary where Micram or wheel type adjusters are fitted. As with leading/trailing shoe units, the linings are not symmetrically fitted in relation to the shoe platforms.

But to continue with the dismantling. Disengage the tie springs from the tips of the pistons. And where steady springs are used, these will also have to be removed. This having been done, one of the springs is levered against the pull-off spring to allow its trailing end to be disengaged from the slotted abutment on the slave cylinder body. This is repeated on the other side, after which the springs are unhooked and the shoes freed from the pistons and the eccentric pegs of the eccentric pin adjusters. Then place elastic bands around the wheel cylinders to prevent them popping out. Carefully clean all metal to metal contact points and lubricate with Rubberlube on the shoe tips and Expander Lubricant elsewhere, both applied sparingly and well clear of the braking surfaces.

Re-assembly is very much a matter of reversing the dismantling procedure. Both expanders should be fully backed off, and the shoes centralised by eye before fitting the drum. With the drum in place the adjusters should be rotated clockwise (viewed from the inboard side of the back plate) until the assembly is locked. Then back off the minimum necessary for free rotation. Depress the pedal, a number of times to centralise the shoes and check the adjustment. If Micram adjusters are fitted, there are no tie springs to worry about. But if the brakes are fitted with these adjusters, check that the recessed ends of the shoes (those adjacent to the exposed parts of the platform) engage with the Micram adjusters and that the flat ends of the adjuster masks are positioned within the projections on the piston dust covers.

To overhaul the wheel cylinders (and this should only be done if the bores are in perfect condition), first uncouple the brake hose and remove the transfer pipe, and the set bolts. You will find a gasket is fitted between the cylinders and the back plate and this should not be re-used. In the case of cylinders using a ring type seal, the rubber boots are disengaged from the cylinder bodies, and the pistons, complete with boots, withdrawn. Remove the old seals and when fitting new ones, *ensure that they are fitted with the lips away from the slotted ends of the pistons.* Great care must be taken not to bend back, or damage, the lips.

Where a full base seal is featured, the piston/dust cover is withdrawn and the sealing ring retrieved. Next apply a low pressure air line to one of the fluid ports, covering the other with your finger. This will eject the cup or seal, after which the cup filler spring can be removed. When reassembling, the spring and cup filler are the first items to be fitted . Check that the small diameter of the spring engages the groove in the cup filler. The next step is to ease the seal, after soaking it in fluid, down the bore, lip leading, until it touches the filler. Again, you must take great care not to damage the edge. The sealing ring is then located on the cylinder spigot near the mouth of the bore. The next step is to coat the dust cover and the outer part of the piston with Rubberlube, after which the piston is introduced into the bore and finally pushed home. Check that the sealing ring enters the dust cover without suffering damage.

The following instructions apply to the cylinders on rear brakes, where the cylinder must be free to slide. With the single acting type, disconnect the handbrake rod or cable from the lever projecting through the back plate, unscrewing the pipe nut spring, and pipe, away from the cylinder. Then tap the retaining plate from the neck of the cylinder, easing it over the raised ends of the spring plate. Work the lever pivot from underneath (the removal of the retaining plate will allow sufficient clearance) and push it through the dust cover to the backplate. Remove the dust cover and slide the spring plate from the neck of the cylinder and remove the cylinder from the back plate. With the cylinder removed from the back plate, take off the rubber band, you, of course, remember to place there, and remove the dust cover. Extract all the internal parts and reassemble.

Changing the pads and overhauling a Lockheed disc brake light duty caliper   The brake pads should be changed when the friction material is less than about $1/8$ in. thick. They are retained by two split pins and a spring steel retainer, so once the wheels are removed, the ends of

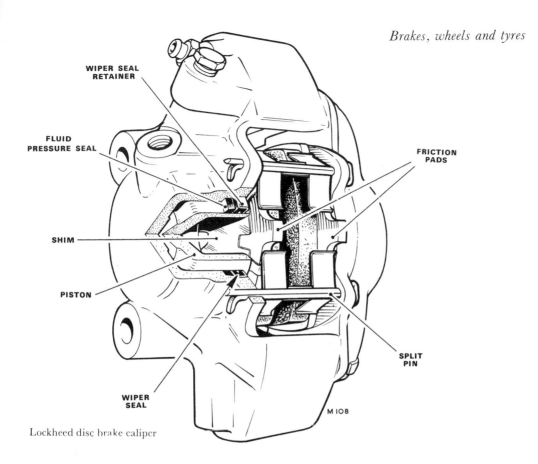

WIPER SEAL
RETAINER

FLUID
PRESSURE SEAL

FRICTION
PADS

SHIM

PISTON

SPLIT
PIN

WIPER
SEAL

M 108

Lockheed disc brake caliper

the split pins should be straightened so that they can pass through the holes in the calipers. The spring retainer is then depressed and the springs withdrawn. The retainer is removed, so exposing the pads.

It is quite likely that corrosion, or a build up of dust is stubbornly holding the pad in the caliper, so if it does display some reluctance it should be levered sideways and then backwards and forwards. Then with a pair of pliers, firmly attached to the lug on the pad, it should be possible to withdraw it without too much difficulty. You may find a shim between the pad and the piston. It is designed to eliminate brake squeal and its position, in relation to the pad should be noted.

Before fitting the new pads, check the condition of the discs and pistons. Any build up of rust on the faces of the disc should be removed, even if it appears outside the path of the pad. If there is any sign of leakage, then the caliper will have to be removed, of which more anon. If all appears well, clean the piston using a non-fluffy cloth and hydraulic fluid, taking care to make sure that the area immediately surrounding it is free from rust. Then push the piston back into its housing using a screwdriver, taking care that the piston remains square in its bore. To reduce the effort, the caliper bleed screw should be opened, though do not forget to close it after the job has been completed. However, if all is functioning well by this time, smear the back of the pads with Lockheed disc brake lubricant. Fit new pads and new retainers and split pins. You are then back in business.

But if you find that the seals are leaking, then the caliper must be removed from the car. Remember, though, that the two halves of the caliper must not be separated. There is nothing to be gained from the exercise, and there is always the risk of mis-aligning the two halves and damaging the internal seals. To take off the caliper, remove the two securing bolts, which are usually locked by a tab washer. At this stage, do *not* disconnect the hydraulic hose, so the caliper should be supported. Clean the exterior of the caliper. Having done this, one of the pistons should be held back with a clamp. Then depress the brake pedal and the opposite piston should pop out.

91

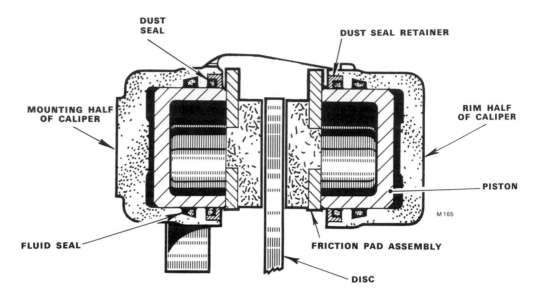

Section through caliper

Repeat, and the other piston should eject. The wiper seal retainer should then be removed, a screwdriver being inserted between the retainer and the seal, taking care not to damage the seal.

Once these parts have been removed, the piston bore and seal grooves should be cleaned with *new* brake fluid. If the pistons and bores are in perfect condition, new seals can be fitted, but if there is evidence of pitting or any other type of surface damage, then a new caliper will be required. Before the pressure seal is inserted, it should be coated with Lockheed disc brake lubricant, and then fitted by hand. The cross section of the seal differs from that of the groove, so that when the seal is correctly seated, the edge farthest from the mouth of the bore should feel proud.

The next operation is to slacken the bleed screws and insert the pistons; the wiper seal is inserted later. The pistons should be liberally coated with Lockheed Brake Seal Lubricant and squarely inserted. It should be pushed smoothly in with the relieved portion of the rim in the correct position. The piston should be left with its rim just proud of the face of the caliper. Now comes the business of the wiper seal. This again should be coated with disc brake lubricant and fitted in its retainer. The assembly is then slid squarely with the seal side first into the counterbore in the caliper. The seal and its retainer should then be pushed right home and the bleed screw tightened. The operation should then be repeated with the other piston. The whole unit can then be re-mounted on the hub carrier and the pads and shim inserted. Reconnect the brake pipe, and as the seals are completely new, use new fluid throughout. Then bleed the system. Check that there are no leaks, top up the fluid level, and you are in business.

Here is a final tip to remember when you are working on hydraulics. When you disconnect any of the aforementioned slave cylinders, and, for example have just fitted fresh brake fluid, and do not want to loose it all again, place a piece of polythene under the cover of the master cylinder, and screw it back into place. Consequently when you come to disconnect the hydraulic pipe, you will hardly loose any fluid. But when everything is reconnected, do not forget to remove that useful piece of plastic.

Wheels and tyres

When it comes to their restoration, artillery wheels are by far the most straightforward to cope with. Make a point of checking the wheels for deep pitting, and if this is particularly bad, get rid of them. In my experience, artillery wheels never seem to be in particularly short supply, but obviously this situation cannot go on forever. Shot blasting is the best way to clean these wheels, followed by stove enamelling. The same goes for wire wheels, though some years ago a friend of mine sent his wheels away for this treatment and was handed back a set of rims and hubs when he went to collect them. In other words, check that the spokes are not badly rusted. Motor Wheel Services and Repair Co., of London W12 can re-spoke wire wheels, and after you have had the job done, the firm advises that you return six months, or 6000 miles, later to have them tightened; rather like torquing down a cylinder head after a decoke. Again, stove enamelling is a practical finish for wire wheels and though chrome looks impressive it is less kind to the spokes. They are much admired, of course, usually by people who do not have to clean them!

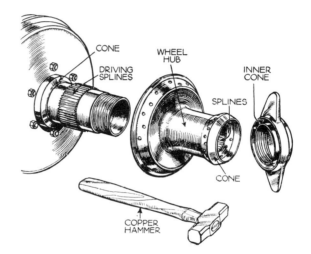

Layout of the centrelock wheel hub. The thread is cut left or right handed, according to the position of the hub. Thus the cap tends to tighten, aided by the coned surface

The Dunlop centre lockhub, a feature on Rolls-Royce cars for many years. The car is a 1932 20/25

If you've any doubts about their condition, get your spoked wheels re-laced. The illustration shows this being done at the Motor Wheel Service and Repair Co., of London W12

Tyres are your next consideration. Fortunately we have Dunlop to thank for manufacturing still, a variety of otherwise obsolete beaded edge and wellbase covers. These are available through Vintage Tyre Supplies Ltd., of London NW10. If you are fitting new tyres to wire wheels then you should protect the tubes from the heads of the spokes with Polyvil PP10 tape which is also available from the same company.

If you are contemplating some reasonably brisk motoring, then it is worth having your wheels balanced, but remember that the job will have to be repeated once the tyres are changed.

Notes on development

1919 – 1929   The Vintage era opened with the vast majority of cars being fitted with rear wheel brakes only, although the Scottish make of Argyll had used Rubury front wheel brakes since 1911. It was not long, however, before front wheel brakes began to appear on most cars from about 1924, and this resulted in the forward end of the chassis frame being stiffened up to cope with the brake torque reaction. Of course, the perky little Austin Seven had sported four wheel brakes (in theory, at least) since 1922. Practically all brakes were on the internal expanding variety, the cruder external type being mainly confined to American imports. (The Model T Ford, which was a law unto itself in many respects, was never fitted with front wheel brakes, despite the fact that it was made right up until 1927.)

Many manufacturers made their own braking systems with varying degrees of success. Austin was one, but the brakes on these Longbridge-built cars were never particularly satisfactory until Girling brakes were fitted in the mid-thirties. By contrast, William Morris over at Cowley, favoured a Rubury system made by Alford and Alder on his 'Bullnose', a reminder that Britain's best selling cars of the 'twenties was an assemblage of skilfully chosen component parts, while Austin endeavoured to make as much as possible himself.

Hydraulic brakes had featured on the Duesenberg and Bugatti racing cars of 1921 and 1922 respectively, and in one case they were hydraulic in every sense of the word, water being employed as the fluid.

We have seen how Malcolm Loughead thought up his ideas for a four wheel hydraulic brake system back in 1914 and after the war, in 1919, the Four Wheel Hydraulic Brake Company was founded in California to develop and exploit Loughead's invention, although it was initially offered as an accessory, as most cars at the time were only fitted with two wheel brakes. In 1923 the company moved its sales department to Detroit, the centre of America's automotive industry, and in 1924 it was decided to transfer the manufacture of the brakes to the Wagner Electric Corporation, though manufacturing licenses were also sold to smaller car producers and axle makers. At this stage an external contracting layout was used, though some intensive development work by Loughead himself and his assistant E. K. Loweke, with active co-operation from Chrysler engineers, saw the creation of the hydraulic drum brake, much as we know it today.

It was while he was in America that Willie Emmott, of a small British company with the somewhat generic title of Automotive Products, noticed the braking efficiency of the Chryslers which pulled up so squarely on Detroit's icy roads. An enquiry revealed that the cars were fitted with the Hydraulic Brake Company's brake (the archaic 'Four Wheel' prefix having been dropped earlier). A five month long wrangle followed, but the outcome was a sensational one for Automotive Products, because they acquired the manufacturing rights of the Lockheed Hydraulic Brake for the whole world, outside the United States. It was a shrewd move because three years later AP would have been too late. For in 1930, Bendix Aviation purchased the Hydraulic Brake Company, and they were then in the invidious position of having to deal with a competitor of their British subsidiary, Bendix Brakes. The only trouble was that Bendix produced an inferior mechanical brake, and the introduction by Automotive Products of the hydraulic brake into Britain hastened its decline.

Automotive Products announced the 'New Improved Lockheed Hydraulic System' in 1927 and two years later William Morris endorsed the concept by fitting his export Wolseley (he had bought the company in 1927), with hydraulic brakes, next to the Morris Isis, and then proceeded to incorporate them through his range. (I recall a leading light in AP telling me of the hectic, behind the scenes goings on, for an early public viewing of a hydraulic braked Morris product. These early components were made in America, and all reference to the country of origin, namely 'made in the USA' were carefully filed off, in view of WRM's 'Buy British sentiments'.)

The detachable steel artillery wheel (so called for its use on gun carriages) shod with a high pressure beaded edge tyre, featured on most mass produced cars after the First World War. A wooden version had first appeared back in 1830 by William Hancock for use on one of his steam carriages, though Joseph Sankey was responsible for introducing a steel version in 1908. However, wire wheels were favoured by more expensive and sporting machinery, often in conjunction with a Rudge Whitworth hub, though the use of wires on the Austin Seven is a reminder that there is an exception to every rule. Low pressure tyres and the well based rim appeared around 1924. By the end of the 'twenties the artillery wheel's popularity began to wain, wires taking their place. Medium sized cars were fitted with 19 in. rims, while 20 and 21 in. covers were favoured by larger vehicles.

1930 – 1940 The adoption of hydraulic brakes by William Morris put his cars streets ahead of his rivals, at least in the stopping department. Then in 1932, A. H. G. Girling began the manufacture of his 'rod in tension' system, a far more efficient rod brake which transferred primary adjustment away from the rods themselves, onto the brake back plate. Riley was one of the first manufacturers to fit this new system and Rover, Austin and Ford soon followed. These Girling brakes were manufactured by the New Hudson Cycle Company of Birmingham until 1943 when it was taken over by the electrical manufacturing giant, Lucas, who also acquired Bendix.

Wheels were getting smaller, with wire predominating until 1937 when the cheap pressed steel wheel from America swept the board of Britain's mass produced cars, 17 in. rims being fitted to many of the smaller horse power models by the end of the decade.

1945 – 1960 The introduction of independent front suspension to cars during the 'thirties was the spur that caused Girling to re-think their rod system. For the independent movement of the front wheels favoured the hydraulic braking layout with its flexible hoses. In 1944, therefore, Girling announced their Hydro-Mechanical system, an arrangement retaining rods at the rear, with hydraulics at the front.

The post-war era also saw the increasing use of the more efficient twin leading shoes, rather than the leading and trailing fitted hitherto. This was achieved by operating each shoe independently of the other with separate hydraulic cylinders. But this layout also led to the development of the twin trailing shoe because the more efficient leading shoes generated a considerable amount of heat, which resulted in brake fade. Trouble was, trailing shoes required more pedal pressure, so they were generally fitted in conjunction with servo assistance. The use of a servo, either mechanical or vacuum, was by no means a new phenomenon. From 1924 Rolls-Royce fitted a mechanical servo driven off the car's gearbox to the Silver Ghost. Although this assistance was only initially applied to the front brakes of this model, it was subsequently applied to all the brakes on later cars. The system was developed from one originally fitted to Marc Birkigt's Hispano-Suiza of 1919, and to whom Rolls-Royce paid a licensing fee. The Clayton-Dewandre vacuum servo was fitted to a number of cars in the 'twenties and 'thirties, but this fairly bulky unit was mounted beneath the vehicle's floorboards. The post-war era saw the development of the more compact vacuum servo, which could be fitted under the car's bonnet.

However, the major braking development of the 'fifties came with the adoption of disc brakes on production cars. These brakes were initially produced by three manufacturers in Britain: Dunlop, Girling and Lockheed. Dunlop crops up in this context because their brakes were a development of their successful aircraft discs. The layouts varied in some degree. Dunlop used three round friction pads each side of the disc to arrest its progress, while Girling built their brakes under Dunlop patents, but incorporating their own Hydrostatic system, resulting in the pads being in rubbing contact with the disc. By contrast Lockheed (who had produced disc brakes for George Eyston's Land Speed Record car, Thunderbolt, back in 1937) favoured segment shaped pads. Many variations are to be found on racing cars of the early 'fifties, namely BRM, Vanwall Specials and Lotus sports racers, discs also appearing on the Jaguar XK 120Cs of 1952 and 1953. These discs were introduced to cope with the problems of brake fade experienced with ever more powerful engines, full width bodywork and the adopting of disc wheels in the place of wires, all of which had the effect of reducing the circulation of cooling air.

Although the Austin Healey 100S of 1955 was fitted with disc brakes as standard equipment, it was, in fact, a sports racer, and the laurels are usually given to the TR3 of 1957 as being the first British production car to be fitted with discs, with the Jensen 541 as a very close second, both of which appeared at the 1956 Motor Show so adorned. Jaguar followed with disc brakes on their XK 150 of 1957, while they appeared on a production MG for the first time; the MGA Twin Cam, of 1958.

At the end of the war 16 in. wheels were normal for medium size cars. Then came the Issigonis designed Morris Minor which appeared at the 1948 Motor Show sporting 14 in. rims. Other manufacturers gradually followed suit, with an increasing number of companies fitting 13 in. covers by the end of the decade. Issigonis again took the initiative by specifying 10 in. tyres for his Mini Minor of 1959. The 'fifties saw the re-invention by Dunlop of the tubeless tyre in 1953 and the appearance of the radial ply tyre, the Michelin X, marketed in the same year.

1960 – 1970 The rapid rise in traffic density and the greater speeds allowed by the improving road network, dictated that, in concert with the suspension, brake performance had to be improved for safety's sake. Thus, the use of disc brakes became more widespread, as did servo-actuating mechanisms.

The radial-ply tyre, having demonstrated its impressively low wear rate and sure-footedness, became almost universal as original equipment on all but some very heavy, luxury sporting and touring cars.

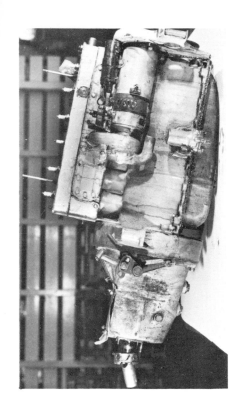

Both sides of a worn Morris Oxford 15 hp engine just as it was when removed from the car. Previous to this overhaul the engine had never left the car

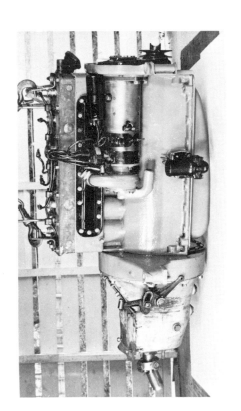

The 1930 six cylinder side valve Morris Oxford engine after rebuilding. Note that the starter motor still has to be added

The Morris Eight Series E engine, as fitted to the Minor from 1948 until 1952. Note that the block and electrical components are all painted (4/1)

Chapter Four

The engine, clutch and gearbox

Things must be kept clean, very clean **Ettore Bugatti**

As the engine is the most complex mechanical item on the car, you should consider your plan of campaign carefully, as far as its restoration is concerned. If the car you have bought is a runner, then you will be able to get a fairly good idea of its condition. Perhaps the best indication is the rate at which the engine consumes oil. But you have first to ascertain whether it is burning it, or if it is simply leaking out of a bad joint. To discover whether lubrication is actually being burnt, check for blue smoke at the exhaust pipe. To do this, first see that the sump is filled to the correct level. Then go for a short run, at around 30 to 40 miles per hour, and get a friend to tell you whether blue smoke is coming out of the pipe. He can either be following behind you, or be placed at a strategic point at the side of the road. To make absolutely sure, allow the engine to idle for around five to ten minutes, and then rev up. If you get an unhealthy blast of smoke you will know that there is oil in the combustion chambers. From this you know, at least, that a recondition is your first priority. Loss of power and high petrol consumption are also associated with high oil consumption.

However, if you find that the engine is not burning oil, but is still consuming it at an unhealthy rate, the alternative is that it is leaking from some point on the engine. If you think that this is the trouble, first thoroughly clean the engine with paraffin or Gunk, taking particular care with the suspect areas around the rocker or cam box, timing chain cover, oil pipes and sump gasket. Then go for a drive, rather longer than the proverbial run around the block, making sure to get up to the usual running temperature. On returning to your garage, place the front of the car over a clean white sheet or white paper, and the leaks will soon show their location. If you have still got any doubts, leave the engine running for 15 minutes. Be certain that the sump is topped up to its correct level for this test, as the fault may only make itself apparent when it is full.

By this time, you will be in little doubt as to whether your engine needs reconditioning, or not. If it does, then the following guide-lines will be of help, but every engine has its own peculiarities, and you would be advised to talk to someone who has already done the job, who can point out any pitfalls. There is always something that is a bit tricky! You will find the engine and gearbox removal details in Chapter Two.

Rebuilding an engine

Remove the cylinder head. This may be a lot more difficult than it sounds. If the nuts are badly rusted, then give them a good soaking with Plus-Gas a good 24 hours before you start the assault. Also, if the engine has been running, and you expect trouble ahead, remove all the nuts with the engine in the chassis, then give it a blib on the starter. The compression may be enough to move it.

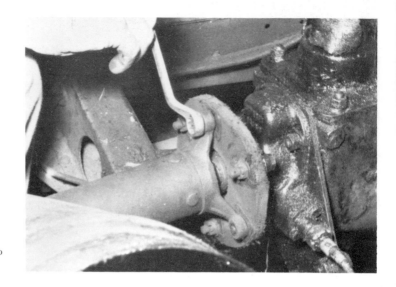

Before disconnecting the
propellor shaft, mark it to
aid re-assembly

A Mark V Jaguar engine
being removed from the
car. The correct angle of tilt
is important. The hoist was
hired, a vital aid

The Mark V engine after reconditioning. Note the length of the engine/gearbox unit. On occasions the components can be fitted separately

Many engines built in the 'twenties featured a separate crankcase/block layout. This is well exemplified in the Austin Seven engine

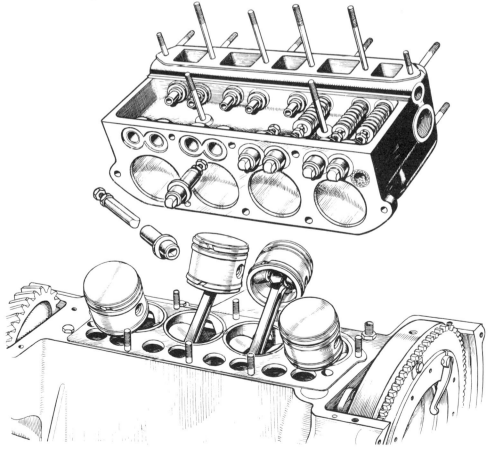

You may have a tussle if you have an engine with a cast iron block fitted with an aluminium cylinder head, secured by long, high tensile steel studs and bolts. There may well be bi-metallic corrosion between the studs and the head, caused by the high chromium content of the studs. You have been warned. . .

If the engine is fitted with a chain driven overhead camshaft, check the chains, gears or bevels for markings. Normally they are intended to coincide when number one piston, (nearest the radiator), is at Top Dead Centre of its compression stroke. This means that both valves will be closed and the distributor rotor adjacent to number one segment. When you come to examine the chain, you should find a connecting link in the form of a detachable side plate with a spring fastener. Usually this coincides with a marked tooth on the camshaft sprocket. If, however, the investigation reveals no such clips, then you can generally remove the sprocket from the camshaft.

When you have taken the head off, leave it intact if its an overhead camshaft or overhead valve type. There is no point in taking everything apart in the first instance. In this way you avoid loosing vital parts. And make a point of putting the cylinder head gasket in a safe place, it may be needed for a pattern. Then remove the flywheel, marking its position on the crankshaft flange. You may need a puller!

Now the pistons can come out. Invert the engine in its stand, having, of course, re-membered to drain the oil(!) and take off the sump. Then undo the big end bolts. You may find that the pistons, complete with rods come out of the top of the bore, though with other varieties, you have to push the pistons out of the bores until the gudgeon pins are exposed and remove the pins, so that the pistons can continue on their upward journey, while the conrods come out at the bottom. As soon as you have the pistons and rods out, reunite them, clean them off with paraffin and label them by number, and, if necessary, which way round they are fitted. Once they are dry, mark them with paint as labels have a habit of becoming detached. These variations are only necessary if the block and crankcase are cast in one piece.

Many pre-war engines are in two distinct parts, which is an advantage when it comes to restoration. First there is the crankcase, usually of aluminium, and on top of that is bolted a cast iron block, and finally, when detachable, the head. Thus it can be seen if the block and crankcase are damaged in some way, a replacement can be affected without having to scrap the entire engine. To remove the pistons and rods with this construction, disconnect the big end caps, unbolt the block, and lift it off, complete with pistons, immediately replacing the caps to their respective rods, the right way round.

The inverted tooth chain, found in many engines built in the 'twenties, and virtually impossible to replace today. The answer is to fit a roller chain in its place

Note the markings on both the cleaned piston head and the cylinder block

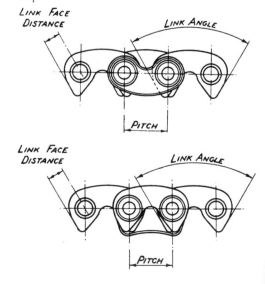

Wet liners have the advantage of being easily removable from the block. These are from a Triumph Renown

It is possible to have engine parts made on a one-off basis. These components (the tappets are for a Riley Nine) were produced by Leonard Reece and Co Ltd., of Carshalton, Surrey

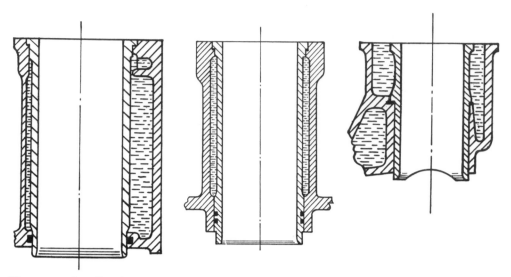

Three types of wet liner found in post war engines

Before dismantling the crankshaft assembly make a check of the position of the timing gears or the timing chain. If you are in the slightest doubt about the positioning of the components, photograph or draw their respective positions. When you come to 'break' an inverted tooth chain on a 'twenties engine, you will find that it is fitted with a pin type joint. However, American cars fitted with these chains used a rocker joint which had a cranked or hunting link attached to it, and is rather more difficult to find. The only way to split the chain is to grind off one of the appropriate pins. These inverted tooth chains began to be superceded by the roller variety by the end of the Vintage era, which have a far more conventional link. In fact, should the inverted tooth chain be damaged, or missing altogether you might be well-advised to convert to the roller type, though the cogs will have to be replaced as well. This is because 'new' chains, these days, are very difficult to come by, and if you do obtain a second-hand example, you have no guarantee just how long it will last, and failure could be an expensive business. Also have a look at the state of the tensioner. If it is the spring variety it might be on the point of disintegration.

Undo the main bearings and lift out the crankshaft, replacing the caps immediately to their respective opposite numbers. Also check the order of any shims that may be present, and if thrust washers are fitted, note exactly where they are positioned and how they are arranged. You are now in a position to clean the block and crankcase throroughly (if they are separate), and the head. The best way to get parts really clean is to soak them in petrol or paraffin. This applies particularly to components which have been running in hot oil, which tends to build up surfaces of impurities. This treatment, followed by some vigorous applications with a nylon brush should break this film down. Clean the internal components in a similar way, paying particular attention to the crankshaft oil ways. If plugs are fitted (and this particularly applies to pre-war engines), then they must be drilled out, if they cannot be moved in any other way. They are usually made of dural or brass. If they are replaced, then the same material must be used or this will upset the balance of the engine.

While on the subject of cleanliness, I cannot stress enough the necessity for scrupulously clean working conditions. All too often one sees engines being rebuilt on dirty benches, cluttered up with tools. If you have not the use of an engine stand, then do your rebuild on a *clear* bench, covered with clean newspaper, or better still, a piece of lino.

Bead Blasting

One of the more recent, and effective, processes for cleaning and burnishing iron, steel, aluminium, glass, plastics, and even wood, is bead blasting. The equipment for carrying out this work is produced by Guysons International Ltd., of Otley, Yorkshire and is to be found in many restoration establishments throughout the country. The item to be cleaned is positioned in a cabinet and bombarded with millions of microscopic glass beads at high velocity. This peening action is also valuable in improving the fatigue life of metals, improving lubrication of moving parts as well as eliminating scratches and other imperfections there may be present on the surface.

The action blasts out all carbon deposits on such items as internal engine parts, leaving a scrupulously cleaned micro-dimpled surface. It gives a new look to rubber moulding too, and even if you want to remove the varnish off a wooden dashboard, then make your way to the nearest bead blasting centre. It is important, incidentally, that the items under bombardment are not wet, greasy or excessively porous. Such engine parts as carburetters, camshafts, pistons, cylinder heads, fuel pump cases, starter motors, clutches and brake shoes can be effectively cleaned by this process, which can save you hours of dirty, boring work.

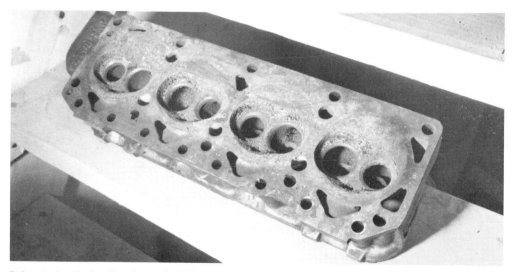

Before (*top*) and after (*lower*). A cylinder head before and after bead blasting at PAO Metal Finishers of Cricklade, Wiltshire

(*Both above*) Bead blasting effectively used on engine parts

The Rolls-Royce 20's
cylinder block has been
bead blasted, followed by
stove enamelling

A damaged block or crankcase

Once you have all the engine parts clean, it is time to carefully examine the block and crankcase, or complete engine unit. If you discover damage on a post-war or popular pre-war engine, then you will find it easier to obtain a replacement, so these foregoing remarks really only apply to Vintage engines, or exceedingly rare ones manufactured after this date.

In the case of small cracks, these can be repaired by drilling and reaming, and inserting a dowell pin, but this is probably a job which should be left to a professional. Bad cracks will have to be welded, and if you should be unlucky enough to find that your engine is so afflicted, it is the time to sit down and do some hard thinking.

Repairs to cast iron and aluminium on an old engine is a highly specialised and expensive business. Your first resort is to try to get a spare part you can use in place of the original. There are a number of exceptions to this rule. You may own an extremely rare vehicle, for which it is virtually impossible to obtain spares. Then you have no alternative but to have the repairs effected. The same applies if the car that you own has a distinguished competition history of which the 'right' engine is an integral part. Also, you may find that the particular part of the engine has cracked as a result of a fault in the basic design, and a replacement is likely to be similarly afflicted.

But whatever you do, do not think that you can take your damaged engine to the garage on the corner, and get them to do a quick and cheap welding job. The chances are that they have not got the facilities, or skill, to cope with your particular problem. As far as cast iron is concerned, there are a number of methods which can be used to repair cracked and damaged parts of which welding is just one. Metal stitching (which is a cold process) provides very successful results, and can be used on such items as gear wheels. The only real limitation is that the part to be stitched must be sufficiently thick, but the metal must also be soft enough to be drilled. If the component has given trouble in the past, and there have been attempts to arc weld it, any hard spots present may prevent stitching. The big advantage of this method is that being cold, there is no distortion and the parts do not have to be re-machined before they can be used.

Arc welding on a cylinder block that hasn't worked. The chalk marks indicate the leaks on this Delage D8S cylinder block

Before (*top*) and after (*lower*). Angell and Williams' repair to an engine from a Connaught. "The difficult we repair at once, the impossible takes a little longer", they say!

The other method of repairing damaged blocks, heads or crankcases is by fusion welding. The part is first pre-heated in a hearth (just this stage of the operation can take two days). Once it reaches the right temperature, it is gas welded. In this way the metal can be fused and puddled to give a fine grain. But one of the problems with pre-heating any part is the cooling process. Here the correct type of oven and the use of expanding jigs to maintain alignment is of vital importance. The repaired parts are then machined. Angell and Williams (Peckham) Ltd., of London SE15 specialise in repairs of this nature, which, as can be seen, is a highly specialist business. For arc welding should not be used for cast iron. "Its like applying a blowlamp to a pain of glass, it cracks all over", Mr. L. T. Duff, the company's general manager told me. When it comes to aluminium, argon arc welding can be used on unstressed parts on the periphery of a casting, but the only way to tackle cracks in large castings is again by fusion welding, *a la* Angell and Williams.

Checking the bores

Assuming that all is well with the block (or if it is not, it will be), now is the time to consider the state of the bores. If you have a cylinder bore gauge, so much the better, for it is usual to refer to bore wear as the difference between the original sizes and the maximum size recorded by the gauge. If you are in any doubts about the original size, clean off the carbon at the very top of the bore, as this part should be unworn. In fact, as a rule of thumb method, the prominence of this ridge at the top of the bore should give a fairly good indication of its general state. If it is barely noticeable, there is obviously little wear, so that the greater the ridge, the greater the wear. Keep a weather eye open for any score marks in the bores. They are often caused by a loose gudgeon pin and blow by, and an increase in oil consumption has probably resulted. Then look out for dark or brown patches in the bore. This could have been caused by an excessively tight cylinder head nut or it might mean that a water jacket is clogged, and is causing a local hot spot.

If maximum wear exceeds 0.010in. in a bore of up to $3\frac{1}{2}$in. diameter, or 0.015in. in a bore over this size, then a rebore or resleeve is the order of the day. Most engines can be rebored up to 0.060in. over size. If the block has already been rebored to its maximum, or the bores are badly scored, then it will have to be re-sleeved. Again, if you have the chance of a spare block with bores in a better state, it will be worth opting for that. A few points on resleeving. This is not always a straightforward job on old engines. For if the sleeves are made an interference fit in the block, there must be sufficient metal to resist the outward pressure and possible cracking. Sleeves can be secured by Loctite, incidentally, with the sleeve being free enough to push in by hand. If the fit is not correct, the sleeve tends to move downwards and a stepped liner and pinning will usually sort this problem out.

Do not worry if you have not got a bore gauge, as your local machine shop will do the measuring for you and tell you the size of replacement pistons you require.

The all important ridge at the top of the cylinder bore. This is a useful rule of thumb method to judge bore wear

Obtaining new pistons

A surprising number of pistons for pre-war engines are still listed in the current Hepolite catalogue. Hepolite is one of the Associated Engineering Group of Companies. They are widely available throughout the country, though the following may be of use: branches of A. E. Edmonds Walker Ltd., Ferraris Piston Services of London NW2, Paul Backhouse Ltd., of Manchester 15 and Pistons and Components Ltd., of Glasgow 4. If you draw a blank there, try F. W. Thornton and Son of Shrewsbury, Salop, as they specialise in obsolete piston sets.

On the other hand, this can be the point when membership of a car club really comes into its own because if there is a shortage of the genuine article, the spares registrar will be able to advise you how to get over the problem. He may suggest another piston that can be modified to fit, or the club could have had some pistons made. Should you wish to have your own pistons manufactured then Omega Racing Components Ltd., of Warley, West Midlands can take on the job.

Dimensional terms relating to pistons, which are particularly relevant if you are attempting to obtain a modern equivalent to an old piston

The piston positioned in its bore, indicating the thrust face

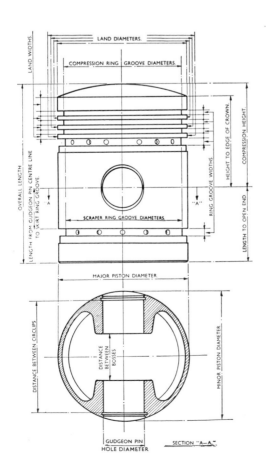

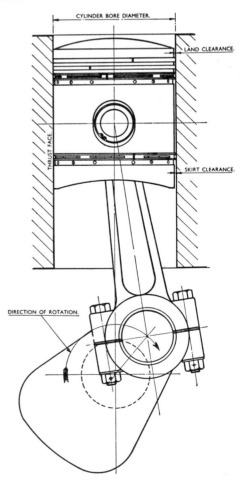

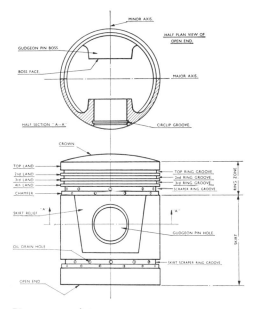

Piston nomenclature

Fitting the piston to the con rod. In this instance a finger push is all that is necessary, though this can vary: circlip and button type, Thumb push; gudgeon pin anchored in piston: Light tap; gudgeon pins up to and including 0.75 inch diameter, clamped in conrod: Finger push; gudgeon pin over 0.875 inch diameter, clamped in conrod: Finger push

On some engines it may well be essential to restore the engine number plate

Bottom end bothers

With the top of the engine sorted out (you hope), now is the time to consider the bottom end. On most pre-war engines, the main bearings and big ends were white metal cast directly into shells. Sometimes solid (die cast) white metal shells were used, these now being unobtainable and the answer is to fit bronze shells and white metal in the normal way. However, thin wall shells do also appear on pre-war engines and practically all post-war ones.

But first you have to check the condition, and ovality of the crankshaft journals. And, quite simply, if they are more than 0.002in. out of round, the shaft will have to be reground. Looking on the black side for a moment, you may have a shaft that is excessively worn, or larger diameter bearings are needed for substitute con rods. (Needless to say this trouble is usually confined to the older type of engine.) There is a choice of reclamation processes available. The first is metal spraying. Preparation is vital for this operation and the resulting finish is slightly porous, though it should wear better than the normal steel crank. But the process contributes no mechanical strength and it is not recommended to pre-war cranks of small diameter as they tend to be rather flexible. As the finish is somewhat brittle, it is easily damaged. Metal spraying is also no good for building up the side faces of journals. Then there is hard chrome plating, but this process does not add to the strength of the crankshaft and, in fact, can lead to weakening, if the shaft is made of a high tensile or heat treated steel.

The crankcase of the restored Morris Oxford engine of 1931. Look at the sharpness of the angle of the oil feed pipe

This big end cap is held by castillated nuts and locking pins

An example of the horrors that can lurk below. These white metal big end bearings are ripe for replacement! In this particular instance the crankshaft was also badly scored

Something else to be farmed out is crankshaft re-grinding

One of the best processes, particularly on Vintage crankshafts, is shield arc welding. This is a type of continuous arc welding under a stream of flux which minimises crank distortion. As the weld metal is selected to suit the crank, the process will, to some extent, have the effect of strengthening it. One of the big advantages of the method is that it is possible to build up thrust faces and fill in surface cracks. However, the crankshaft will have to be straightened afterwards. And while on the subject of straightening, its absolutely essential that a pre-war crankshaft is checked for straightness before grinding takes place.

When new white metal bearings are required they have to be specially cast . . .

. . . and the block (in this case from a 1935 SS), mounted in this Cuthbert line borer and machined to the correct clearance

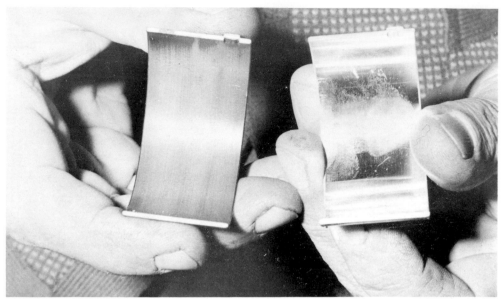

Replacement shell bearings are a far more straightforward cup of tea. The new shell is on the right

The lip in the edge of the shell fits into a similar recess in the bearing cap

While on the subject of regrinding, it should be noted that old and spindly crankshafts have a generous journal radii (as opposed to modern shell bearings that have a tight radii), and this must be maintained, otherwise strength is lost. These remarks particularly apply if the crankshaft is an old or rare one. Usually it is cheaper to get hold of a replacement, if the existing shaft is not up to the job in some way or other. But if you really are stuck for a crankshaft (some of the pre-war two bearing cranks are getting scarce, due to fracture), then the Allen Tool and Engineering Co., of Slough, Berkshire can make a new one for you.

The state of the oil pump is of considerable importance as all the moving parts depend on it for lubrication. The most likely places for wear are at the end of the gears or at the end plate. In the latter case it is possible to make some correction by surface grinding, but if the clearance is still present, then new gears and housing may be needed. The same applies if the drive shaft is loose in its housing, or when the idler gear is slack on its pin.

The bottom end of a Rolls-Royce 20 hp engine. This type of work is undertaken by a variety of specialists, though this particular job was carried out by the Jarrot Engine Company of London SE19

Also remember this: the vast majority of lubrication systems employ a pressure relief valve, and it is quite likely that it has been re-adjusted at some time in the past to compensate for bearing wear and to so increase the pressure. When the engine is run after reconditioning, the oil pressure should be checked and if it appears excessively high, then the valve should be re-adjusted. Otherwise you may run the risk of sheering the pump drive or bursting the oil delivery pipes.

And talking of pumps, one component that is bound to be in a bit of a state is the water pump. They are often made of aluminium, and corrode horribly. These days many one-make car clubs are having new aluminium bodies cast. If this does not apply in your case, then the only answer is to try and make one up from a variety of parts. If the impeller is badly rusted, then a new shaft should be made from stainless steel and fitted with brass impellers. The packing used in pre-war water pumps can be obtained from James Walker Ltd., of Woking, Surrey.

You are probably now in a position to send the crankshaft away to be reground and new main bearings and big ends cast, or shells supplied. If the former is the case, then you must supply the crankshaft, all the bearing caps and conrods *together with* the block. With all these large pieces of engine out of your way, you can now turn your attention to the cylinder head, though if you are dealing with a side valve engine, some of what follows will have to be done when you have the block in your workshop.

115

Reconditioning the valve gear

If the engine has been burning oil it is quite likely that a certain amount has been getting into the combustion chambers by way of worn valve guides, if an overhead valve or overhead camshaft head is fitted. Before removing the guides, it is important to check their position in relation to the block (in the case of a side-valve engine) and in the head (of an overhead valve one). They can usually be removed with a drift. As a rule for side valve engines, the guides are generally driven down from the port end into the tappet chamber, while with the ohv type, the guides are usually pushed out through the port. This is a job that can either be done in your own workshop, or by a specialist. If you do the job yourself, make sure that the new guides are pressed into their correct position and clear the top of the block (or port) by the same distance as the old ones. It may be necessary to reamer the guide to eliminate any distortion caused by the fitting. A solid type valve guide reamer will make the hole slightly larger than the diameter of the reamer and as valve stems are ground about 0.002in. to 0.003in. under a standard guide size, the correct clearance will be a arrived at automatically. If you lack facilities, have the job done by a specialist.

The valves themselves must obviously be in good condition and have not become unduly thin round the outer edge. It is advisable to fit new ones throughout. If you cannot obtain originals for your engine, then it may be possible to modify a modern example, but if not , then go and see G and S Valves Ltd., of Godalming, Surrey and they will make a set for you. But, of course, there is little sense in fitting new valves if the seats are in bad condition. Slight pitting can be removed by the use of carborundum paste, but the chances are that the seats will be badly worn. If this is the case, the head (or block) should be sent to a component engineering firm who will fit new valve seat inserts.

Another important point to consider, as far as the head is concerned, is the business of distortion. Any efficient engineering works should be able to check this with a surface plate. As a rough guide, distortion of the head, and the top of the block should not exceed 0.004in. If the figure is greater than this, then both components should be refaced, otherwise gasket blowing may result.

If your engine is fitted with an overhead camshaft(s), now is the time for checking. Should there be any evidence of wear or damage to the case hardening, then the camshaft should be replaced or the existing one reconditioned. If the bearings are worn, then there are two ways round the problem. The journals can be cleaned up by grinding and new bronze bushes made, or the existing bushes can be white metalled and then remachined. If the cams themselves are worn, then these should be reprofiled. Leonard Reece of Carshalton, Surrey can undertake this work. This, of course, also applies to a side valve engine.

One of the most oft neglected items on a vehicle's valve gear are the valve springs, and the chances are that the ones on your car have seen better days. Replacements are available from Herbert Terry and Son Ltd., of Redditch, Worcestershire or Quality Springs Ltd., who also hail from the same town. The rocker shaft and rockers should also be examined for wear, and replaced if suspect.

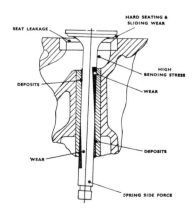

Some of the shortcomings associated with valve failure

Fusion welding a cylinder head at Angell and Williams' works at Peckham, London SE15

After welding, the appropriate part has to be machined. Here an MG PB cylinder head is having its valve seats re-cut after repair

Don't forget the time consuming job of grinding in the valves. Here a Ford V-8 engine is being given the works

The exception rather than the rule. An Austin Seven side valve racing engine being restored by the Donington Collection, the chassis of which was featured earlier. Note the 32 cylinder head studs and thickness of the valves

Balancing

It is well worth having the engine balanced, prior to reassembly. This applies to all types of engine, and is particularly rewarding on a small power unit, such as the Austin Seven. But if you decide on balancing, then weigh the conrods, before they are remetalled. For if the weights vary drastically, then its possible to build up the caps, or rods with braze to equalise them. Another alternative is to fit special big end bolts with large heads, or extra washers can be fitted under the nuts. Laystall Engineering Co Ltd., of London SE1 can undertake balancing. They will require the crankshaft, flywheel and clutch cover plate, conrods and pistons.

Gaskets and seals

Before launching into the rebuilding procedure, some thoughts on gaskets, would, I think, be appropriate. If you want to get the best possible joint between components, it is important to clean thoroughly the respective surfaces. Make a point of getting rid of such irrelevances as pieces of ancient gasket and old jointing compound. Aim for a clean and smooth surface, the sort that can be attained by the use of fine emery cloth. But what you do not want is a polished surface, so do not overdo it. It is vital, of course, that the parts to be joined are completely flat, the most likely culprit being the cylinder head, which I dealt with earlier.

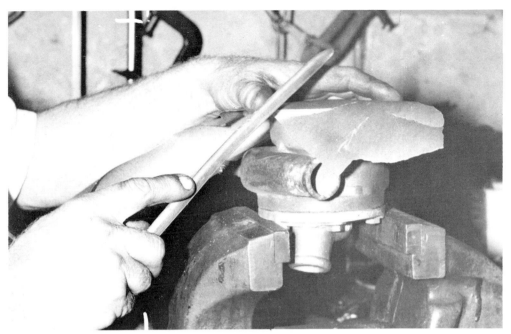
Making a water pump gasket

If you can buy all the gaskets you want, fine, but if not, with the possible exception of the cylinder head gasket, you can make them yourself. Gaskoid, by James Walker Ltd., of Woking, Surrey is ideal for this purpose, being a lot better than the more usual brown paper, as it is impregnated for oil resistance and toughness. It is best used in 0.006in. thicknesses and is available in 36 × 72in. sheets, and is ideal, for instance, for positioning between the oil pump and its mounting.

To make gaskets of this material, place it on top of the component in question, and using a small fibre hammer, beat out a silhouette, starting with the bolt holes. Do not use a conventional hammer, or you may damage the mating surfaces.

Gaskets for pressed steel sumps should be made of 0.0625in. Nebar Standard grade from the same manufacturers, being available in 48 × 48in. sheets. This is a bonded cork material, combining the advantages of cork with the resilience of rubber. Nebar Standard, of the same thickness, is ideal for such items as the timing case cover, external oil filter flanges, tappet case covers, gearbox lids and the like, for any service, in fact, relating to oils, solvents and grease. However, when used with water, 0.03in. is advised, this thickness being available in 48 × 36in. sheets. This is ideal for water jacket plates and water take offs. Unlike Gaskoid, you will need a sharp knife and a punch to make joints of this material.

Rocker box gaskets have to retain a high degree of resilience, but also have to be fairly thick. Lioncelle CS in 0.18in. and 0.25in. thicknesses is ideal for this task.

Should the engine you are assembling have a separate block and crankcase, you should use the aforementioned Nebar Standard of 0.03in. thickness, but if the block is providing rigidity for the crankcase, then 0.006in. Gaskoid should be favoured.

James Walker Ltd., can also provide you with a new copper/asbestos cylinder head gasket, providing you supply a pattern, and the same goes for any difficult exhaust manifold gaskets that may be required. However, a perusal of the current Payens catalogue will show a surprising number of cylinder head gaskets for pre-war cars, from Austin Seven to Ford and Morris Eight, which are available from Hall and Payen stockists. Again check with your club spares registrar if you are in any doubt.

Make a point of replacing any oil seals, as part of your rebuild. While felt washers are fine for retaining grease, they must be soaked in oil overnight prior to fitting. Where possible, replace with the modern spring loaded Neoprene variety. The concave side must face the oil source, though.

Re-assembling the engine

Now comes the business of putting the engine back together. If white metal bearings are used, check that the oil grooves are at least 0.25in. short of the bearing edge, to avoid oil leakage.

Also, after remetalling and crank grinding, the rods should fall under their own weight when attached to the crankshaft. Fitting the crank is your first priority, and it is probably again an appropriate moment to underline the importance of cleanliness. Do not forget to oil all the work surfaces prior to re-assembly.

The fitting of new shells, is fortunately a very straightforward business. Most shells bearings are fitted with a lip, stamped out of the steel back, which should be fitted in the appropriate slot in the crankcase, bearing cap or connecting rod. The oil hole also should line up with its opposite number in the bearing housing. Always use new big end nuts, bolt and tab washers. If split pins are used, and the castle nuts do not line up with the hole, file the bottom of the nut until they do.

After fitting the crank, it is important to check the end float at the thrust bearings, which on the majority of engines is reckoned to be between 0.004 and 0.006in. To check the end play, the crankshaft should be prised as far as possible to either the front or the rear. You will have to find which is the more convenient, as the position of the thrust bearing varies from engine to engine, as the thrust may be taken on the rear, centre or front bearing. Should there be a collar on the crankshaft, in line with thrust surface of the bearing at one end, the total clearance is easily measured with a feeler gauge at the other.

It is absolutely vital that you get the crankshaft thrust washers (if they are fitted), positioned the right way round. Note that the *relieved* side always goes towards the outside, that is the crankshaft web side.

Always replace the rear crankshaft oil seal as it is a favourite area for oil loss

Post-war bottom end. This sturdy crankshaft is a feature of the S1 Bentley engine. A vital check when assembling all engines; the con rod small ends should *not* be touching the gudgeon pin bosses

The routine of fitting the crankshaft first certainly applies in a pre-war engine when the block is separate from the crankcase, but if the the engine is constructed in one piece, then you are better off fitting the pistons to the rods, and positioning them in the bores, *before* fitting the crank. When you take the new pistons out of their box, you will probably find that the gudgeon pins stubbornly refuse to move. Emerse the pistons in boiling water and the pins should drop out easily enough, though make a point of carefully drying everything before assembly. Also thoroughly oil the bores before fitting the pistons; you will need a piston cuff to compress the rings before they will fit into the bore.

Many engines are fitted with the gudgeon pin located by a pinch bolt. Always fit a tab washer on this all important bolt, otherwise the pin can loosen and score the bore. The longer tab should be bent down the side of the rod, while its shorter opposite numbers should be bent round the head of the bolt. Spring washers are *not* recommended for this application. The other principle method of securing the gudgeon pin is by a circlip (one each side of the piston). You will need a pair of circlip pliers for this particular job; check that the clips are well and truly in position, for a loose clip can wreck an engine. If the correct piston for the engine is the split skirt variety, make sure that it is fitted the right way round, with the split on the non-thrust side. If you are not clear which side this is, turn the engine slowly round on the starting handle until the piston is positioned half way down the bore. Check the position of the conrod's small end; it will be pointing towards the thrust side. Incidentally, the split pinch bolt con rods should also face away from the thrust side. Some engines are fitted with gudgeon pins which are offset from the centre line of the piston to avoid piston slap. These, as well as the split skirt variety, are marked 'front'. This indicates that this side must face to the front of the engine. The conrods may be also so marked, and the same procedure applies.

121

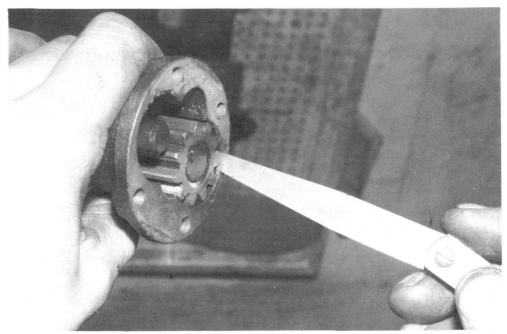

Clearance between the cogs in the oil pump and the casing must be checked, as must the end float

Gapping the piston rings is another vital aspect of any engine re-build

The engine can be fitted to its chassis without its cylinder head. Here a 1930 overhead camshaft Morris Minor engine is being assembled

A piston cuff is usually needed to compress the piston rings when fitting the pistons to a re-bored block

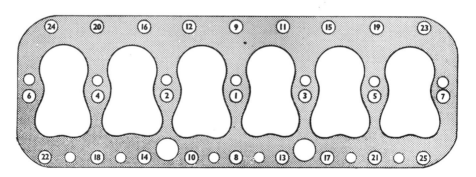

Typical orders for tightening down cylinder head nuts. *Top*, side valve six cylinder engine;

Lower, four cylinder overhead valve engine

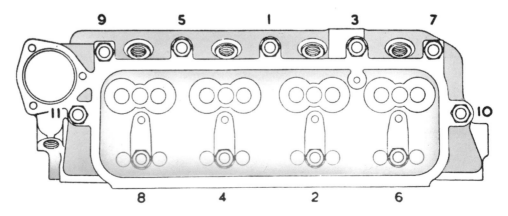

Whether you are fitting new pistons, or are just reringing, you must remember to gap the rings correctly. Carefully remove the rings from the pistons and position them in the top of the bore. You must allow a gap of 0.003in. for every inch of bore on water cooled engines and 0.005in. for air cooled engines. Check this clearance with a feeler gauge, filing the end of the ring to obtain the correct clearance. Carefully replace the rings on the pistons in their correct order, remembering to stagger the gaps, so that the oil does not find a direct route to the combustion chamber.

Wet liners

If you are dealing with a wet liner engine, your main concern is to ensure that the seals at both the top and bottom end of the replacement liners are sound. The bottom seal is usually made of one or more rubber rings fitted into grooves round the liner, although they can be positioned in the block itself. Yet another variation locates the lower end where there is a flange and gasket, but no sealing ring. At the top end, a soft copper or composite gasket is sandwiched between the top of the bore and the head.

You may find when you extract the old liners that the block is badly corroded around the bottom flange. This can be corrected by welding, or by boring and fitting an insert, but this is a specialist job. Otherwise, clean the surfaces with a medium soft emery paper, taking care to remove all traces of the old ring, if it was located in the block. You may find that the top edge of the hole through which the sealing ring might pass is unduly ragged and sharp; this should be cleaned up with a file.

Before fitting the new liners, check that they can be easily turned by hand, *without* the sealing ring. If there is any tightness at this stage, the liner could be distorted in service. If all is well, fit the sealing rings in position.

Remember that the top of the liners should stand proud of the top of the block by equal amounts all round. If this is not the case, then gasket blowing can occur.

Setting the valve timing

Should you find that you have mislaid the notes you took when the engine was dismantled, you can reset the valve timing, basing your calculations on the inlet valve of the number one cylinder.

First turn your attention to the back of the engine and to the rim of the flywheel. If you are dealing with a four cylinder engine, you should find a mark reading 1/4, or 1/6 if it is a six. This indicates that the front and rear pistons are at Top Dead Centre, which is the maximum extent of their travel. Your car's instruction book may well tell you the correct valve timing, but if not, your friendly club spares registrar will.

But let us assume, for the sake of argument, that the timing specifies that the inlet valve on number one cylinder starts to open five degrees BTDC (that is Before Top Dead Centre). Right. You know where Top Dead Centre is by the 1/4 and 1/6 marks on the flywheel, so mark the back of the engine immediately above the position, if it is not already done. But now you have to find five degrees before that. Measure the circumference of the flywheel, To make the calculation easy, let us assume that it is three feet. Now there are 360 degrees in a circle, so reduce your circumference to inches, that is 36 and divide by 360. The answer, according to your mental arithmetic, or pocket calculator is 0.1. Then multiply by five (remember five degrees BTDC) which will give you 0.5, which then expressed as a fraction is exactly half an inch. Measure 1/2 in. back from TDC on the periphery of the flywheel, and make a mark. Then turn it through its normal direction of rotation until the mark on the flywheel is opposite the one on the back of the engine. Now you can turn you attention to the camshaft.

Set the tappet on the inlet valve of number one piston at its specified clearance but remember that some makes (such as Rolls-Royce) have a special valve setting tappet clearance, so check with 'Those Who Know'. Now turn the camshaft in its normal direction of rotation (if gear driven, the opposite direction to the crankshaft, but if chain driven, the same). As soon as the tappet starts to move the inlet valve, lock the valve timing and all should be well.

It's obviously essential to have the valve timing right first time. It's hard to have to unlock all those gears for a second time

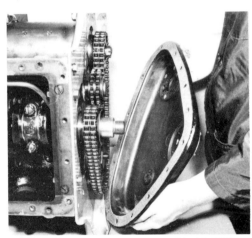

Gaskets proved little problem even with this 1930 Morris Oxford engine

Getting the valve timing right is aided by marks on the crankshaft and timing gears, as in the case of the Austin Seven

Side valves have to have their clearance set in much the same way as overhead valves. Sometimes, as in this case, it's much easier

Setting the ignition timing

With the valve timing established, you can now set the ignition. Turn the engine over until the piston of number one cylinder is at Top Dead Centre on the compression stroke. You can tell this by the position of the valves (they should both be closed), or even easier, remove the spark plug and place your thumb over the hole. You will soon be able to tell when it is blowing! You can also confirm this by the $1/4$ or $1/6$ marks on the flywheel.

Now position the high tension leads in their correct order in the distributor cap. The most common firing order for four cylinder engines (number one cylinder being the nearest to the radiator) is 1-3-4-2, while 1-2-4-3 was also used. Six cylinder engines are 1-5-3-6-2-4 or sometimes 1-4-2-6-3-5.

With the piston in its correct position attach the distributor (or magneto) to the engine, so that the rotor arm is pointing to the electrode of number one plug and the points are just opening. You will find that a distributor fitted with a gear drive is a little more tricky to position than one fitted with an offset dog. Then bolt up. The engine will now run. Detail ignition adjustment can follow.

The timing marks on the flywheel indicate that the pistons one and four are at top dead centre (TDC)

On with the head

Of course, everyone has their favourite products when it comes to rebuilding an engine. One such is Loctite Stud and Bearing Fit. If you have removed the cylinder head studs from an engine, prior to having it rebored, coat the threads with this product, prior to re-assembly to prevent future corrosion. Do not worry, that it is not a permanent seal. The product's other use is to make the refitting of ball races easier. In this way, bearing housings that have worn can be reclaimed, to some degree, permitting the slip fit of a bearing, instead of a press fit. In this way the expensive business of building up an aluminium housing can be eliminated.

Another useful jointing product is Wellseal, developed by Rolls-Royce, and manufactured by Associated Engineering Group, it can be used for sealing without the need for gaskets or joint washers, being usable in the temperature range of −55°C to 200°C. If permanent joints are required, then Green Hermatite does a very satisfactory job.

You should now be in a position to fit the cylinder head. As a general rule, when you come to position the cylinder gasket, the beading, or throw over, around the bores should be placed face down on the block. If this is not the case then the gasket will be marked 'Top'. On a new gasket, it is generally sufficient to apply a light film of oil or grease to the mating surfaces. Then bolt up, using a torque wrench. If you have not got a plan of the correct tightening order, start at the centre of the head and work outwards. After a hundred miles of running, retighten the nuts, though remember to do this when the head is *hot* with a cast iron head, though aluminium heads should be tightened down when the engine is *cold*.

And should you wish to paint the block, then Trinite is a good engine paint.

The exhaust system

The chances are that your car's exhaust system is probably on its last legs; resist the temptation to throw the whole lot away. First check whether you can obtain a replacement system. This is not as unlikely as it may sound, even for a pre-war layout, but if you cannot, then you may have to have a new one made. This is where your salvaged system comes in, because various flanges can be grafted onto the new layout. TDC Components (Kingston) Ltd., of Kingston upon Thames, Surrey will make a new exhaust system for you. Of course you may opt for a long lasting stainless steel layout, and these are available from P. J. Langford Ltd., of Eastgate, Nottinghamshire.

Whether you retain the old system, or have a replica made, you may want a special finish. One process is metal spraying. This employs a system where any metal or alloy, which is available in wire form, can be fed into a flame, where it breaks down into fine droplets, then being sprayed on to a cold surface. The result is a slightly porous metal layer. Sprayed aluminium can be used to considerable effect on exhaust manifold and pipes.

Another process which has attained recent popularity is an aerosol, Sperex SP 100 Very High Temperature Coating, which is available in white, black, silver-grey, aluminium and (wait for it) green. Efficient bonding is essential and ferrous metals should, ideally, be shot blasted with 60 grit and then rinsed in trichlorethylene. The official instructions sound a trifle alarming. '15 minutes at 250°F (120°C), followed by one hour at 600 – 650°F (315 – 344°C). Operation and/ or curing under continual rising heat to 850°F (455°C) will provide a superior coating resistance. For maximum resistance to solvents and fuels, curing should be continued to 1000°F for a short period.'

In practice, you can spray on the VHT coating and run the engine up gradually to achieve the same effects. However, under stressed Vintage engines may not rise to the occasion, so the answer is to pre-heat the manifold, or pipe with a blow lamp or welding torch. A Sperex finish is visually acceptable and long lasting. Always use brass nuts on exhaust system fittings.

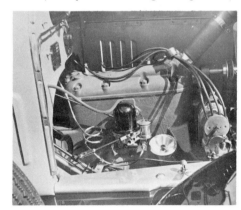

Most popular power unit of the 'twenties. A nicely restored Bullnose Morris engine

A re-built Sunbeam Twin Cam engine, complete with re-profiled cams

This 1927 Austin Seven engine is all ready for the chassis

A 1926 3 litre Bentley engine re-built by the Jarrot Engine Co.

You won't find one of these in a barn! This twin cam R1 Anzani engine fitted in a rare 1936 Squire shows how effective bead blasting can be when applied to aluminium parts. Jarrot Engine Co. again

129

Where the water works

On a Vintage car, the radiator must not only work effectively, it must also look right as well. This is because it is the most impressive feature on the front of the car, and should respond well to polishing. Nearly all radiators built during the 'twenties were nickel silver or nickel plated, chrome only starting to come in a big way in 1929. Radiator restoration is very much a job for a specialist, and as might be expected, this type of work does tend to be expensive. Of course, it does to some extent depend on what sort of radiator your car is fitted with. On many Vintage makes, the radiator and shell are soldered together, and if a new core is required, everything must first be unsoldered. Fortunately, some manufacturers, Austin being the main one, simply bolted the shell to a frame containing the core which was a completely self-contained unit. Restoring this type of radiator is considerably cheaper as you can dismantle it yourself, getting the shell replated when any other items are being seen to, sending the core off to Marston Radiator Services of Coventry who run a Vintage radiator reconditioning service. This company manufactures the original Honeycombe radiator core, though the alternative diamondal airway type is, at present, unobtainable. Radiator restoration is a vital part of any rebuild because the core is so visible. I have seen otherwise perfect Vintage cars spoilt by the owner using a modern cutdown core (which was never intended to see the light of day), so completely ruining the front of the car. If you have a rare car, and it is impossible to obtain a spare radiator, then Marston will actually manufacture you one, but it is naturally a highly skilled and pricey business. For example, a Vintage Bentley radiator has no less than 40 pieces, and all these are faithfully reproduced.

If you run a 'thirties car with the radiator core tucked out of sight, then your local branch of Marston Radiator Services may well be able to repair it on the spot, if you provide them with the old core. They will simply remove the old header and bottom tank and solder them to a new core. This will cost a lot less than replacing the old tubed type. If, on the other hand, you run a post-war car, you may well be able to get a new radiator off the shelf. In any event, it is certainly worth checking first.

Should you have lost your old radiator badge then Marston may be able to provide a new one, while I. Markovits Ltd., of London W12 can re-enamel your old one if the original colouring is chipped.

Another item that is worth checking in the water works department is the radiator pressure cap, if one is fitted. Most British cars operate at 4 or 7lb pressure, and you will find this stamped on the top of the cap. Being such a basically simple item, checks are straightforward, looking out mainly for corrosive damage. Pay particular attention to the condition of the locking diaphragm and sealing gasket. And make sure that the vacuum release valve is neither stuck, or hanging loose.

You will find that all important item, the thermostat, positioned around the water inlet pipe of the cylinder head. If possible, fit a new one.

Variations of radiator construction used in the 'twenties and 'thirties. *Left to right*: gilled tube, flat plate, false honeycombe, true honeycombe

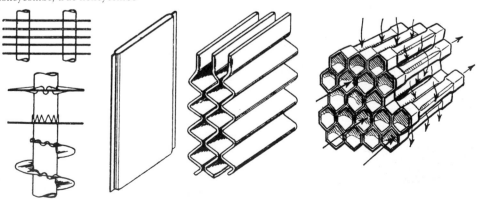

Water pump corrosion. Wear on the impeller and shaft indicate the need for replacement

A replica Alvis radiator, produced by Marston Radiator Restoration Unit of Coventry. The company faithfully reproduce the original honeycombe matrix

Badges and other trim fittings can be a problem these days. These Jaguar badges are examples of some of the excellent replicas now available

131

A Bentley radiator under restoration at
Marston's Coventry works

An Austin radiator being replated at T.
Smith and Co's premises in London EC1

The flywheel and clutch

The flywheel should be fitted fairly early on in the rebuild, particularly if you are going to have to reset the valve timing. Not an awful lot can go wrong with it, the main failing being damaged teeth on the starter ring. If you cannot get a new ring then Gwynne Townsend can build the old teeth up with weld. Another dodge is to turn the wheel round, in relation to the crankshaft, as engines always stop in the same places, but remember this when setting the timing. On a four-cylinder engine, give the wheel a quarter of a turn, and on a six, a sixth. In this way the worn teeth will not come into contact with the Bendix gear. Also check the condition of the pilot bearing in the flywheel, and replace it if you are doubtful.

Now comes the business of reconditioning that hard working component, the clutch. From around the mid-thirties the Borg and Beck single plate clutch was fitted to practically all British popular cars. These coil spring clutches ruled the roost for about 30 years, but now have been replaced by the diaphragm operated clutch. Linings are still obtainable from most old Borg and Beck clutches, but in case of difficulty write to Automotive Products Ltd., at Banbury, Oxfordshire. When you take the clutch to pieces, take care that you do not distort the cover, so slacken the retaining bolts off a little at a time. With the cover removed, check the condition of the driven plate. If the linings are worn down to the rivets, then the chances are that they have scored the flywheel and the pressure plate. If replacements are not available then these parts can be skimmed to remove any scoring, but no more than 0.010in. of metal should be shaved off. The presence of any lubricant on the lining will tell you whether any oil is leaking from the engine, but the rear crankshaft oil seal should be renewed as a matter of course during the engine rebuild. Oil can also contaminate the clutch from the gearbox, if the oil seal on the input shaft has failed. While on the subject of gearboxes, it should be noted that their correct alignment with the clutch is particularly important if the two units are separate. If it is not right then the clutch will prove difficult to operate and wear will be accelerated in the gearbox bearings.

However, to return to our clutch rebuild. Examine the thrust springs, and check that they are all the same height. If there is evidence of the clutch having overheated at any time (the coils will be discoloured if this is the case), then they should be replaced. When re-assembling the clutch with its new driven plate, this must be centralised with the bearing in the flywheel. A dummy first motion shaft is an ideal guide, though I have heard of a cut-down broom handle being used to great effect! Before fitting the new clutch plate, do not forget that most new linings are covered with preservative, and this should be washed off with petrol and dried before fitting. Tighten the cover plate bolts progressively, doing them up a couple of turns, then transferring your attention to the one directly opposite, and so on. When this job is completed, the cover plate should be firmly attached to the flywheel with the driven plate centrally located. (New cover plates can also be obtained from Automotive Products).

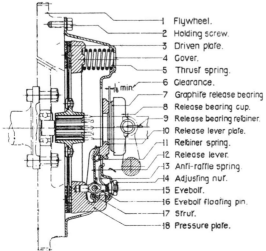

1 Flywheel.
2 Holding screw.
3 Driven plate.
4 Cover.
5 Thrust spring.
6 Clearance.
7 Graphite release bearing
8 Release bearing cup.
9 Release bearing retainer.
10 Release lever plate.
11 Retainer spring.
12 Release lever.
13 Anti-rattle spring.
14 Adjusting nut.
15 Eyebolt.
16 Eyebolt floating pin.
17 Strut.
18 Pressure plate.

Cross section of a pre-war Borg and Beck single plate clutch (knife edge fulcrum type)

The clutch lining has, in this case, worn down to the rivets and scored this pressure plate. It should be replaced, though skimming is an alternative

The carbon thrust race should always be replaced when the clutch is renewed. They are available from Automotive Products Ltd., of Banbury, Oxfordshire in case of difficulty

When replacing the pressure plate, its essential to use a dummy main shaft or universal mandrel to centralise the driven plate

There are two other hard working components that must be replaced, or reconditioned, before your clutch service is completed. The first is the clutch release bearing which on earlier cars will be a ball race (that required lubrication) and on later ones a carbon thrust race (that did not). You may well find that if you have the ball race variety, it has suffered from lack of regular greasing. The ball thrust races should be replaced if the tracks are at all pitted or rusty. If unavailable, they can be reground and new balls fitted into the cage. You should be able to replace the carbon thrust race easily enough, (again from AP) though the chances are that wear will have taken place on the fingers of the withdrawal arm assembly, and if you cannot obtain a replacement then these can be reclaimed with stellite.

With some variations of the Borg and Beck clutch, these fingers have to be correctly set up. This is done by varying the position of the adjusting nut. Larger clutches used shims to achieve this clearance, which does vary from car to car.

There must also be 0.06in. clearance between the thrust bearing and the release fingers. For as the linings wear, the pressure plate will gradually move closer to the flywheel, the release levers will move backwards and the clearance will be taken up. With a hydraulic clutch layout, the system may be self compensating, though there may be adjustment on the pushrod of the slave cylinder. The usual clearance is about 0.125in. between the pushrod and the withdrawal lever.

With mechanically operated clutches, the adjustment is usually made between the pedal and the withdrawal arm. There should be about an inch free movement at the pedal, which is in keeping with the 0.06in. clearance in the clutch itself.

Gearboxes

If, during your test drive, the gearbox proved itself perfectly satisfactory, was quiet, had efficient synchromesh and did not jump out of gear, then you would be well advised to drain it, and replenish with fresh oil and leave well alone! If, on the other hand, the box is obviously about to succomb to the rigours of old age or misuse, you may be well advised to save yourself a lot of time by obtaining a second hand unit. Should this not be possible, for a variety of reasons, then you may consider it worthwhile to strip the box down yourself. The following information should be regarded as a guideline and nothing more. I would strongly advise that if you do undertake a gearbox rebuild that you obtain the appropriate workshop manual for your car. A gearbox's internals vary in important details, and it is an unwise man (unless he is particularly well acquainted with gearboxes) who takes on the task without being adequately prepared. Fortunately, not every gearbox shortcoming requries a complete rebuild and I will consider these first. One of the most common difficulties with a box that is getting a bit long in the tooth, is that it will jump out of gear. Although this can spell out some internal malady, it can be caused by wear in the selector forks, particularly if the gears are of the sliding, rather than the constant mesh variety. The problem can be resolved by building up the appropriate area of fork with weld. Weak selector springs, that are positioned at the top of the box, can also cause the same shortcoming; so renewing them can cure the trouble. If none of these alternatives work, then the culprit is either worn splines or bearings (or both), or worn gears, and stripping the box is your only alternative.

You will require a few special aids for the task. A good set of circlip pliers is an absolute must, and where the gear clusters run in that most frustrating of arrangements (as far as the rebuilder is concerned), uncaged needle roller bearings, a dummy layshaft is also necessary. By contrast, the first motion shaft is usuall ball bearing mounted.

So, remove the top of the box and then lock it by sliding two sets of gears into mesh at the same time, though with a synchromesh box, make sure that you do not push the outer parts of the synchro units too far after moving the selectors, or they may fly to pieces! Once the gearbox is locked up, unscrew the nut at the back of the box securing the universal joint coupling flange. You will probably need a hub puller to get the flange off. This means that you can then take off the cover or tail shaft, which will reveal the layshaft spindle (or bearings), and the primary shaft (and bearings). Removing the layshaft is the next item on the agenda, and if needle rollers of the uncaged variety are favoured, you will need a dummy shaft, though this must be the same length as the layshaft, but not as long as its spindle. Push out the layshaft spindle with the dummy shaft endways, having removed the front cover of the box. The layshaft itself will be consigned to the

135

A familiar wear point on a gearbox which will prevent the appropriate gears being selected with accuracy

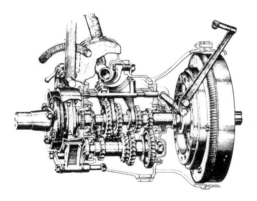

Gearbox of the 1928 Austin 12. The gate change is a delight to use, even if the changes are somewhat slow! There is, of course, no synchromesh. A transmission brake is fitted at the rear of the box

bottom of the box, and you can continue with the business of removing the mainshaft. Next out comes the short clutch shaft, which often runs in a spigot bearing in front of the mainshaft. It is often secured by a locking device in the third gear pinion. The shaft can then be removed. On the other hand, the clutch shaft may be freed by careful application of a hide hammer to the prop shaft end of the main shaft. This will push the front ball bearing out, but check that it is not secured to the gearbox casing in any way. Then tap the mainshaft rearward; it should take the bearing with it. These bearings are often secured with circlips, so make sure that you remove them first! You can then remove the layshaft which has been sitting at the bottom of the box out of the way.

I do not intend to itemise the why's and wherefores of synchromesh replacement, this should all be detailed in your workshop manual. Examine the gears for chipping, and if they are blue in colour, this may indicate that the box has overheated at some time, probably through lack of oil. Check the ball bearings for wear as well as thrust washers on the layshaft gear cluster. New gears, should spares not be available, can be made by Schofield and Sampson, of London WC1.

Re-assembly is the reverse of dismantling, though remember to smear the layshaft needle rollers with grease. Fit new oil seals, making sure that if the cup type seal is used, the inner edge of the cup faces the source of the oil.

Universal joints

The Hardy Spicer needle roller Hooke joint has been fitted to practically all British cars since 1934, prior to that the IG (Improved Grease) variety, by the same manufacturer, was used. Vintage cars generally used a combination of leather universal (behind the gearbox) on the prop-shaft, with a sliding pot type joint at the rear axle end; the latter being remarkably trouble-free, providing it is regularly greased. Replacements for the leather universal are available

The Hardy Spicer universal joint can be easily dismantled

The needle rollers should be re-packed with grease

Rebuilding these joints is remarkably straightforward, and it is well worth remembering that the pre-war joints were not fitted with a grease nipple, though until about 1963, post-war ones were!

To dismantle these joints, remove the four circlips, then hold the joint in one hand and hammer the radius of the ear with a copper hammer. The needle rollers should gradually emerge and can be removed with the fingers. Be sure to hold the bearings in a vertical position, and when free, remove the race from the the bottom side to avoid dropping the needle rollers. Then do the same to the opposite bearing. Support the two journal pegs and tap the ears of the flange yokes to remove the race. Reverse the assembly and repeat the operation. You can now wash all the parts in petrol. Repack the bearings with gear oil and re-assemble. Remember to replace the cork washer which is fitted between the ends of the cage and the flanged portion of the trunnion journal.

137

Lubrication

Oils have, of course, improved considerably over the past years. Modern lubricants have good detergent qualities to clear out sludge, dirt and water. In the past, oil stayed clean and the engine got dirty, while today the reverse is true! However, the old fashioned 'straight' oils are still available today because some select specialist, air-cooled engine manufacturers specify them. They tend to be cheaper, in fact, but a straight 20 grade is fine in winter, but is not anything like as efficient as a 20W50 multigrade which remains equally versatile throughout the year. Most engines will now run happily with oil and filter changes every 6000 miles (there are, needless to say, exceptions, so check with your own make club first).

One important point to remember about modern multigrades is that they do not behave at their best in an over-cooled engine. In these circumstances, a lot of water vapour is produced in the combustion process, most of which ends up in the oil. Although the oil can cope with this emulsification, it makes a lot of mess around the oil filler, breather and inside the rocker cover.

Notes on development

1919–1929 The design of British engines between the wars was dominated by the imposition of a horsepower tax in 1921, but we must briefly return to 1906 to see how this came about. It was in that year that the Royal Automobile Club set down its 'RAC Rating Formula'. This was defined as $D^2N/2.5$. D represented the cylinder bore, N the number of cylinders, while 2.5 was arbitrarily arrived at, 'and will be found reasonable and sufficiently accurate for comparative purposes'. For this was, quite simply, the reason for setting down the formula, 'so that the public may arrive at the approximate power of any given engine in *comparison* [my italics] with others'. The Club rightly stressed that 'it is not to be considered as an accurate or scientific calculation of actual horse power'.

However, the RAC had not reckoned with the politicians! For in his Budget of 1909, the Chancellor, David Lloyd George, announced a new graduated car tax, based on the RAC horsepower rating. Prior to this date vehicles had been taxed mainly on weight. The new law was duly implemented (together with a tax on petrol), so, for instance, a car over 12 'horsepower' paid four guineas a year tax, while a 60 'horse power' monster paid £21.

This state of affairs continued until 1921 when the aforementioned, new system was introduced, still based on the old RAC formula, but now taxing cars at a rate of £1 a horsepower. This was very damaging to the big bored American imports, such as the model T Ford, which in 1919 had accounted for no less than 41 per cent of British new car registrations. Under the old system it paid six guineas tax, though its RAC rating was 22.5, so the new law meant an annual tax of £23. By contrast, the home produced Morris Cowley (11.9 RAC horsepower) cost a modest £12 to tax. Although this served to protect the home market, it did little to help the country's colonial car exports, where the small bored British cars had to compete with big engined American opposition. This was because, as we have seen, the RAC's formula of $D^2N/2.5$ took no account of an engine's stroke, only the bore and number of cylinders. This legal straightjacket had a far reaching effect on design, because manufacturers, in an effort to keep their RAC rating as low as possible, (and thus the customer's road fund licence) opted for narrow bores and long strokes, which were favoured by the formula. Consequently, the RAC rating was often emphasised when marketing a car, for example, Austin Seven, Ford Eight, Singer Nine and so on, even though this bore little relation to the actual horsepower developed by the engine.

Some of the cars which appeared immediately after the Armistice were essentially updated versions of pre-war designs, with often the head and block cast in one piece. This layout was a reminder that the internal combustion engine used in the car had evolved from the fixed head gas engine, and was unsatisfactory from a maintenance point of view, to say the least. The gearbox was usually quite separate from the engine, power being transmitted via a short drive shaft.

As it happened, the Americans were not so hide bound by such traditions, as Henry Ford proved to such devastating effect in 1908. His model T had a cylinder block and crankcase cast in one piece, and consequently the cylinder head was detachable; the prototype of all mass produced car engines. For the gearbox was also 'in unit' with the engine, so obviating the need for a sub

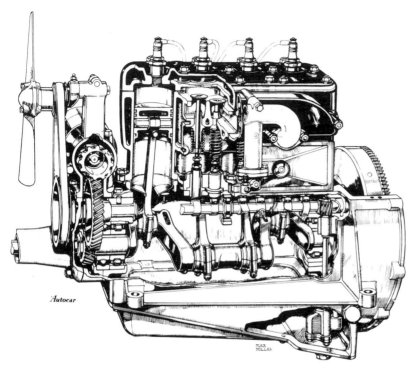

A coil ignition Austin Seven engine, circa 1928. The roller bearing crankshaft is unusual for a cheap car. Like all Austins of the vintage era, the block and crankcase are cast separately. Introduced in 1922, the Seven remained in production until 1939, the only major modification being the introduction of a centre main bearing in 1936

The engine of the MG Midget Double Twelve replica illustrated in Chapter One

frame, and streamlining the process of manufacture.

In the immediate post-war era two British manufacturers, Herbert Austin and William Morris dominated the mass market by sound designs and exploiting this American thinking. (British engineering concerns such as Crossley and Napier had favoured the unit construction of engines and gearboxes, prior to the First World War, but they were hardly providing 'motoring for the masses'.)

William Morris had been selling cars since 1913, and was wedded from the very first to unit constructed White and Poppe engines and gearboxes. During the First World War he fitted the American U-type Continental Red Seal engine, produced in Detroit, in much the same way as the model T, having a one-piece crankcase/block arrangement and detachable cylinder head. As might be expected, the gearbox was in unit with the engine and, horror of horrors, the gear lever was in the centre of the car, when everyone knew that the only 'U' place for it was on the *right* of the driver. When supplies of this unit dried up, Morris got Hotchkiss of Coventry to copy the engine. This, with a few modifications, they did with great success, the engines powering the Morris Cowley and Oxford which were the best-selling British cars of the 1920s; but they were Yankees at heart!

In the same way, Herbert Austin took careful note of trans-Atlantic design trends, endorsed by his running of a Hudson 16 during the First World War. His Austin 20, of 1919, bore unmistakeable signs of American ancestry. Although the engine used the traditional separate crankcase/block arrangement the cylinder head was detachable and the gearbox was mated directly to the engine with a centrally mounted gate change. All this added up to a design philosophy that had germinated many thousands of miles from his factory at Longbridge, Birmingham. Many manufacturers were reluctant to follow suit immediately, probably because the unit layout rendered the then tiresome business of clutch adjustment rather more difficult. Bentley, for example, always kept his engine and gearbox separate, up to the mighty 8 litre of 1930.

But the traditional cone clutch soon gave way to the dry plate variety, though a notable exception was Morris's cork faced unit which ran in oil, one of the few contributions he made to detail engine design!

As far as the rest of the engine design was concerned, crankshafts generally ran in white metal bearings cast directly into shells in the main bearings and big ends. This Babbitt metal (invented by Isaac Babbitt in 1839) described a wide range of white metal alloys, and was used in practically all engines of the Vintage era. (The Austin Seven was a notable exception, its crankshaft being ball and roller mounted). Connecting rods were usually H section steel stampings, though dural of which more anon, with its strength and low weight began to compete with the more traditional material from around 1923. Although W.O. Bentley had fitted aluminium pistons to the French DFP of 1914, cast iron pistons were almost universally employed until about 1924, when the lighter material took over. Although some of the cheaper engines favoured inverted tooth chain driven internals, gears predominated at the more expensive end of the market. Most engine ancilliaries such as the dynamo, magneto and water pump were, in the main, positively driven from the engine, the fan belt being just that!

Improvements in combustion chamber shape, carburation induction and progress in oil refining all tended to benefit engines during the 'twenties. Also in 1920, in America, Thomas Midgeley and T. A. Boyd discovered the use of Tetr-Ethyl lead as an anti-knock agent. The addition of this lead to petrol allowed compression ratios to be increased without the danger of pre-ignition, though these benefits mainly showed themselves in the following decade. This is shown by the fact that in 1929, the average British touring engine had a compression ratio of just over 5:1, while by mid 1936 this had risen to 6 : 1, with 20 brake horse power per litre being the power developed by the average engine of the Vintage years, and by 1935 30 bhp per litre was easily attainable.

The advances made in the production of case hardened steel during the First World War resulted in a great improvement in the quality of gear wheels used in the gearboxes of cars built in the 'twenties. The decade also saw the advancement of the multi splined gearshaft, which replaced the earlier square shafting. Improvements in the design of ball bearings also contributed to the reliability of gearboxes, but it was necessary to double de-clutch when changing gear, both up and down the box; otherwise it would make noisy protests. This shortcoming led to the adoption of helical gears in constant mesh in place of straight cut gears, in some gearboxes. The open gate change was featured on many cars during the 'twenties, the notable exceptions being American imports and, as we have seen, American inspired designs. Nevertheless the trend towards the cheaper, though less satisfying (from a gear changing point of view) ball change became increasingly popular towards the end of the decade, though this, and the traditionally positioned right hand gear lever, lingered on with the more expensive cars.

A 'remarkable mechanism' as *The Motor* put it, appeared in 1928 on the Armstrong Siddeley Twenty and Thirty models, being a pre-selector gearbox designed by Major W. G. Wilson. This box was derived directly from Dr Frederick Lanchester pre-selective compound epicyclic system from the early days of motoring; there was no need for double de-clutching and no noise! The box allowed the driver to completely separate the action of depressing the clutch pedal and engaging the gear. With the pre-selector system he selected the gear by a stubby lever, usually mounted on a steering column quadrant, but it was not engaged until, the 'clutch' pedal was depressed.

The side valve four cylinder engine ruled the roost at the cheaper end of the market, Austin, Morris, Clyno and Bean all favouring this layout. Overhead valves, operated by pushrods were rather fewer, at least, during the early 'twenties, though Rolls-Royce, Riley, Aston Martin and Alvis were some manufacturers who followed this trend. This arrangement did, however, increase in popularity from 1926 onwards.

Valves actuated by a single overhead camshaft were somewhat fewer, Wolseley, Bentley, Napier and, rather surprisingly, Morris (with the Minor of 1929) opting for an 'upstairs' cam. A twin overhead engine was a rare bird indeed (having first appeared on the Grand Prix Peugeot of 1912), Sunbeam upholding this desirable, though expensive, variant.

Although four cylinder engines predominated in the early 'twenties, they were strongly challenged by the six, half way through the era until the end of the decade when it was the more popular of the two. The rarer straight eight surprisingly increased in popularity at the end of the 'twenties, which is significant in the knowledge of the Wall Street crash of 1929.

Radiator construction changed remarkable little, the principle types being made up of round, or honeycombe ended tubes, soldered together at their extremes, so that water could run between them, while air passing through the centre would exercise a cooling effect on the water. Another variation on the theme was the diamondal airway film type core.

Most industries benefit from technological spin off in one form or other, and the motor industry in the 1920s was no exception. Much valuable metallurgical research was carried out in the course of developing the British aero engine industry, though ironically, one of the better known aero alloys used on cars hailed from Germany. Dural, being an abbreviation of duraluminium, was discovered in that country by Dr. Alfred Wilm in 1906. He later presented this aluminium alloy to the Durener Metal Works, hence its name. It was soon seized upon by Zeppelin engineers, who recognised that this ultra light, age hardened material could help revolutionise airship design. Duraluminium was manufactured in Britain by James Booth and Co, being used in car conrods from the early 'twenties onwards. Another aircraft alloy which also crops up in cars from the 'twenties is electron, being a magnesium alloy, though is more often remembered in the industry for its inflammable machining properties, than its weight saving advantages!

1930 – 1940   The 'thirties saw a sophistication in engine production methods, to the benefit of the manufacturer. Popular engines also became smaller, for while the 11.9 hp market had dominated the 'twenties, it was the 8 hp car that typified the 'thirties. Also the dreaded horse power tax was reduced from £1 per hp to 15s in 1934, (though it was upped to 25s in 1940).

The most significant step forward in engine production came around the mid-thirties, though it is doubtful whether many motorists were even aware of the change at the time! And like so many other innovations, this one also hailed from the USA. As we have seen, practically all engines used white metal for their main and big end bearings. This was cast directly into the bearing shells, line bored and often hand scraped to give the correct clearance. But in 1928, the Cleveland Graphite Bronze Company of Cleveland, Ohio, provided an alternative to this time-consuming operation, with the invention of the 'thin wall' bearing, first used on the 1930

One of the famous engines of the inter-war years: the Riley Nine first appeared in 1926, remaining in production until 1938. The twin camshafts mounted high in the block actuated short pushrods which prodded the inclined valves in the hemispherical cylinder head, so beloved of the tuning fraternity. The layout persisted into the post war era, the last car to feature it being the 2½ litre Pathfinder which ceased production in 1957. Coil ignition replaced the magneto shown here in December 1932

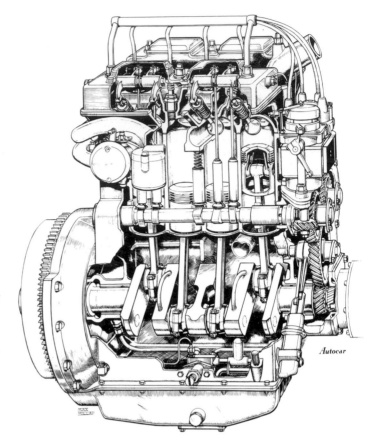

Autocar

This series one Morris Eight engine has been restored by Mike Finnigan

Studebaker. This had the great advantage that it could be manufactured from a continuously rolled, thin composite strip of metal with a steel back and (initially) a Babbitt surface; later lead bronze and copper lead mixes were used instead of the more traditional material. These thin, usually semi circular shells, about 0.06in. thick, together with the accurate machining of the crankcase, was destined to completely eliminate the earlier process.

In 1932, Guy Anthony Vandervell became the first manufacturer outside the United States to purchase the production rights. After trials, the new thin wall shells were first used as a production item on the Austin 10 and Hillman Minx of 1935, being followed by Standard in 1937 and Vauxhall in 1938. Mass production had received a vital shot in the arm.

Another trans-Atlantic influence that appeared in the early 'thirties was the arrival of the synchromesh gearbox, which had featured on the Cadillac of 1928. In 1932 it appeared on the Vauxhall Cadet, as might be expected from a General Motors' satellite, and a few months later on the 20/25 Rolls-Royce. In both cases, synchromesh was offered on third and top gears. The Alvis Speed Twenty of 1934 was the first British car to be fitted with an all synchromesh box; the gearbox cost the same as a complete Ford model Y!

Yet a further contribution from the New World came in 1931 when Automotive Products Ltd., who had already acquired the licence to produce Lockheed hydraulic brakes in 1927, purchased the manufacturing rights of the Borg and Beck single plate clutch. The 1932 Humber 16 was the first British car to be fitted with this unit, which by the end of the decade had been adopted by practically all manufacturers.

Not that it could be used in conjunction with the pre-selector gearbox (a fluid flywheel or centrifugal clutch were the usual couplings), but the box was very much in vogue in the early 'thirties, before synchromesh managed the business of quietly changing gear cheaper and easier. Unfortunately, the pre-selector's tendency to absorb too much power (particularly noticeable on smaller engines), its weight and high manufacturing costs were contributory factors in its decline from the middle of the decade.

The cheap manufacturing appeal of the side valve four cylinder engine continued to be reflected at the lower end of the market, despite the popularity of the small six in the early years of the 'thirties. Ford, Morris, Austin, Hillman and Standard all stuck with the dependable side valve four, though the exception was again provided by Vauxhall who offered overhead valves with their R type of 1928, and have remained wedded to them ever since. Although he had a brief flirtation with the overhead camshaft with the Minor of the early 'thirties, Morris did not again succumb to ohv in a big way until 1938, while MG less desirably went from overhead camshaft to pushrod ohv engines from 1936, as did Wolseley (which was also part of the Morris stable). Single overhead camshafts were also to be found on the Singer Junior, and at the sporting end of the scale, on the Aston Martin produced during the decade. Mention should also be made of the classic Riley design which featured two camshafts set high in the block actuating the inclined valves in a hemispherical head via short pushrods, which first appeared on the Monaco of 1926, the configuration lasting right up until 1957 when the Pathfinder model was phased out by BMC. Twin overhead camshafts were confined to essentially expensive machinery, though Lagonda offered twin cam motoring for a chassis price of £270 with their Rapier of 1934. Other twin cam engines built during the era were the Blackburne unit fitted to the Frazer Nash and the R1 Anzani fitted in the visually appealing Squire, and even more esoteric Triumph Dolomite of 1934.

Belt driven dynamos and water pumps became increasingly popular, as did air and oil filters, reflected by Automotive Products production of the Purolator oil filter, later in the decade. There were also changes on the radiator scene, the traditional tubes being replaced by fin and tube radiator blocks. The core by this time was modestly relegated behind a stone guard, grill or even *false* honeycombe, out of public view.

An aircraft alloy, hiduminium, joined the other aviation inspired alloys during the 'thirties. Hiduminium was an aluminium magnesium alloy developed by Rolls-Royce for their R type aero engine, used to power the victorious Schneider Trophy Supermarine S6B of 1931. Manufactured by High Duty Alloys of Slough (hence its name), it was first used extensively in the automotive sense in the Armstrong Siddeley Sports Special of 1933. Other manufacturers did not grasp the new material with such alacrity, but it often crops up in the brake parts and axles of the more sporting

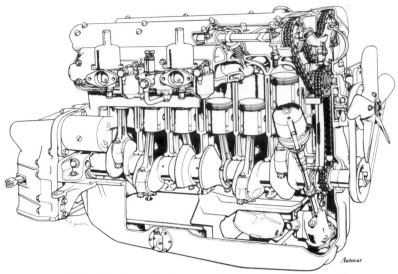

The most successful British twin overhead camshaft engine ever produced: the Heynes, Hassan, Baily six cylinder 3442 cc XK Jaguar engine of 1948, and still in production. The block/crankcase is cast iron and the cylinder head aluminium. The lack of studs at the front end of the cambox covers identifies this early engine

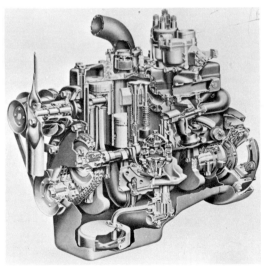

Ford continued making this side valve engine right up until the early 'sixties. Although it was the same capacity (1172 cc) as that used in the earlier 10 hp side valvers, it was a completely re-designed engine, having a new block, larger valves, bigger bearings, integral water pump and adjustable tappets. It powered the trusty 100E model between 1953 and incredibly up until 1962

machinery of the 'thirties, the idea, no doubt being to reduce the unsprung weight.

1945 – 1960   The post-war era saw the infamous horse power tax at last abolished, and from 1948 all cars were taxed at the same rate. This relaxation resulted in the appearance of over square engines by Ford and Vauxhall in 1951, designers no longer being penalised for the size of the bore. Very gradually side valve engines were phased out, being replaced by pushrod overhead valve variants. Austin built their last side valver in 1947, Morris in 1954 while Hillman lingered on one year later, while Ford incredibly perpetuated the archaic design until it was finally dropped when the Ford 100E ceased production in 1962.

Single overhead camshafts continued to be the sign manual of Singer and, briefly Wolseley, while AC soldiered on with their single overhead camshaft, aluminium, wet liner six that had been in production since 1922 and remained so until 1963. Aston Martin, as benefited their sporting traditions, adopted the W.O. Bentley designed twin overhead camshaft six from 1950, though the most outstanding and reliable and successful twin cam six of the post-war years came from Jaguar with their famous XK power unit that first appeared in the XK 120 sports car of 1949.

Improvements to combustion chamber shapes and the disappearance of pool petrol, saw

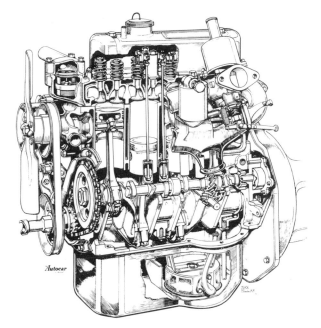

Autocar

Another famous engine which is still in production, the A series developed by Austin and first used in the A30 of 1952. This 803 cc example is fitted with an SU carburettor (replacing the original Zenith unit) and made possible by the merger with Morris to form BMC in 1952. Note the unusual mounting of the oil pump at the end of the camshaft

The engine of Bill Clark's 1953 MG TD. The model was produced between 1949 and 1953

compression ratios rising again in the early 'fifties to around 7 : 1 for the average touring engine. the power unit producing around 40 bhp per litre. Many of these engines, although gradually improved over the years are still in production: the BMC A and B series date back to 1951 and 1947 respectively, the current pushrod four cylinder Triumph unit first saw the light of day in the Standard Eight of 1953, while the larger Hillman pushrod four dates from 1954.

Gearbox design did not alter much during the 'fifties, even if the location of the gear lever did; the vogue for bench type front seats seeing the adoption of the column change gear lever. The Laycock de Normanville overdrive also put in a welcome appearance, the 1950 Standard Vanguard being one of the first models to offer this petrol-saving extra gear.

Automatic transmission had first appeared on General Motors Olsmobile, back in 1940, though the system was available for export Rolls-Royce and Bentleys from October 1952.

While clutch actuation remained mechanical until the early 'fifties, hydraulics took over in a big way, the 1954 Standard Eight, being one of the first cars to feature this layout.

145

1960 – 1970 The trend of getting more from less continued with the use of increasingly high compression ratios, more common use of the ohc and the further refinement of cylinder heads, porting and camshafts. Power/weight ratios benefited further from the greater use of aluminium alloy in many engine components formerly using cast iron.

Front-wheel-drive, often used with a transverse engine installation, pioneered by Citroen before the war, gained popularity after the impetus given to it by the introduction of the Mini.

Little change occurred in gearbox design other than that synchromesh became universal on all, even 'sporting', models, and automatic gearboxes, once the province of powerful luxury cars, became available as an option on even the humblest Mini.

An underbonnet view of the 1500 MGA produced between 1955 and 1959. This is a left hand drive example

Probably the best looking British post-war engine; the twin overhead camshaft six cylinder XK Jaguar unit. The black stove enamelled exhaust manifold effectively complements the polished aluminium cam boxes. This is an early Mark II saloon

The 3 litre Triumph Stag engine is a good example of engine development of the late 1960s

The compact Series-A engine from BMC, in transverse configuration with underslung gearbox, being inserted into a Mini

Chapter Five

Fuel systems

The motorist should endeavour to get the best mixture possible, and to explode it at the right time
R. J. Mecredy (The Motor Book), 1903

Carburettors will soldier on for years, although worn, but by contrast the pumps which deliver the petrol will soon let you know that all is not well by failing to deliver the stuff! I will be dealing with the business of checking and overhauling the pumps later in the chapter, but first some thoughts on reconditioning carburettors are appropriate.

There are three main makes of carburettors fitted to cars in the era under consideration. Solex, SU and Zenith. The SU is of the constant vacuum variety, thus differing from the other two makes which are of the fixed jet type. Despite this, *all* types of carburettors are vulnerable to four types of wear of:
(i)   The throttle spindle
(ii)   Jets and needles
(iii)   The inlet flange
(iv)   Gaskets and washers

The way round (i) is to have an oversized spindle fitted (0.005 and 0.010in. oversize is usual), but this is a specialist job, because the mounting holes must be bored exactly in line, so as not to upset the positioning of the throttle butterfly. Jets and needles vary according to type and will be dealt with individually. Refacing the mating flange with the inlet manifold is a straightforward job for anyone competent with a file, while as far as gaskets and washers are concerned, they are reasonably easy to make if replacements no longer exist. When you come to strip the carburettor down, you may find that it is coated with a hard gluey deposit. You should be able to remove this by immersing the component in cellulose thinners, but if this proves ineffective, then use concentrated paint remover. With all carburettors, the float should be checked for leaks; submersion in hot water will tell you whether all is well for there will be a stream of bubbles if there is a puncture. Repair, using the minimum amount of solder, so as not to upset the weight if you cannot obtain a replacement.

I will now consider the three makes of carburettor in greater detail.

SU

The most likely areas for wear are the needle, to a lesser degree the main jet and the throttle spindle. Let us look at the needle first. There are two essential points to be checked. Look at the shoulder of the needle on which you will find a code number stamped. Check with your one make car club or manufacturer's handbook that the carburettor is fitted with the right needle. Then closely examine the actual taper to see whether there are any score lines which will show that the needle has been coming into contact with the jet. If there are any marks, particularly near the

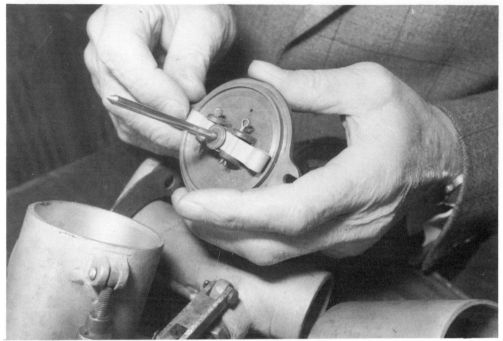

New weights and needle valve for an SU 'Sloper' of the 'twenties by BG Carburettors of Hillingdon, Middlesex

shoulder, then the needle must be changed. If this is the case then a new jet must be fitted at the same time. There are a variety of jets available so it is not a bad idea to take the old one along with you, when you get a replacement. Both needles and jets are available from about 1929 onwards from the SU Carburetter Co., of Erdington, Birmingham or from BG Carburettors of Hillingdon, Middlesex. The latter company will also fit oversized spindles and give the entire carburettor a thorough overhaul.

We now come to the next wear point of the SU; the throttle spindle. Open the throttle and feel for the amount of side play that may be present. If it is noticeable, undo the screws that secure the throttle, then withdraw the throttle and spindle. The wear is usually found in the spindle, rather than in the carburettor body on the more recent units, so fitting a new spindle can often cure the problem.

Tuning the SU is a basically simple job. First warm the engine up to a normal temperature. Then switch off the engine. Unscrew the throttle adjusting nut until it is just clear of its stop and the throttle is closed. Now set the nut one and a half turns open. Mark the piston/suction chamber assembly with a scratch mark to make sure that it is in line with the rest of the carburettor assembly. Then unscrew the three securing screws and remove the piston/suction chamber unit. Disconnect the choke cable.

Having done this, go to the bottom of the carburettor and screw the jet adjusting nut until the jet is flush with the bridge of the carburettor, or fully up if this position cannot be attained. Now replace the piston/suction chamber, lining it up with the scratch mark you made earlier. Check that the piston falls freely on to the bridge when the lifting pin is released. It should do this without a click, but if it does not and only does when the jet is lowered, then the jet unit requires re-centring.

This is carried out by removing the jet control linkage and swinging it to one side. Mark for reassembly, and withdraw the jet, remove the jet locking spring and replace the adjusting nut, and screw it up as far as it will go. Replace the jet, keeping the slot in the jet head in the correct relative position to the control. Now slacken the jet locking nut until the assembly is free to rotate. Turning to the top of the carburettor, remove the piston damper, and apply pressure to the top of the piston rod with a pencil. Tighten the jet locking nut, keeping the slot in the jet head in the correct position and the jet hard against the adjusting nut. Then check the procedure with the lifting pin again; the piston should freely fall on to the bridge when the lifting pin is released. Re-assemble the rest of the parts. If the needle does not fall freely, then go through the jet re-centring procedure again.

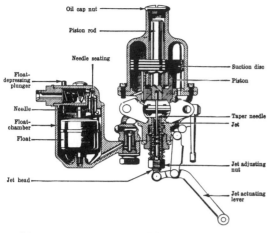

An SU carburettor of the mid 'thirties

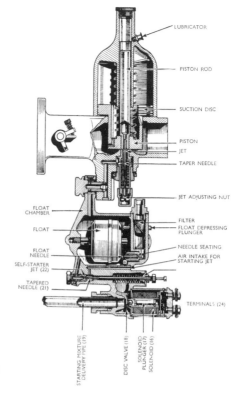

A 'thirties SU downdraught carburettor, fitted with thermostatic starting device, with actuating solenoid

The jet assembly of the SU thermostatic starting carburettor

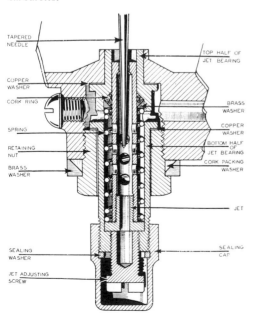

The post war SU H type carburettor. *Key* 1, jet adjusting nut; 2, jet locking nut; 3, piston suction chamber; 4, fast idle adjusting screw; 5, throttle adjusting screw; 6, piston lifting pin

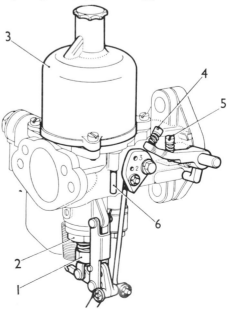

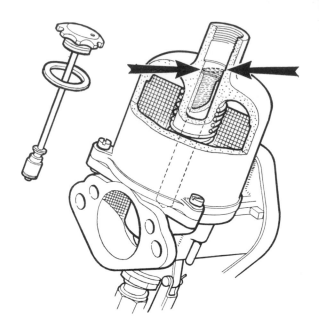

Thin oil (SAE 20) should be used to top up the piston damper, until the level is .5 in. (13mm) *above* the top of the hollow piston rod

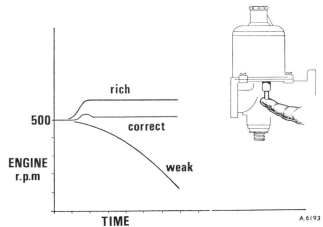

Check for correct mixture by gently pushing the lifting pin up .0625 in. (1mm). The graph illustrates the effect on engine rpm when the lifting pin raises the piston. This indicates the mixture strength
RICH MIXTURE: rpm increases considerably
CORRECT MIXTURE: rpm increases slightly
WEAK MIXTURE: rpm immediately decreases

A.6193

Adjusting the mixture control on an SU carburettor

The SU piston and needle assembly

If, on the other hand all is well, turn the jet adjusting nut back two turns. Re-start the engine and adjust the throttle adjusting screw to give the desired idling as indicated by the glow of the ignition warning light. Turn the jet adjusting nut up to weaken, or down to richen, until a faster idling speed consistent with even running is attained. Readjust the throttle adjusting screw to give correct idling, if necessary.

To check whether the correct mixture has been achieved, gently push the lifting pin up about $1/32$in. If the engine speeds up considerably when this is done it indicates a rich mixture. This will also be shown by a blackish exhaust smoke and a regular or rhythmical misfire. If, on the other hand, the engine speed decreases and the exhaust note is irregular with a splashy misfire and colourless, the mixture is too weak. A correct mixture will result in the engine's RPM rising slightly when the lifting pin is raised. The choke wire can now be re-connected with about $1/16$in. free movement before it starts to pull on the jet lever. Pull the choke knob until the linkage is about to move the carburettor jet, and adjust the fast idle screw to give an engine speed of about 1000 rpm when hot. Finally, top up the piston damper with thin engine oil grade SAE 20 until the level is $1/2$in. above the top of the hollow piston rod.

Make sure that your SU is fitted with the correct type of piston spring, as they are available in different strengths. If, for example, your carburettor is fitted with too weak a spring for its type, it can be a reason for the engine running weak, while too strong a one will result in the mixture being over rich. The following colour identifications refer to horizontal carburettors up to $1^3/4$in. throttle, and downdraughts up to $1^1/4$in. throttle. A red spring is regarded as being an average fitment.

Colour identifications of piston springs

Paint on end coil	Load
Blue	$2^1/2$oz
Red	$4^1/2$oz
Yellow	8 oz
Green	12oz
White	18oz

Special only to H1 type $1^1/8$ in. throttle horizontal carburettors

Green and Black	5oz

SU throttle sizes

Throttle diameter	Caruburettor type
$7/8$in.	HV0
1in.	UB, OM, HV1
$1^1/8$in.	HV2, H1, D2
$1^1/4$in.	MC2, HV3, H2, D3, HS2
$1^3/8$in.	HV4, H3, D4
$1^1/2$in.	H4, D4L, HD4, HS4
$1^5/8$in.	U5, HV5, H5, D5
$1^3/4$in.	H6, DU6, HD6, HS6
$1^7/8$in.	HV8
2in.	H8, HD8

Solex

The Solex carburettor is of the fixed jet variety. When it comes to removing the jets, the petrol and air ones can be removed without touching the other parts of the carburettor, this also relates to the economy and accelerator pump jets and pump non-return valve. On the other hand, the pilot jet air bleeds can only be removed after the float chamber cover has been taken off. You can probably expect to find sediment in the base of the bowl and this will have to be cleaned out. If the needle valve is leaking, then there is no alternative but to fit a new one.

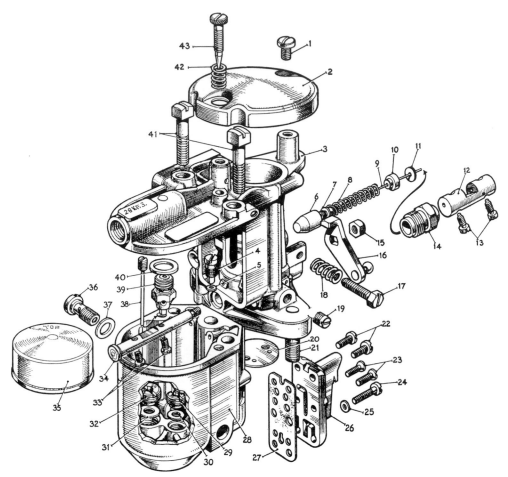

Zenith 26VF-3 carburettor, as fitted to the 8 hp Ford engine 1935-51. *Key* 1, screw fixing cowl; 2, cowl; 3, carburettor barrel; 4, slow running jet; 5, washer for same; 6, suction valve (includes item 9); 7, screw fixing wire in valve; 8, spring for distributor valve; 9, see item 6; 10, gland piece; 11, packing piece; 12, connector; 13, screw for connector (two off); 14, plug for distributor; 15, nut for throttle spindle; 16, throttle lever; 17, throttle stop screw; 18, spring for same; 19, plug over progression hole; 20, throttle; 21, stud for carburettor flange (two off); 22, screw fixing emulsion block (short, cheese head – two off); 23, screw fixing emulsion block (instrument head – two off); 24, screw fixing emulsion block (long, cheese head); 24, screw fixing emulsion block (long, cheese head); 25, washer for same; 26, emulsion block; 27, gasket for same; 28, carburettor bowl; 29, main jet; 30, fibre washer for same; 31, fibre washer for compensating jet; 32, compensating jet; 33, screw fixing throttle (two off); 34, throttle spindle; 35, float; 36, starter jet; 37, washer for same; 38, dip tube; 39, needle and seating; 40, washer for same; 41, screw fixing bowl (two off); 42, spring for air regulating screw; 43, air regulating screw

Standard setting. Choke tube, 19; main jet, 70; compensating jet, 65; S.R. jet, 60; needle setting 1.5mm; starting venturi, 4.0mm; jet, 100; dip tube, 140

Slow running is effected by turning the volume control screw, so weakening the mixture, clockwise, while anti-clockwise will naturally have the opposite effect. When carrying out this adjustment, make sure that the throttle control screw is set for an idling speed of about 500rpm.

To get the best results from a simple and basic Solex, remember that the main and correction jets virtually act independently of each other. Therefore, to richen up the lower end of the mixture curve, the main jet can be increased in size without effecting the correction jet. Similarly, wide throttle settings can be adjusted by changing the correction jet, the reverse principle, in fact, to the Zenith carburettor.

These carburettors can be overhauled by The Carburettor Centre of London N6.

If you wish to identify a Solex carburettor of the 'fifties, then the following information may be of help:

Size and type available

26mm diam. throttle bore, sidedraught, downdraught and updraught
30mm diam. throttle bore, sidedraught, downdraught and updraught, also twin bore
32mm diam. throttle bore, downdraught
35mm diam. throttle bore, sidedraught, downdraught and updraught
40mm diam. throttle bore, sidedraught, downdraught and updraught
46mm diam. throttle bore, updraught and downdraught

Type and code letters

F & BF	: Die cast carburettors
H	: Horizontal throttle bore
V	: Vertical throttle bore
I	: Downdraught model
R	: Regulator (governor) assembly in throttle tube
D	: Float chamber on right-hand side of air intake on horizontal carburettors, or starter unit on right-hand side of vertical carburettors
G	: Float chamber on left-hand side of air intake on horizontal models or starter on left-hand side of vertical models
L & LS	: Heavy commercial models
A	: Bi-starter
Z	: Dustproof
O & OS	: Special 'Zero' starter
T	: Thermostatically controlled starting device
P	: Accelerating pump (discharge direct to choke tube)
E	: Accelerating pump (discharge to base of well carrying jet assembly)
AA, FF, etc.	: Indicates dual or twin bore carburettor

Zenith

Fixed jet Zeniths are very straightforward to maintain, though on occasions it will be necessary to clean the jets which are screwed into the float chamber bowl. You can remove the main and compensating jets using the squared end of one of the float chamber bolts, while the slow running jet will probably have a screwed slot, as will the progression and accelerator pump jets if these are fitted. On occasions, the main and compensating jets are situated beneath external sealing plugs below the float chamber bowl. To obtain access to the pump discharge jet, the emulsion block, which contains the spraying beak, must be removed from the float chamber. It is vital to use a new gasket when refitting the block, incidentally.

With the jets removed, the ideal way of cleaning them is with a jet of compressed air, though an alternative (and this applies to jets of all makes of carburettor) is to use an aerosol spray like WD40. Never use wire though, as this can enlarge the orifice.

To adjust the idling, turn the air regulating screw, that you will find mounted fairly high on the carburettor, clockwise to enrich the mixture, while if you turn the volume control screw in the opposite direction, you will reduce the amount of mixture entering the engine. This latter control is found close to the mounting flange. Setting the slow running mixture slightly on the rich side will produce the best results.

Remember that the maximum power of the engine is influenced by the size of the main jet, though the compensating jet determines the mixture strength when the engine is working hard at low speeds.

The Zenith Carburetter Company report that they have a fair range of replacement parts for carburettors manufactured from 1945. Where common parts are used on old and new carburettors, they may still have some parts suitable for pre-war units as well. The company also keep many old carburettors in stock, so it might be worth getting in touch with them if you are in need

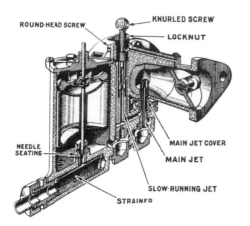

A side draught Zenith carburettor of the 'twenties, as fitted to the Austin 12. Standard setting: main jet 95; compensating jet 95; choke tube 21; slow running tube 26.5

Adjusting the mixture control on a Zenith carburettor of the 'fifties

The Solex AIP carburettor of the 'thirties

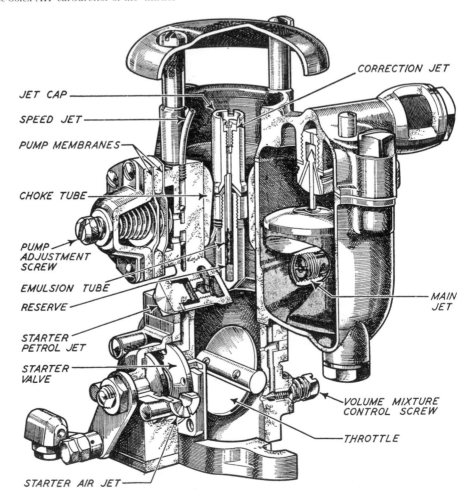

of a complete post-war carburettor. If it is just parts, or an overhaul, then go through the aforementioned Carburettor Centre.

If you wish to identify a Zenith of the 'fifties then the following information may be of help:

Size and type available

13mm diam. throttle bore, sidedraught
24mm diam. throttle bore, sidedraught and updraught
26mm diam. throttle bore, sidedraught, downdraught and updraught
30mm diam. throttle bore, sidedraught, downdraught and updraught
36mm diam. throttle bore, sidedraught, downdraught and updraught
42mm diam. throttle bore, sidedraught, downdraught and updraught
48mm diam. throttle bore, updraught and downdraught

Type and code letters

VE : Basic design letters, also used to denote updraught model
I : Added to VE reference to denote inverted (or downdraught)
H : Horizontal
G : Left-hand float chamber on side draught models when looking at air intake; also indicates anti-clockwise (or left-hand rotation) of throttle lever in updraught and downdraught models
A : Throttle spindle at 90° drawn through centre line drawn through bolt holes in fixing flange
F : Fixing flange centre line turned through 90° to normal
M : Often used to indicate a monobloc or combined casting

Deletion of letter E from any type reference, indicates that an accelerator pump is fitted

Weber

In addition to being fitted to much exotica, carburettors of Weber manufacture were finding their way, as original equipment, even onto the humble Ford during the 1960s. If the SU is the epitome of functional simplicity then the Weber is very much at the other end of the spectrum, not only in philosophy of construction but in the myriad types and configurations available. In view of this, and the space limitations here, no attempt is going to be made to lay bare the Weber mysteries in this book. If you have a Weber fitted to your classic, it is strongly recommended that reference be made to the Haynes Owners Workshop Manual which covers these animals in great detail.

Essentially the Weber is a fixed jet carburettor, often with twin chokes, and as such shares many of the adjustment procedures and wear problems of the Zenith and Solex.

I will now deal with some of the various petrol delivery systems that were available, beginning with the Autovac, which was fitted to many cars during the Vintage era.

The Autovac

The Autovac is always mounted under the bonnet on the vehicle's bulkhead, utilising suction from the engine to draw petrol from the tank, delivery to the carburettor being effected by gravity. It was made in the following sizes:

Type	Diameter	Tank length	Hp range
AV.7	4½in.	4¾in.	7 – 10
AV.1	4½in.	6in.	10 – 12
AV.21	4½in.	8in.	12 – 20
AV.31	5½in.	7in.	12 – 20
AV.41	5½in.	9in.	20 – 40

Although, as can be seen, the units differ in external dimensions, the internal working parts are identical. It is worth remembering that the unions are not the usual pipe threads, but are ½in. ×

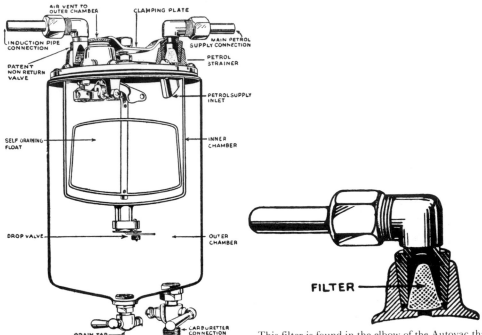

The Autovac. These worthy instruments are fitted to a wide variety of vintage cars

This filter is found in the elbow of the Autovac that leads to the main petrol tank, and should be checked at regular intervals

26 TPI (cycle) ones. Incidentally, it is not at all uncommon for the backfire valve in the suction elbow to carbon up. And should the elbows loosen, they should be lapped into their tapers with Brasso. Rolls-Royces using Autovacs are fitted with a restrictor valve in the suction elbow, which is also prone to carboning up and must be cleaned.

The system is remarkably fool proof, but if for some reason, petrol fails to appear in the carburettor, and you have not run out, then the following checks should be made. First see that the gauze filter mounted in the top of the unit in the elbow which leads to the petrol tank is clear. Also check that the air vent hole in the petrol tank filler cap is not choked. Make a point of checking all the unions and pipes for leakage. If the trouble is not caused by any of these factors, then take the top off the unit and see whether the valves, operated by a float within the Autovac, open and close alternately by hand and are not both open at the same time. Always use a new cork seal on the top flange. Another common cause of trouble is with the gravity flap valve at the bottom of the inner chamber, which can become pitted. This should be ground off flat on a sheet of carborundum paper on a piece of glass and lapped in with Brasso. Owners of cars fitted with Autovacs are fortunate in that a spares service still operates for these worthy components. Parts are available from Vintage Racing Cars (Northampton) Ltd., of Northampton.

AC mechanical pump

The parts most likely to wear on these pumps are the rubber diaphragms and valves. AC's recent catalogue still lists pump kits going back to the early 'thirties, so do not assume that because you have an old pump, you cannot get parts for it.

Basically the pump consists of two die castings, the body (which is mounted on the engine) and the upper casing. These are joined by a ring of screws round their flanges which pass through a diaphragm held between the two units. The diaphragm is actuated by an arm driven off the camshaft. For testing the pump, remove the feed pipe where it enters the carburettor bowl and turn the engine by hand. For each two turns of the engine, a spurt of petrol (about half an egg cup full) should be delivered. If this is not the case, the fault finding chart below may be of assistance.

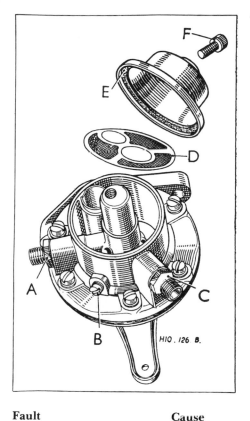

An AC mechanical pump of the early 'fifties *Key* A, delivery pipe; B, sediment drain plug; C, inlet union; D, filter; E, cork joint gasket; F, retaining set screw

Fault	Cause	Remedy
Starving at high speeds	Loose pipe unions.	Tighten.
	Broken or overcompressed filter gasket.	Replace gasket.
	Worn parts.	Recondition pump or exchange.
Difficult starting – slow priming	As above.	As above.
	Faulty valves or springs.	Replace.
	Incorrectly fitted diaphragm.	Refit.
	Leakage from carburettor bowl.	Stop leakage.
Carburettor flooding	Faulty carburettor needle valve.	Clean or replace.
	Pump pressure incorrect.	Check with specification. In some cases it is permissible to fit one or two extra gaskets between pump and crankcase to check flooding – not so many as to affect volume of pump delivery for max. power.
Excessive wear on moving parts	Lack of lubrication and corrosion due to: blow-by, inefficient crankcase ventilation.	Recondition engine. Improve breathing if possible.
Noisy operation	General engine noise.	Check with pump removed.
	Worn parts or broken rocker arm spring.	Replace.
Gum deposits from fuel	Vehicle standing unused.	Clean out fuel system completely.

159

Vapour lock	Fuel pipe near exhaust system.	Reposition or lag.
	Pump overheating.	Fit heat shield, improve ventilation if possible.
Excessive fuel consumption	Ignition, carburation or mechanical fault.	Excessive fuel consumption cannot be attributed to fuel pump, except in rare cases of diaphragm puncturing or splitting, and allowing fuel leakage to waste or into sump.

To dismantle the pump, first disconnect the unions and remove the nuts or setscrews securing it to the engine. Then clean the exterior of the pump and mark the flange of the body and the upper casing with a file or hacksaw blade to ensure correct re-assembly. Now you can remove the screws and separate the two halves. Then turn the diaphragm through 90 degrees and remove. Also undo the screws retaining the valve cage, trapping the valve discs and springs. Remove the filter cover and gauze and take out the circlip retaining the pivot pin, and push it out, releasing the rocker arm, spring, link and washers.

Wash the valve discs in paraffin, as this aids seating. The new (or original valves) should be replaced in the following order: outlet valve and spring, inlet valve on seat, spring in centre of disc, valve plate and retaining screws. Make certain that the inlet valve seats on the valve plate.

Also note that the 'U' type pumps have separate valve units fitted with 'spectacle' gaskets and retaining plates. The inlet valve spring should project into the pump chamber, with the outlet spring into the air dome.

Place the filter gauze on top of the casting, then fit the cork gasket, fibre washer and set screw, and assemble link and packing washers, rocker arm and spring in the pump body. Then insert the pivot pin and fit new springs. Where fitted, thread the oil seal washer spring and its washer onto the pull rod and turn the washer through 90 degrees to retain it. Now the diaphragm spring and diaphragm assembly can be placed in position.

Turn the diaphragm until the tab on its edge is at the '11 o'clock' position. Now press downwards on the diaphragm, turning the assembly to the left until it slots into the pull rod and engages with the forked end of the link. Finally, turn it one quarter turn to the left, to seat the pull rod in its working position at the same time as aligning the holes in the diaphragm with those in the body. The tab should now be in the '8 o'clock' position.

Now push the rocker arm towards the pump until the diaphragm is level with the body flange. Place the upper casing in position, bearing in mind, the score marks you made earlier. Replace the cover, screws and lock washers, tightening until the screw heads touch the lock washers. Continue to hold the rocker arm towards the pump and finally tighten the screws diagonally and securely. The edges of the diaphragm should be perfectly flush with the clamping edge.

The following information may help identify the various types of AC pumps, fitted to vehicles up to the mid 'fifties:

Type of pump	Body	Filter bowl or cover	Use
A	With detachable horizontal lower cover.	Glass	In general use to 1931 inclusive.
B	With detachable sloping lower cover.	Glass	Used on engines 10 hp and upwards, 1932-34.
M	With detachable sloping lower cover	Metal (ribbed) on top of pump.	Used on small cars, 1932-33.
Y	Single piece body.	Metal (plain) on top of pump.	Used on small cars, 1933 onwards.

T	Single piece body.	Metal (domed) on top of pump.	In general use, 1934 to to 1947.
TF	Single piece body, special engine flange.	Metal on top of pump.	Used on Ford (ex 8 and 10 hp) 1936-43.
TQ	Single piece body.	Glass (or metal) held by stirrup on top of pump.	Used on Vauxhall (ex 10 and 12 hp) and Bedford 1940-44.
U	Single piece body, detachable valve assemblies.	Metal on top of pump.	In general use, 1945 onwards.
UF	Single piece body, detachable valve assemblies, special engine flange.	Metal on top of pump.	Used on Ford (ex 8 and 10 hp) 1944 onwards.
UG	Single piece body, detachable valve assemblies.	Glass (or metal) held by stirrup on top of pump.	Vauxhall 6 cyl. 1945-51. Bedford 5 cyl. 1945-53.
UE	Single piece body, detachable valve assemblies.	Glass at side of pump.	In general use 1952 onwards.
WE	Combined fuel and vacuum pump.	Glass at side of pump.	Used on Ford Consul and Zephyr, Bedford 8 after March 1952, Bedford TA.

SU Petrolift

If this unit does give trouble, the chances are that the pump plungers are sticking, due to dirt or grit, between them and the pump body. If the pump fails to respond to a sharp tap, remove the bowl and foot valve, together with the top cap of the pump and the cork float. You will then be able to push down the plunger and remove it. A clean rag can then be drawn through the bore of the pump.

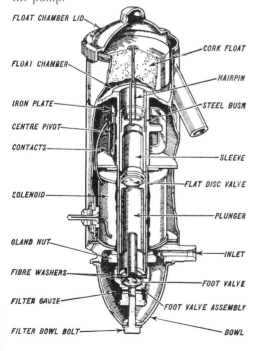

The SU Petrolift electric petrol pump, showing the construction and internal parts

However, if this does not do the trick, then remove the float chamber lid to see if the chamber contains petrol (if the Petrolift is fitted to a car when the fault occurs), and if it does, then the trouble does not lie in the pump. On the other hand, if the pump continues to make the right noises without producing any petrol, the trouble can be found in other areas.

First, check whether there is fuel in the main petrol tank! Another possibility is an air leak which may be between the bowl and the casing. If tightening the filter bowl does not have any effect, then fit a new washer. Another alternative suspect is the washer at the base of the filter bowl bolt. A rarer cause of trouble is caused by the foot valve being held up. To remedy this, remove the filter bowl, filter and foot valve by pushing a tommy bar through one of the holes. It is then possible to clean the valve. Remember that you will find a second filter in the foot valve, underneath the priming tube.

On the other hand, if the pump works slowly though without delivering any petrol, this could be due to blocked pipes; these must be cleaned out. If your battery is on the low side, you can prime the float chamber with petrol and start the engine by hand. Should you be faced with the situation that the pump will not work at all, and you are sure that the plunger has not stuck, a bad electrical connection is the probable culprit. To ascertain this, remove the terminal from the pump, and check that you have power, with a test bulb.

In the event of the electrical part of the pump failing, the filter bowl will first have to be removed, followed by the foot valve. Then the large hexagon gland nut which holds the inlet ring should be undone. The casing can then be drawn off, revealing the solenoid. You should take particular care that the cork gland washer makes a good petrol tight connection between the inlet ring and the electrics. If you have any doubts then you will have to have a new one made, or obtain a spare. You must take particular care when removing the casing that you do not break the wires, and the top wire does not foul the rocking plate (marked 'iron plate' on the accompanying diagram). To test that the contacts are in working order, providing the bottom plunger has not jammed, remove the float chamber cover and then lift the float up and down its full length. Should you require a new float, then a replacement can be made by Charles Cantrill Ltd., of Birmingham. Listen carefully and you should hear the rocker plate click as it breaks contact.

Having re-assembled the pump, and it works, it should be primed by pouring a little petrol into the top chamber.

SU L-type electric pump and its variants

If you find that the pump is not working, disconnect the fuel delivery pipe, and if the pump then works, this indicates that the carburettor's needle valve is sticking. But if it does not work, disconnect the feed wire, and with the use of a test bulb, check that it is live. If you have power then remove the pump's cover and touch the feed terminal with the live wire. If the points are closed, but no sparks occur, then suspect dirty points, which can be cleaned by drawing a piece of cardboard between them.

With the pump connected, the carburettor tickler depressed, and the delivery pipe unions slackened, and the pump still does not work, suspect a blocked suction pipe. But if the pipe is clear then the fault can lay in the pump itself, being a stiffened diaphragm or dirty guide rollers.

When you come to examine the all-important points, armature travel is suspect if they are not making contact. Check that the diaphragm is not stuck to the solenoid housing by slackening the assembly screws and passing a small knife blade between the surfaces. If the toggle is still not operating, then you will have to dismantle the entire pump.

To do this remove the filter plug and washer, then the inlet union and washer, followed by the outlet union and its washer with the valve cage and washer, suction valve, and in some cases, a spring. Remove the spring clip from the valve cage to gain access to the delivery valve. Then undo the cheesehead screws and the earth terminal. (Early examples of these pumps have five screws and one earth mounting terminal while later examples have six retaining screws and an earth terminal.) Now unscrew the diaphragm assembly from the trunnion, taking care not to lose the all important guide rollers (there are 11 of them).

Remove the nut retaining the contact breaker cover and take off the cover, and then take off the retaining nut on the terminal screw.

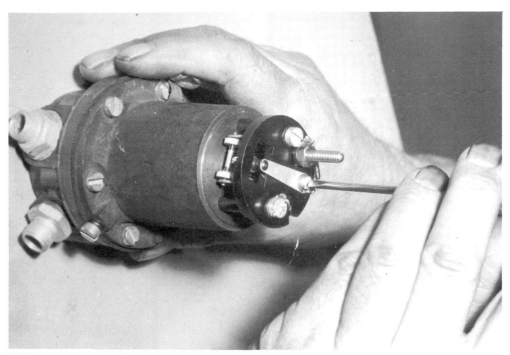

Fitting new points to an L type pump

Undo the 5BA screw retaining the contact blade terminal tag, spring washer and then the blade. Remove two long 2BA screws retaining the pedestal, and spring washers. Take off the toggle assembly, carefully sliding the coil end tag over the terminal, then push out the hinge pin and remove the rockers. But do not touch the solenoid core.

When you come to re-assemble the pump, make sure that the disc valves are fitted with the smooth side on their seatings, ensuring that the retaining clip is well and truly home in its groove. A thin hard fibre washer fits under the valve cage with thick washers over the cage, above the filter plug and inlet union.

Assemble the contact breaker toggle so that the rockers are quite free without any side play. You may find it necessary to square up the outer rocker with pliers. Fit the contact spring blade with the coil tag on top. You must now adjust the points. The blade should rest on the projection on the pedestal when the points are open, and they should connect when the rocker is in the mid position. The tension of the blade should not impede the action of the rockers, the gap being 0.03in. Hold the blade against the pedestal and insert the feeler between the body of the pump and the rollers on the outer rocker.

However, should you fit a new diaphragm, adjust the armature. To do this, swing the contact blade to one side, fit washers into recess in armature; screw armature in position in trunnion, place the guide rollers round the armature, remembering that no jointing compound should be used on the diaphragm, and holding the solenoid assembly nearly horizontal, push the armature in firmly and steadily. It should be screwed until the toggle does not operate, then unscrewed a sixth of a turn (one screw hole) at a time until the position is found where the toggle just operates. Then unscrew the armature two thirds of a turn (four screw holes). The setting is now correct. Place the solenoid body on the pump body, with the drain hole in the solenoid in line with the filter, and all the rollers in position. (Misplaced rollers will, incidentally, puncture the diaphragm.) Insert the cheese headed screws and the earth terminal, but do not tighten them until the diaphragm is flexed by placing a match stick under the outer rocker rollers to prevent toggle action and energise the solenoid by connecting the terminals to the supply. This will flex the diaphragm fully. Tighten the screws and terminals evenly and in rotation, and remove matchsticks.

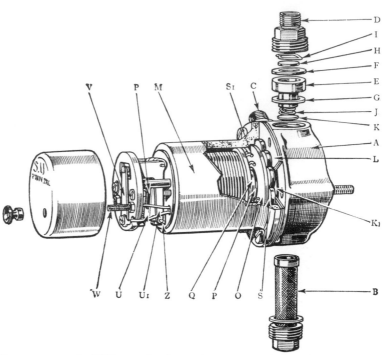

That familiar component, the SU L type electric petrol pump. A mid 'thirties example is shown here. *Key* A, pump body; B, filter; C, inlet union; D, outlet union; E, valve cage; F, fibre washer (thick); G, fibre washer; H, delivery valve disc; I, spring clip; J, suction valve spring; K, suction valve disc; K 1, retaining plate; L, diaphragm assembly; M, solenoid housing; O, armature; P, bronze pushrod; Q, solenoid iron core; S, guide rollers; S 1, volute spring; U, U 1, rocker mechanism; V, contact blade; W, stud terminal

Variations on a theme of SU

In addition to the aforementioned L-type, the pump is also available in a number of variants: the HP which operates at a high pressure and the LCS which has a larger capacity. The L and HP are also available in double forms, sharing a common base. All these pumps are very similar, but the HP can be identified by its longer solenoid housing, having a different spring and diaphragm assembly, while the LCS has a rectangular base and different diaphragm layout.

The 12 volt pumps are identified by the fact that they are fitted with black or red covers and red insulation, while the six volt variant can be identified by a brown end cover and green insulation.

A word of warning about fitting these pumps to vehicles that previously relied on gravity fed carburettors is necessary. High pressure pumps should *not* be used, as the extra pressure will overcome the weak needle valve and raise the float level causing a rich mixture and flooding. High pressure pumps will not deliver a greater volume of petrol unless small bore pipe work is fitted.

The following applications of the various SU electric pumps described in this section, may be of help:

Type	Recommended mounting position	Petrol pipe outside diameter	Maximum output gal/hour	Suction lift (approx)	Output lift (approx)
L	In region of engine, at approximately carburettor level.	$5/16$in. single $3/8$in. dual	8	48in.	24in.
HP	Amidships or over rear tank, at carburettor level or just below.	$5/16$in. single $3/8$in. dual	10	33in.	48in.
LCS	Amidships or over rear tank, at carburettor level or just below.	$3/8$in.	$12\frac{1}{2}$	33in.	48in.

Maximum outputs of 'double' types of L and HP pumps are just over double those of single types.

Petrol tanks

Things like petrol tanks have a horrible habit of leaking, but it is not possible to repair them yourself as you do run the risk of blowing yourself up. A much safer and quite 'cold' process is to apply Petseal* to a dry tank. This gives a long term repair and also seals up any rust, or loose particles in the old tank.

However, if the base is beyond repair, Raymond Radiators of London NW1 can make a new bottom for you, and if you require a completely new tank, then this can be made by Marston Radiator Services Restoration Unit, of Coventry. The important thing is that the metal used must be zinc or lead coated to prevent it from rusting internally.

This fuel gauge sender unit has clearly been leaking. A new gasket will probably be required

Petrol tank floats are either cork or metal. The latter should be checked for leaks

Notes on development

Practically all cars built in the 'twenties relied on gravity to supply petrol to the carburettor(s). This either took the form of a scuttle mounted petrol tank, on the cheapest cars, or the phenomenally reliable Autovac, patented by J. Higginson and H. Arundel in 1911. (Higginson was, incidentally, the first customer for Vauxhall's magnificent and legendary sports car, the 30/98.) The Autovac is basically a small feed tank mounted high enough above the carburettor to give a head of fuel. By tapping suction from the inlet manifold, fuel is drawn from petrol tank into the Autovac to an inner chamber, which when sufficiently full, passes the fuel into an outer chamber, and so by gravity to the carburettor.

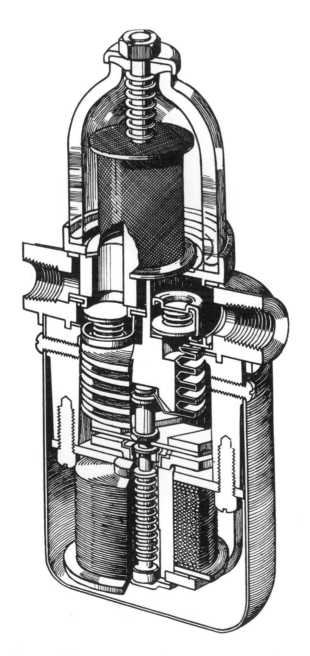

The American Autopulse electric pump put in a brief appearance on British cars at the end of the 'twenties and early 'thirties

But it was this reliance on gravity, that led to the disappearance of the Autovac in the 'thirties, although it lingered on for many more years on commercial vehicles. For the introduction of downdraught carburettors rendered the difference in height (so necessary for gravity feed) almost neglible. Consequently in 1928, the American AC Sparking Plug Company produced their mechanical pump that was driven off the engine's camshaft, and was available in this country from 1929 onwards. The American Autopulse electric pump also appeared here at about the same time, though a British built electric pump, the Petrolift, produced by the SU Carburetter Co., designed by J. N. Morris and M. D. Scott, appeared in 1929. This lasted until 1933 when it was replaced by L-type electric petrol pump, designed by Morris (of Petrolift fame) and R. L. Kent, and is still with us in substantially the same form today. This, and the continual refinement of the AC mechanical unit resulted in the Autovac's fate being well and truly sealed!

Carburation has changed little over the years, the two principle types being the fixed jet (exemplified by the Solex and Zenith) and the constant vacuum variety typified by the famous SU. This carburettor was invented way back in 1904, though it was not patented until the following year, by two brothers, G. H. and Carl T. Skinner (hence Skinners Union). The single jet carburettor used a tapered needle connected to a piston which rose when the throttle was opened, thus utilising the suction produced by the engine. The original SU used leather for the carburettor bellows; the brothers connection with the shoe firm of Lilley and Skinner presumably proving useful! The design was refined over the years, the famous G5 'slopers' being fitted to the three litre Bentley, though the company's most significant customer was William Morris, who fitted SUs to his 'Bullnose' cars for the 1922 season. Although he swapped to Smiths instruments the following year, he was obviously impressed with the SU and in December 1926 he bought the company.

By contrast, both the Solex and Zenith carburettors hailed from France before the First World War. The Solex, invented by Messrs Renee and Jouffret, and produced by Maurice Goudard and Marcel Mennesson, soon became available in this country after the war, being sold by Messrs Wolfe and Co., of Southwark, and in 1925 Gordon Richards, left Wolfes and started Solex in England as a manufacturer of carburettors, rather as an importer of French parts and components. Solex in Britain remained independent until 1964 when it joined forces with Zenith, though carburettors are now longer manufactured under this name.

The Zenith carburettor was invented by one Francois Baverey in 1907, and right from the start was a truly international component, one correspondent in the early 'thirties noting that it was being manufactured in Germany, France, Italy and America. Although Zenith now embraces the constant vacuum type of carburettor, they are probably known during the era under review for their fixed jet instruments. The Zenith fitted to my 1928 Austin 16 has practically no wear after nearly 50 years use, but it is made of bronze, which is perhaps a reminder of one of the changes in the manufacturing processes that dominated carburettor production in the 'thirties.

For up until the early 'thirties practically all carburettors used sand cast bronze bodies, which made them virtually indestructable, but expensive to produce. (In fact a Solex might cost between £8 and £9 cast in bronze, which is not much more than a small unit of the present day.)

The answer to this problem (as far as the manufacturer was concerned) was to adopt die-casting, which was already well established for this purpose in America by the late 'twenties. The process involved a mould, machined from high quality nickel chrome steel, receiving a shot of molten zinc alloy injected under pressure. It was not long before die casting became a feature of British built carburettors, although sand cast throttle bodies were often retained in view of the metal's hard wearing qualities. Also SU electric fuel pump bodies were originally sand cast, but die cast zinc bodies appeared in the late 'thirties.

The archetypal Weber, the 40DCOE, fitted to the Lotus Twin-Cam engine of an Elan

Chapter Six

The overhaul of the electrical system

Any electrical apparatus is usually regarded by the average person with fear or as somewhat of a mystery . . . **Sir Herbert Austin (1926)**

Although Austin wrote these words for an excellent three part work on car electrics, which he hoped would remove some of the 'mystery', there is little doubt that electricity in general, and a car's in particular, is still approached by many with considerable trepidation. This is no doubt because you cannot *see* the wretched stuff (a live and dead wire look exactly the same) for only the *results* of current passing through a cable indicate that power is flowing.

If you are embarking on a complete restoration, it is a good idea to overhaul all the various electrical components, even if they appeared to be functioning correctly when you gave the car its test run. Far better to overhaul the dynamo, starter and distributor in the relative comfort of your own workshop than at 3am in the middle of Dartmoor, which is the sort of occasion when the volts department can start playing up!

I will be dealing with the individual components later on, but first some general observations on the subject of tracking down electrical faults, might be appropriate. For when dealing with car electrics your best friend is a simple, though very effective, test lamp. Purchase a 12 or 6 volt lamp and holder (depending on the voltage of your car), and connect two lengths of wire, each about three feet long, to the socket. Then attach a crocodile clip to the end of each wire. You are now in business.

To discover a fault in a circuit, connect one wire to the car's body or chassis. Then, with the current switched on, touch the other end to the feed terminal. The bulb will light if current is present. You can then try it on the other side of the switch to check continuity. Should you find that everything is working at that particular point, but the component is still dead, try earthing it with a separate earth wire. If it then works, then the original earth is at fault. But if it does not, you will know that the breakdown is in the component itself.

If you find that as a result of these checks that you have to replace a length of wire, make sure that you use the proper grade, and correct colour coded type, and that you insulate the connection well. The business of using the correct coloured cable may not sound important, but think of the poor chap who might have to sort out a future failure. I remember I once ran an Austin Seven which was completely wired in one colour, yellow! Fortunately the electrics never gave any trouble, but I shudder to think of the problems that could have arisen with a luckless owner having to sort out those cables, using the aforementioned test lamp.

The electrical wiring used in cars is specially graded, and is usually referred to first by a number, indicating the number of strands, and then followed by a decimal reading of the thickness of a single strand. Therefore a 28/0.012, indicates that there are 28 strands, each one having a diameter of 0.012in. When replacing cable, you should strictly adhere to the following grades:

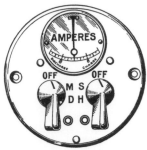

Lucas switch panel, 1928. The left hand switch turns on the magneto, then the dynamo, while the right hand one operates the side and head lamps

Lucas switch panel, 1933. On the left, the half and full charge positions indicate a 'third brush' dynamo

Grade	Application
14/0.012	Side and rear lights, interior and dashboard lamps
28/0.012	Headlights, windscreen wiper motor, dynamo charging circuit, horn
37/0.036	Main battery lead and starter motor supply
61/0.036	lead. The longer the lead the thicker the
61/0.044	cable required

Many Vintage and some early 'thirties cars were fitted with armoured electrical cable as original equipment. This was for many years manufactured by Ripaults Ltd., but is now produced by Paul Beck of Norwich, and is available from him, in 30 metre rolls in the following grades:

14/0.012	Single, double and triple core
28/0.012	Single and double core
37/0.036	Battery cable (10 metre coil)

From about the mid 'thirties, colour coded cables (also known as the Lucas Colour Code) began to appear, which has grown in size and complexity over the years. Feed wires (such as ignition, lights, etc.) carry only one colour, while switch wires have the main feed colour, with a coloured tracer. Return, or earth leads, are black. In the following table, the main colour is given first and the tracer second.

Colour	Circuits
Brown	Main battery feed to control box and equipment supplied direct from battery. Lighting and ignition switches
Brown/blue	A1 on control box to ignition switch
Brown/green	Control box (F) to dynamo field coil
Brown/yellow	Dynamo to control box (D) also ignition warning light
White	Ignition circuit, and all associated when ignition is switched on, but are not fuse protected
White/red	Ignition switch to starter solenoid
White/black	Distributor to CB contact on coil
White/blue	Ignition auxiliary terminal to fuse
White/red	Starter switch to solenoid switch
Green	All accessory feeds through ignition switch, protected by ignition auxiliary fuse
Green/purple	Stop light feeds
Green/red	Left hand indicator feed
Green/white	Right hand indicator feed
Light green/brown	Flasher unit to direction indicator switch

Light green/purple	Direction indicator dash warning light
Blue	Headlight circuits
Blue/white	Dipswitch to headlight main beam
Blue/red	Dipswitch to headlight dipped beam
Purple	Circuits protected by auxiliary fuse, not normally controlled by ignition switch
Purple/black	Horn push to horn
Red	Side and tail light circuits
Red/white	Panel light feeds

Of course, you have to consider whether you are going to completely rewire your car. Modern wiring, with its PVC insulation, certainly does a much better job than the rubber insulated wire of the past, which was subject to perishing. The wiring of Vintage cars is obviously a lot more straightforward than that fitted to cars in subsequent decades, though the job is somewhat complicated by the fact that you cannot really use colour coded cables, as they will not be in keeping with the rest of the car. Before removing the old cable, take careful sketches of the positioning of the wires, particularly those found behind the dashboard. It is difficult to generalise on how much cable you will need, but around 100 feet is average (compared with anything up to 200 feet on a modern car). You can get some idea by measuring the amount of wire in the old loom. Do not throw this away, because you will probably need many of the special clips and connectors attached to it. And if you use the aforementioned armoured cable, remember that you will have to whip the ends to prevent the aluminium armour unwinding. To identify the wiring, when you are carrying out the actual job (bearing in mind that the cables will usually only be coloured red and black), attach loops of suitably inscribed masking tape to the tags, so that you know 'what' comes from 'where'. They can be removed after the wiring has been connected up, and the system is working correctly. If the cables have to pass through metal, always fit a rubber grommet to prevent the sharp edge of the hole chafing the wiring.

Rewiring a 'thirties car is rather more complicated because there is so much more wire, although replacement looms for a wide variety of cars from the post-vintage years onwards are available from Auto Sparks Ltd., of Hull, Yorkshire. However, you do have the advantage of the colour coding system to help you. Nevertheless, go through the same procedure of making drawings of the wiring before you tear everything apart. When you write down the colour of the cable, make sure to put the main colour first, followed by the tracer, not the other way round. Auto Sparks' looms are fitted complete with their end terminals (there are often about 100 of them), but you will find that the entire system is finished in PVC tape, rather than the traditional cotton braided covering. While you are carrying out the rewiring, it is not a bad idea to make a minor alteration to the loom's layout, if it originally ran underneath the car. If possible, try and re-route it *inside* the car where it will not be vulnerable to the rigours of the climate.

There are a number of different ways by which wires can be attached to components. One of the most common is the tag terminal. This is essentially a washer, extended in one direction so that the jaws, when gripped judiciously with a pair of pliers, close and secure the bared cable, though it is often advisable to use solder as well. I expect you are familiar with the grooved washer with a ring of claws round the edge, which are depressed once the hook of stripped wire and a washer are placed within them. This is rather grandly known as the Ross-Courtnay terminal. The Lucar connector is probably the best known push-on-spade terminal. With this variety, only a very small amount of insulation needs to be removed from the cable, the strands being stripped under the bridge piece of the terminal and then soldered in place. The adjacent jaws are then crimped into position on the wire, thus removing any strain from the connection. Finally, a rubber shroud is pulled over the joint which serves as an effective insulator. A very simple method of joining one, or more cables together is to use a bullet connector. This is a hollow section of tinned copper. The appropriate cable is stripped and the bared wire inserted until the strands project through the hole in the end. They are then soldered in place, cleaned off with a file and attached to a similarly attired opposite number with an insulated spring connector.

Before leaving looms and their component parts, some mention should be made of fuses, as from the early 'thirties onwards, they played an increasingly important role. The amount of fuses on cars varies considerably. However, on average, one fuse rated at 35 or 40 amps protects the accessory circuits, which only operate when the ignition is switched on. This includes the fuel gauge, windscreen wiper and direction indicators. Also a 35 amp fuse is used on the horn, interior light and fog and spot lamp circuits, those in fact, which operate regardless of the ignition. The following fuses are to be found:

Fuse rating (Amps)	Identity colours (Lucas, other makes vary)
5	Red printing on yellow paper
10	Green printing on black paper
15	Black printing on light brown paper
25	Black printing on pink paper
35	Black printing on white paper
50	Purple printing on yellow paper

If a fuse should blow, discover what the fault is by checking each component in turn with your test lamp. Do not just replace the fuse, it will probably just blow again!

I will now consider the individual components that make up the car's electrics, starting with the heart of the whole system: the battery.

Battery care and maintenance

If you have the slightest doubts about the age and efficiency of the battery in your car, get rid of it because a dodgy battery is far more trouble than it is worth. I know, I have suffered with some!

Considering the amount of hard work they do, batteries require surprisingly little maintenance. Keep them regularly topped up with distilled water (about 0.125in. above the top of the plates). Also ensure that the terminals are clean, and stop copper sulphate deposits from building up there. In my experience, I would definitely advise against using the battery connectors which are secured by a single screw to the top of the post. Either the thread strips, or the screw breaks off through corrosion. The clamp type connectors, fitted with a pinch bolt, give you a far tighter and longer lasting connection. If your car is fitted with a battery of unusual shape (MG and Riley are two examples), then it is possible to obtain replacements from L.G.Batteries of Luton, Bedfordshire. Should you have any doubts of the ability of your battery to retain a charge, then buy a hydrometer (they are quite cheap) to measure the specific gravity of the electrolyte.

Although I am the first to underline the importance of originality, there are exceptions to every rule and in the battery department I think that modifications are quite acceptable. Many old cars (and even some modern ones) use a 12 volt system, produced by wiring two six volt batteries in series. You will save yourself a lot of trouble if you convert the system to a single 12 volt battery. By doing this, you will eliminate connection problems and while six volt batteries are still available, they are becoming increasingly difficult to locate.

Overhauling the dynamo

Dynamos are, on the whole, very reliable pieces of equipment, and the following overhaul is normally all that is necessary to ensure that they continue to function correctly. These instructions essentially refer to the more modern two brush components, though obviously much of the information can be related to the earlier three brush type.

Lubrication is obviously an important factor with any dynamo, and this should be carried out every 10,000 miles. A lubrication hole is provided at the end of the commutator end bracket, and a few drops of oil should be injected there. The oil is absorbed in a felt washer which acts as a reservoir. If, on the other hand, the example on your car is fitted with a lubricator on the end of the same bracket, unscrew the cap and lift out the felt pad and spring and half fill the lubricator cap with high melting point grease.

Unfortunately the chances are that your dynamo will be suffering from more than lack of lubrication. The brushes are the most likely parts to be worn. On some dynamos the brush gear can be reached via windows in the dynamo yoke, which are usually covered by a thin metal cover. But on some later examples the windows are located in the rear plates. To get at the brushes, it will be necessary to partially dismantle the instrument. But before doing so, mark the end plate and yoke to ensure correct re-assembly. Once you have done this, unscrew the two long bolts running through the dynamo, and remove the end plate. You will now see the commutator brushes, secured in their brush holders by leaf springs. Pull off the springs and take out the brushes. On more modern cars, if they are worn down to 0.25in., or less, fit new ones. The minimum brush lengths on older units vary, and if you cannot obtain the correct replacement brush then modify a modern equivalent. The minimum brush lengths tables for some models may be of use:

Lucas generator model	Brush minimum length (in.)
C35 (third brush type)	
Main brushes	0.31
Control brush	0.25
C 39	0.34
C 45	0.43
C 47	0.31

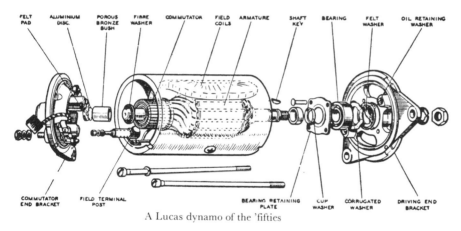

A Lucas dynamo of the 'fifties

A typical 'third brush' dynamo of the 'twenties. *Key* A, brush spring clip; B, brush; C, face of commutator

The brushes on this dynamo are ripe for replacement!

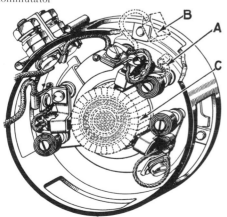

173

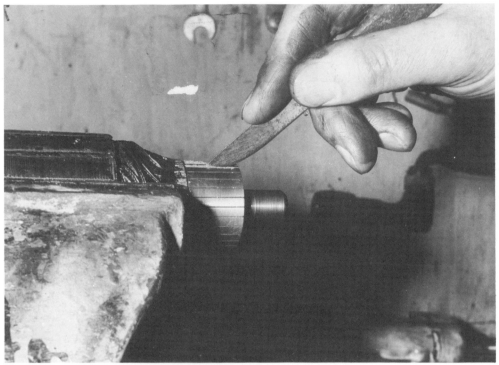

Undercutting the commutator on a dynamo. This should *not* be done on a starter motor

Having dealt with the brushes, you can continue with dismantling the dynamo. Remove the armature and end bracket, and then place the unit in a vice fitted with soft jaws. Undo the nut securing the pulley, remove the pulley and take out the Woodruff key, followed by the bearing locating ring. The end plate should then be supported in the jaws of the vice, and then gently tap the armature through the bearing, using a suitable drift. If you have any doubts about the efficiency of your dynamo, now is the time to take the armature along to your local auto electrician to check the armature windings and the field coils.

The next stage is to clean the commutator on the armature with a rag soaked in carbon tetrachloride (you can buy it at Boots). The surface should be completely free from burn marks or pitting, but any minor damage of this nature can be removed by using a strip of glass paper wrapped round the commutator. The insulators between the segments should *not* be level with the surface. If this is the case, they should be cut back 0.03in. below the face of the commutator. An old hacksaw blade is ideal for this purpose. If, on the other hand, the surface of the commutator is badly pitted then it will have to be skimmed. An auto electrician can do this for you.

The other likely wear points on the dynamo are the bearings. The one in the 'brushes end' is usually porous bronze, fitted in a blind hole. The best way to get it out is to screw in a 0.625in. tap a couple of turns and pull! Some liberally applied heat to the outside of the cover may also help. The new bush should be soaked in oil for 24 hours prior to fitment. Then press the new bearing into position using a vice and a drift.

Unfortunately the ball bearing at the drive bracket end is rather more difficult to sort out. Have a look at the drive bracket and you will see that the bearing is lurking behind a retaining plate, secured by rivets. These will have to be drilled out to free the retaining plate. Once the plate has been removed, turn the bracket over and knock out the bearing with a drift; it is only a press fit. Then out can come the corrugated washer, followed up by a felt washer. Now you can clean the housing, and fit the new bearing, packing it with high melting point grease. Replace the felt washer in the housing, then the corrugated washer. Using a drift to fit the inner ball race, tap the bearing evenly into position. New rivets will have to be used to resecure the retaining plate. Split the end with a cold chisel, then use a ball pein hammer to spread them. You are now in a position to fit the end bracket on to the armature spindle, so mount the armature vertically in a vice and use a hollow drift to tap the inner race of the bearing onto the shaft. Then on goes the spacer, Woodruff Key, pulley, spring washer and nut, in that order.

Make sure that the brushes move freely in their holders. If they seem a trifle on the stiff side, lightly sand them down and clean the holders with carbon tetrachloride. Check that the securing springs are so positioned that the ends bear on the *sides* of the brushes, so holding them firm, prior to completing the re-assembly of the dynamo. After checking the marks we hope you remembered to make, refit the end cover and tighten the through bolts. Now, using a piece of hooked wire, lift the ends of the brush springs into contact with the back of the brushes, thus pushing them into rubbing contact with the commutator. This completes your overhaul. You may wish to give the dynamo a lick of paint at the completion of your work.

Starter motor overhaul

Overhauling the starter is not quite such a straightforward job as working on the dynamo. This is because although two brushes are also connected to the end bracket, two others are soldered to tappings on the field coils. You can get round the problem by cutting off the old brushes, making sure to leave a couple of copper 'pig tails' behind them. Then new brushes and flexible leads can be soldered in the normal way.

On the starter unit, two porous bronze bushes are used, and the new ones must be soaked in oil for 24 hours before assembly. The other main difference between the dynamo and starter, as far as reconditioning is concerned, is that on the latter component the insulation between the segments on the commutator must *not* be undercut. The remaining dismantling and reassembly procedures are otherwise straightforward enough.

You can clean the commutator with a length of glass paper

Commutator wear on a
starter motor

Fitting a new bush in a
starter motor using a vice
as a press

Re-assembling the motor.
Note that the brush springs
against the *sides* of the
brushes during this stage of
the operation. Once the end
plate has been replaced,
they can return to their
customary position on top
of the brush

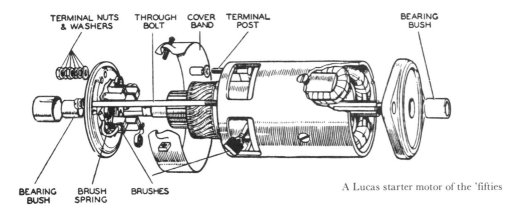

TERMINAL NUTS & WASHERS   THROUGH BOLT   COVER BAND   TERMINAL POST   BEARING BUSH

BEARING BUSH   BRUSH SPRING   BRUSHES

A Lucas starter motor of the 'fifties

Worn brushes, a failing in both starters and dynamos

The dynastart was a feature of the 'Bullnose' Morris, the best selling car of the 'twenties. This bulky unit combined the roles of starter and dynamo and consequently was in constant mesh with the engine

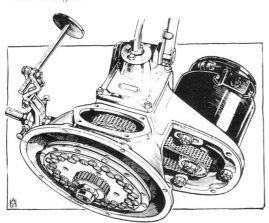

Always try to restore electrical components so that the names and numbers can be read

The Bendix spring, providing it has been working efficiently, should not require much attention, other than giving it a thorough cleaning, but make sure that it is perfectly dry when it is refitted to the car. Do not, whatever you do, oil the Bendix as there is sufficient vapour under the car's bonnet to keep it lubricated. Oil simply collects dust and dirt and prevents the component from working properly. Faults are associated with a bent shaft, broken spring or damaged cog. Taking the spring apart requires special tools, so let your auto electrician sort this one out for you.

All these jobs, including complete rewiring, can be undertaken by Bob Krafft of Auto Services of London SE27.

Distributor overhaul

The distributor is a very important, though fortunately a somewhat simple instrument. When dismantling the device, take care to note the order of the various parts, this particularly applies to the insulating washers and bushes. Also remember that it is easy to re-assemble the unit with a cam sleeve 180 degrees out, so do not forget to take note of the direction of the slot.

It may be necessary to replace the bearings, which are made of bronze and should be oil soaked in the same way as those fitted in the dynamo and starter. It is possible to drift the old ones out, while the new ones should be replaced in a vice using a distance piece. If they are available, make a point of replacing the small springs which control the centrifugal advance mechanism. You may notice that on some distributors, one of the springs appears to be loose on its mountings. This is quite intentional as it allows a rapid degree of advance to build up against one spring, before the second one comes into play. In the same way, one spring may appear thicker than the other.

Make a point (sorry!) of fitting new points and also a new condenser. The latter item is particularly important if the old points seem well worn and 'bluey' in appearance. Now is the time to set the points at their correct clearance, and this can be achieved with the aid of a feeler gauge. On Lucas distributors made prior to 1952, the correct gap is 0.010 to 0.012in. while units made after this date should be set at 0.014 to 0.016in. Check the distributor cap for cracks and for any evidence of tracking inside the cap, and if present, then replace.

The coil

With its lack of moving parts, the coil will soldier on for years without giving any trouble, though it is vulnerable to deterioration if the car is left standing for any length of time. If you have any doubts about its state (a doubtful coil can be a reason for a bad misfire), and you have an ammeter available, then take a reading of the current produced. If you get three amperes exceeded on a 12 volt coil, or six for a 6 volt one, then a partial, or complete short circuit is quite likely. If you have not got an ammeter, then the simple answer is to replace your coil with a proven substitute. If this cures the misfiring, then you have found the answer to your problem.

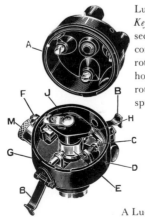

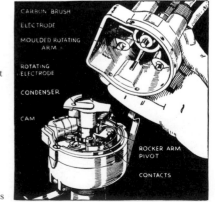

Lucas distributor, type DS4, 1929. *Key* A, distributor moulding; B, securing spring for moulding; C, contacts; D, locking nut; E, rotating cam; F, terminal; G, oil hole for wick lubricating cam; H, rotating distributor arm; J, contact spring; M, greaser

A Lucas distributor of the mid-thirties

A check point in any distributor cap. Always examine the conditon of the central electrode

A typical Lucas distributor of the post war era and a straightforward item to overhaul

Many starting problems can be put down to worn points. Pitting is the most usual shortcoming, as can be clearly seen in this photograph

179

A distributor stripped down. The centrifugal advance weights are readily apparent

Little has changed by way of distributor basics. This 1930 Morris Oxford fitment is close to any modern car with some exceptions

Note how on this distributor body the cap clips are fixed by the most enormous nut

Magnetos

There is a great temptation to pack the magneto off to the appropriate expert if there is any doubt about its overall condition. One definite indication that it is in need of attention is whether you can press your finger nail into the shelac coating of the armature. If you can, then do not hesitate to have the magneto overhauled.

Adjusting the contact points on a magneto is a straightforward enough business, though you will need a small set of spanners which are still, appropriately enough, called magneto spanners. One of the points is usually carried on a threaded spindle and held in place with a lock nut. To remove the contact breaker, undo the central screw and lift it out. If pitted, the points should be cleaned with a carborundum stone or fine emery paper. Later types of magneto used a contact breaker system similar to those found on coil ignition distributors, and should be dealt with similarly.

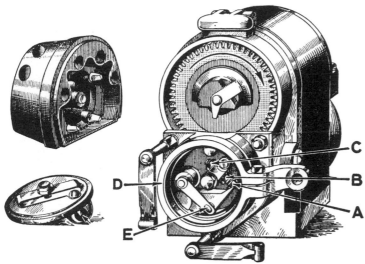

Practically all magnetos of the 'twenties used this layout, with the notable exception of the ML. *Key* A, fixed platinum points; B, adjusting screw; C, lock nut; D, cam cage ring; E, bell crank retaining strip

Another straightforward maintenance operation is to clean the magneto's slip ring. You will find the high tension collector brush beneath the removable cover. Like most brushes, it should slide freely in its socket. Black lines on the collector brush housing shows that high tension current has been tracking. Providing this is not too bad, you can preserve the smooth surface by using fine emery paper, following up with a going over with Brasso. Also carefully check the slip ring flanges for signs of tracking. Where a wipe brush distributor is favoured, check the condition of the brush itself with the segments in the cap. The state of the insulating material between the segments is particularly important. A build-up of carbon, coupled with scoring, can result in tracking between these close set contacts.

If you do have occasion to remove the vernier coupling from the magneto, you will find that a puller will bend the coupling. *Never* tap the shaft. The best method is to position a soft metal bar in a vice and use it as an anvil, placing it on the flange at the back of the coupling, the magneto itself being well supported. Then position another piece of metal on top of the flange, and gently hammer. The coupling should then slide off.

The magneto's points should be set to between 0.012 and 0.015in.

Spark plugs

As explained in the Notes at the end of this Chapter, up until 1933, 18mm plugs were almost universally fitted to British cars, though from this date, the smaller 14mm plug gradually gained complete dominance. Fortunately 18mm plugs are still readily obtainable. Obviously engines vary considerably in type and performance, so you would be advised to speak to the spares registrar of your one make car club to see which plug he usually recommends for your particular engine.

If your engine uses magneto ignition, then set the plug gap to between 0.015 and 0.018in., while plugs used in conjunction with coil ignition should be between 0.022 and 0.025in.

Contrary to popular belief, there is no need to tighten spark plugs with the sort of vigour you usually reserve for big end bolts. Do them up to finger tightness and then nip them tight with a good plug spanner, though be particularly careful with an aluminium cylinder head, as you run the risk of stripping the threads.

The cut out and CVC unit

This is one of those departments best left to the experts. You can confine your activities to taking the covers off and cleaning the contacts, ideally by drawing a stiff piece of card between them. Again, Auto Services will be able to help you out in this respect.

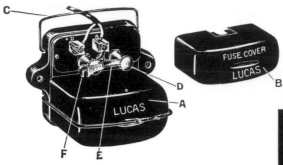

A Lucas cut out and fuse box, circa 1928.
Key A, cut-out cover; B, fuse cover; C,
wire securing fuse cover; D, fuse securing
nut; E, fuse strip; F, spare fuse strips

Cut out and fuse box, type CFR 2 of the mid
'thirties

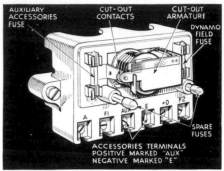

Lamps

If you own a pre-war car, then the lamps will make an important contribution to the appearance of the front of the vehicle. The lamp shells themselves are generally made of brass, but should *not* be stripped or polished. They were originally nickel (later chrome plated) or painted black.

Should the lamps have any dents, they should be dealt with by a professional panel beater, particularly so because the brass can be very thin in places. Remember that the slightest imperfection will be accentuated when the plating is carried out. You can also reckon that most lamps suffer from hinge cover damage (if one is fitted), so this should be attended to at the same time. You will also probably find that the reflector has dulled with age and this will have to be resilvered.

A Lucas headlamp, the reflector of which is ripe for
re-plating

The solenoid that dips the reflector
shell. The other headlamp is
extinguished at the same time

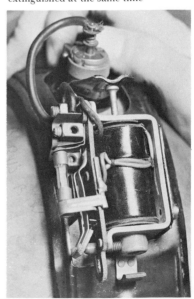

Parts of a Lucas headlamp of the 'thirties, following restoration

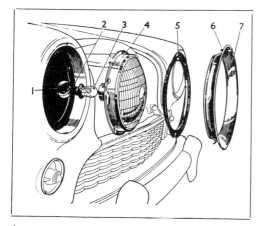

Headlight assembly, 1955. *Key* 1, bulb backshell; 2, adjustment screws; 3, bulb; 4, light unit; 5, rubber dust excluding ring; 6, headlight rim securing screw; 7, headlight rim

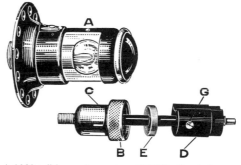

A 1929 tail lamp, Lucas type TF 201. *Key* A, lamp front; B, coupling nut; C, cable covering shell; D, cable plug; E, rubber washer; G, cable securing screw

Rear number plate light, 1955 *Key* 1, light cover; 2, securing screw; 3, light glass; 4, rubber joint ring; 5, bulb

A number plate and tail light, circa 1935

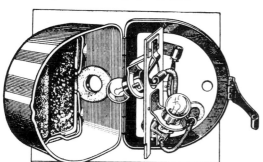

Should your lamps be fitted with a particularly distinctive lens, and one is broken or missing, then the only answer is to hunt around for a replacement, which can often be a lot more difficult than it sounds. However, many Vintage cars were fitted with a diffuser type glass and a virtually indistinguishable modern equivalent is, despite its ecclesiastic overtones, Chance's 'Plain Cathedral'. Make sure that you fit it the right way round in the rim though, with the serrated side on the *inside*, otherwise you will pick up a lot of unwelcome dirt. You will also need this frosted glass for the side lamps, incidentally.

As far as the rear lamps are concerned on a Vintage car, Rubberlite Model 8 by Flexible Lamps Ltd., of Epping, Essex is a good substitute, and they are available with provision for double filament bulbs, so this could be a good opportunity to fit brake lights. A motor cycle stop light switch can easily be modified to work on most systems. On later vehicles, try and retain the original rear lamps and do not be tempted to fit a modern equivalent. Invariably they look ghastly.

The whole question of legislation in relation to lighting on elderly motor cars is ably dealt with in Appendix One.

Wiper motor

Although this item does a tremendous amount of work, the chances are if it does stop, the fault is nothing more crucial than brush failure. To get inside the motor, unbolt the mounting pillars and remove the five screws on the gearbox cover. The conrod on the final gearwheel can then be disconnected from the end of the rack and the motor and rack can then be parted. Fitting the new brushes is a simple enough operation. The two through bolts come out first and then the end covers can be removed, and the yoke pulled off the armature. While the motor is in this state, it is a good idea to give the interior a thorough cleaning, particularly if the brushes have worn right away and everything is smothered in a shower of carbon dust. The commutator will usually benefit with cleaning in carbon tetrachloride and a brush up with a strip of sandpaper.

To fit the new brushes, first study the location of the old ones and make sure that you fit the new ones in exactly the same way. This usually means linking the two brush holders with a spring. They are clipped into position and then locked with a composition plate. Make sure that you get the *right* bushes for the job though. Cut down dynamo ones will not do. Then reassemble the unit.

Another problem you may experience, which can be sorted out at the same time, is the dreaded 'over wipe' characteristic. This usually involves the wiper blades overshooting the windscreen and giving the bodywork immediately beneath the screen an unwelcome brush. This shortcoming is caused by wear in the wheel boxes. A perfectly satisfactory way round the problem is to dismantle the wheelboxes and turn the gear wheels through 180 degrees to bring an unworn sector into contact with the rack.

The electric petrol gauge

This is made up of two principle parts, a sender unit in the tank and a gauge mounted on the dashboard. The three most common faults occurring with this type of gauge are broken resistance wires in the tank unit, burnt out coils in the gauge itself or bad contacts between the wiper arm in the tank and the resistance winding. While in the case of the first two faults the only alternative is to fit new units, the last named problem can be remedied by bending the wiper arm so that it presses more firmly on the winding. However, when carrying out this adjustment, take care not to bend the float arm, otherwise a false reading will result.

When the ignition is switched on and the gauge does not move, this shows that no current is reaching the gauge winding. This can be due to a broken connection between the ignition switch and the gauge, or a short in the two circuits. If the gauge should register 'empty' all the time, it is either due to a sticking float, a break in the tank unit's resistance windings, or a burnt out control coil in the gauge.

With the pointer on the 'full' mark all the time, the break in the circuit will be on the coil in the gauge, or the float is sticking in the 'up' position. Another reason for a low reading is a heavy float. Cork and metal floats are usually used, and a puncture in the latter type will make the float heavy, while the former variety can be 'soaked' by petrol and the same can happen.

Trafficators

Semaphore indicators were fitted to cars from the early 'thirties, even lingering on until 1961 on the faithful Morris Minor! One of their most common failings is the failure of the trafficator arm to light (a three watt festoon type bulb). More often than not, this is due to the flexible wire, which connects the lamp to the solenoid circuit, breaking in one or more places. You can replace the wire, but care must be taken to ensure that there is sufficient wire to loop round the pivot arm.

The trafficator arm itself is highly vulnerable and being a die casting, tends to get damaged easily. If you have occasion to replace the arm, the pivot pin will have to be knocked out. When refitting, it must be rivetted lightly to prevent it from coming out, at the same time taking care not to damage the arm itself.

In two terminal trafficators, you will find that the earth is generally secured to the chassis, rather than the body. However, if a bodywork connection is adhered to, it may account for the unit's erratic operation. Then if the failure is caused by a faulty bulb, it is advisable to raise the arm by means of the indicator switch, holding it out by hand having turned the ignition off. This will prevent you causing a short circuit when you remove the bulb from its holder.

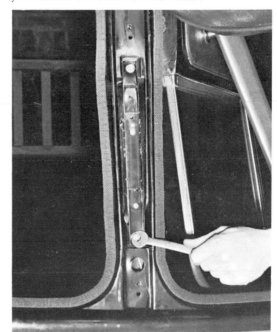

On some cars, the only way to get at the trafficators is on the inside

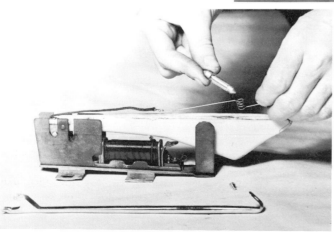

The festoon bulb being removed from a Lucas trafficator. Note the vulnerable spring loaded connector and the wire soldered to it

185

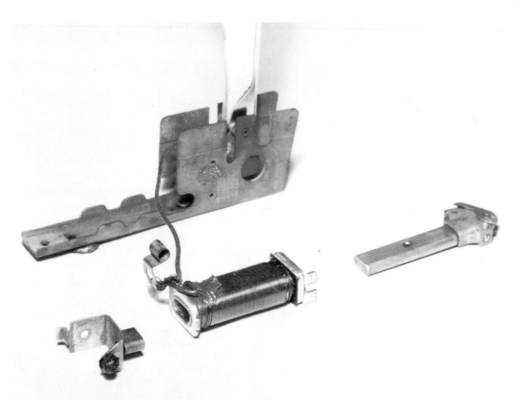

A trafficator stripped down. The main body is in the background with (*left to right*) end piece, solenoid and armature

Sluggish and uncertain arm movements can be caused by grit clogging the moving parts or rust in the solenoid plunger. It is worthwhile smearing thin grade oil on the plunger, but do it sparingly as the oil will gather dust and you will be back to square one. If the arm does not fully return to its housing, a slack connecting wire is the most likely cause. A worn pivot pin and linkage will also cause the arm to stick. This can be prevented by oil, but again be sparing with its application.

Notes on development

1919 – 1929 The main difference in the electrical components of a British car built before the First World War, and after it, was the addition of a starter motor and the standardisation of electric lighting, both items demanding an efficient dynamo and battery system. Ignition was, in the main, by the well established high tension magneto and the vast majority of vehicles were fitted with two pole electrics, which did not harness the chassis as an earth return system. But by the end of the decade the magneto was on the point of being ousted by the coil with the wasteful twin pole wiring also on the way out though some manufacturers like Singer, Riley and Standard stuck with it longer than most.

But to go back to the appearance of that all important component, the starter motor. Charles F. Kettering of America's Dayton Engine Laboratories Company (hence Delco) is usually credited with the design of the electric starter motor, having previously done work in a similar field designing an electric motor for the National Cash Register Company's tills. His starter was fitted as *standard* equipment to Henry Leland's 1912 Cadillac, though initially the starter pinion was engaged in mesh with the teeth on the flywheel by mechanical means. It was not until Vincent Bendix invented the spring that still bears his name the following year, that the starter motor emerged much as we know it today. Apart from electric starting the Cadillac also standardised electric lighting and coil ignition, both of which sprang from Kettering's fertile brain. He invented a mercury type voltage regulator to get over the charging problems associated with electric lighting, while coil ignition had been occupying him since 1908.

186

A 'wipe and contact and trembler coil' had been used by Lenoir as far back as 1860, though the layout was considerably refined by George Bouton (of de Dion Bouton fame) in 1895, with a make and break layout which was the antecedent of the modern contact breaker. However, the appearance of Bosch's H.T. magneto of 1903 resulted in the instrument's almost universal acceptance. Kettering's experiments differed from Bouton's in that instead of a shower of sparks being produced by a flexible blade, he favoured a rigid spring loaded contact breaker arm in a distributor which produced one single accurately timed spark. And he fitted his new component with a condenser to prevent arcing at those all important points.

From this time, Europe and America struck out in different directions, the Old World favouring and developing the efficient but costly (in manufacturing terms) magneto, while the New concentrated on refining of the coil and its attendant battery. These diverse paths were not reunited until the end of the 'twenties when a combination of the rigours of the world economic depression and a trend towards small six cylinder engines (which required more expensive six cylinder magnetos) saw the coil achieve practically universal acceptance, for it offered by that time, consumer reliability and manufacturing economy: an unbeatable combination.

As we have seen, the high tension magneto was born in Germany and up until the outbreak of the First World War, Britain was almost dependent on the ZU series Bosch magneto, though the outbreak of hostilities saw the import of these magnificent instruments and their attendant spark plugs, cut off. Thus the British magneto industry was given something of an induced birth. For by the time that the war came to an end, the exhaustive demands of the aircraft, and to some extent, the motor industry had resulted in the infant growing into a robust and healthy child. Then, in 1920, the Japanese announced the results of their experiments to improve magnet steels, which the British were quick to recognise. It was thus possible to produce smaller magnetos, than hitherto.

Consequentially magnetos were fitted to many British cars during the 'twenties, even the cheapest ones. Morris retained the system on his Cowley until 1929, while the Austin Seven was fitted with magneto ignition until 1928. Coil ignition was fitted to some cars, however, just two extremes being the 1920 Leyland Eight and the two cylinder Jowett!

Dynamos at the beginning of the decade were of the constant current type, being scaled down versions of those used for railway lighting sets. But the third brush system, invented by Dr. Hans Leitner and R. H. Lucas in 1905 and featured on early Delco units, soon gained almost universal acceptance. For this arrangement gave the driver some element of control over the charging rate of the dynamo. The third brush was used in conjunction with a resistance in the circuit so the driver could vary the charge by a 'summer' and 'winter' setting, being low and high charge rates respectively. He did not know it, but there was a third setting as the resistance was completely eliminated when the car's headlamps were turned on. The lamps themselves were handsome affairs, finished either in nickel or painted a sombre black. A variety of dipping aids were tried, the more expensive cars favouring a mechanical system, though pneumatic layout was to be found at the cheaper end of the range. Side lamps often resided on the wings or were mounted high on the scuttle in front of the doors, a traditional position, inherited from the days of horse drawn carriages.

The basic principle of the spark plug had changed little since Lenoir produced his first plug in 1860, it being a brass nut into which was cemented a porcelain body containing the electrode. An 18mm thread diameter with 1.5mm pitch was standardised (first used by de Dion Bouton, incidentally) although mica took the place of the brittle porcelain and zinc coated steel for brass for the plug body, which carried 9/16 Whitworth flats.

Most cars fitted 12 volt electrics, except at the lower end of the price range, where 6 volts predominated. By contrast, practically all American cars used a 6 volt system, some makes only converting to 12 after the Second World War! The dynastart did not last anything like as long. This combination of a starter and dynamo had few champions in this country, with the notable exception of William Morris. This bulky instrument also appeared on George Roesch's Talbots of the 'thirties.

Electrical accessories were few and far between, though the end of the 'twenties saw the electric windscreen wiper begin to challenge the cheap, but erratic vacuum type while semaphore indicators began to make their presence felt, albeit in small numbers.

1930 – 1940   The main changes in car electrics during the 'thirties were the phasing out of the third brush dynamo, the introduction of the colour coded wiring system and the change from negative earth wiring to positive.

As we have seen, the third brush constant current system gave the driver some control over the dynamo charging rate, but the introduction of the constant voltage system around 1934, with its two brush dynamo and CVC unit made the whole business completely automatic. For with the third brush layout, the speed of cutting in was dependent on the speed of the machine and the demands of the battery in large vehicles, such as coaches, made the weakness of the system more apparent. (It is perhaps only of historical interest, but although the new arrangement had been used on the continent prior to its introduction into this country, it already existed in positively jumbo form in power stations. For it appeared in principle in the Tirrill Regulator system, established before the First World War by British Thomson-Houston Company Ltd., in power station generators!) The driver probably did not notice much difference with constant *voltage*, as opposed to constant *current* control, though it did give manufacturers an excuse to dispose of the ammeter, as the change made its readings slightly more difficult to interpret.

Electrical equipment manufacturers had toyed with colour coding on their electrical cables for years, but around 1934 Lucas introduced their colour code, which is still going strong today. Although initially the wiring remained black, coloured sleeves were attached to the ends, being blue for the headlights, red for the side and tail lamps, yellow for the dynamo cables and purple for the horn feed. By 1937 coloured cables had been introduced, the system being extended by incorporating a tracer colour into the cable.

Britain had, for many years, remained faithful to the negative earth system, but in 1936 manufacturers changed over to positive earth which was done initially to effect a reduction in plug voltages and so prolong plug electrode life. Another reason for the change was to reduce corrosion between the battery terminals and on other contact points throughout the car.

1933 saw the introduction of the more compact 14mm spark plug, while from 1938 onwards, mica was replaced by sintered materials as the insulating medium.

Yet another step along the road to eliminating driver control over his electrics came in 1939 when an automatic vacuum advance mechanism was introduced. (Since the earliest days of motoring, the driver had been able to 'advance' and 'retard' his ignition manually, which was particularly important when the engine was started by hand. Too much 'advance' could give the motorist a nasty jolt!) At the same time a micrometer adjuster was introduced which permitted fine adjustment of the ignition timing.

As we have seen, the magneto was vanquished from the vast majority of British cars, though it continued to be used on some more expensive, sporting marques and on racing cars where its ability to efficiently produce sparks at high speeds was unchallengeable. Magnetos were again reduced in size, through further Japanese and British developments, though the advance mainly favoured aircraft magnetos where weight was an ever present consideration. A major advance in magneto design was exemplified by the Scintilla Vertex magneto of 1931 which hailed from Soleure in Switzerland. This featured the elimination of gear wheels and introduced the conventional distributor and contact breaker cam, more associated with the battery/coil system. This had the advantage of eliminating the necessity of periodic cleaning with the older carbon brush type. Also the magnets rotated (though this was not altogether new), but it did mean that the appearance of the magneto was dramatically altered, which had not really changed much in shape since 1897.

The increasing use of solenoids to actuate such components as semaphore indicators, headlight dipping mechanisms, starter motors and petrol pumps, together with the popularity of electric windscreen wipers led to the fitting of fuse boxes under the bonnets of many cars during the decade.

1945 – 1960   Electrics changed remarkably little during this era, the emphasis being on refining the system, rather than breaking new technical ground. Significant advances included the disappearance of the headlight dipping system which tipped one reflector bowl, while the other light was extinguished; this being replaced by double filament bulbs.

The hard working system had to cope with yet another component in the shape of an electric motor for the newly introduced heating units. Windscreen wiper motors disappeared from their traditional position over the windscreen to be tucked under the car's bonnet, the drive being transmitted by flexible cable, a trend that had started in the late 'thirties.

1960 – 1970 The post 1960 era is of historical interest, for the introduction of the alternator from America (with its greater low speed efficiency in our traffic-jammed towns and cities) has rendered the dynamo as obsolete as the magneto became, back in 1930. It has also meant that wiring has reverted to the negative earth system, which is where we came in!

A general increase in the complication of the electrical system went hand-in-hand with early moves towards the 'fully-equipped' car that was to appear first from the Japanese manufacturers in the early 1970s. In addition to a greater array of 'warning' paraphernalia, the standard fitment became more commonplace of such things as heated rear windscreens, hazard lights and even electrically-operated windows.

A more ergonomic approach to driver use saw the start of the migration of many control switches from dashboard (and floor) to clusters around the steering wheel.

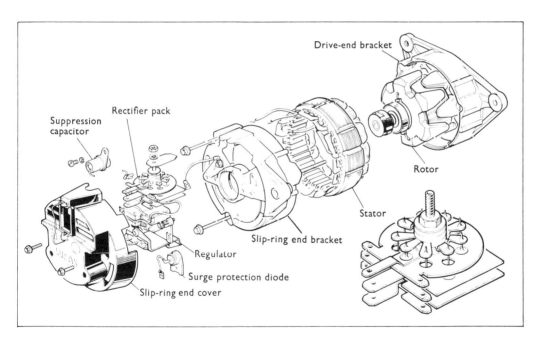

Lucas alternator with integral regulator and rectifier

Sunbeam-Talbot 90, 1944 cc and 2267 cc 1948-54. Sunbeam Mark III, 2267 cc 1955-57. The 90 first appeared in 1948 being fitted with the smaller capacity 1944 cc engine and cart sprung front end. The Mark II, by contrast, used independent front suspension and the 2267 cc engine from the Humber Hawk. The car was further revised, the Mark IIA having engine improvements and larger brakes, remaining in production until 1954, though 'Talbot' was dropped from the title from thereon. The main rust point is around the forward rear spring hanger, though also check the headlamp surrounds and front wings, where there are rubber splash guards which tend to hold water. The picture shows Sheila Van Damm in a 1955 car

Chapter Seven

Bodywork maintenance, repair and construction

For the car to look and keep its beauty and smart appearance, the coachwork must be given its share of attention; it must not be neglected. **Handbook of the Austin Sixteen Light Six (1928)**

One of the most wasteful things on earth is rust. **Professor A. M. Low (Science in Industry)**

It is probably an appropriate moment to consider the whole business of bodywork restoration. But let us look on the bright side for a moment, there might not be much to do! As I mentioned at the start of Chapter Two, if you are lucky enough to discover a car which has retained its original paintwork, then keep it in this condition, though unfortunately such vehicles are few and far between. Cars of all ages rust to a greater or lesser extent, and there is bound to be some body repair work to do. This type of work is often outside your scope, which is why it is so important to get a car with a good body if your resources are limited, as farming out these repairs can be an expensive business. However, there are some things that you can tackle yourself and in this chapter I will be dealing with coping with limited rust damage, repairing dents and holes, respraying and, for the more ambitious, what is involved in building your own bodywork, though this can obviously only apply to the traditional ash frame construction.

Rust attacks cars of different ages in different ways. In Chapter One, I mentioned that saloons were usually in better bodily shape than tourers, mainly because when all the doors were closed, the 'box' was effectively sealed, while a tourer was particularly vulnerable to the effects of our damp climate.

During the 'twenties we have seen that cars were often fitted with 19 and 20in. wheels, which meant that they were fairly high off the ground, and consequently the underside was not so vulnerable to bombardment by mud, rain and slush. In many cases the bodywork was aluminium. This can oxidize, of course, but it is a much rarer phenomenon than our familiar old enemy: rust. Steel wings were generally fitted to the more popular cars, and apart from being vulnerable to bangs and splits were prone to rusting where they joined the chassis, or valances, both being water traps. Most wings will respond to restoration, providing they are not too badly damaged, though their renovation, which can involve a fair amount of panel beating and welding, can be said to be a specialised job; it depends so much on the type of work, your facilities and abilities.

Smaller wheels bringing the bodywork nearer to the road, plus the almost universal adoption of pressed steel bodywork during the 'thirties, meant that cars were more vulnerable to rust; on the plus side the separate chassis continued to do a reasonable job from the structural point of view, though this box section structure was itself susceptible to corrosion.

Post-war cars tend to be the worst rusters of the lot. Let me again underline that if you are faced with a monocoque structure, with its load bearing panels, suffering from an advanced case of 'tin worm', then avoid it unless it is a particularly rare beast. For here the only answer is to cut out metal and weld in new, which requires the sort of equipment that the average DIYer does not have in his garage. But before discussing the various ways of repairing and maintaining your bodywork, I will offer a few words about rust and why it occurs.

Rust is a motor car's most implacable enemy, and it is essential that you take every effort to eliminate it and keep it at bay. I am sure that nobody needs any introduction to the wretched stuff, but it is worth pondering for a moment on just why rust occurs. In pure air, a thin film of oxide forms on metals such as iron, steel, nickel and aluminium which inhibits further corrosion, and a similar protective film occurs in pure water. The trouble is that our air and water (in the form of rain) is by no means pure, being contaminated by industrial fall-out which helps to form weak acid solutions. In addition, salt laid on the roads during the winter months, when aided and abetted by slush makes up a lethal, corrosive paste, which lodges in a car's crevices, setting up an electrochemical action, as in a battery (a fact, incidentally, that was not appreciated by scientists until the 'thirties).

In a wet cell battery you have two electrodes, the anode and cathode in touch with the electrolyte. This liquid contains electrically charged particles called ions. The difference in the electrical potential between the anode and the cathode provides the driving force which causes the negatively charged ions to flow to the anode (positive), while the ions which are positively charged, flow to the cathode (negative) pole. The outcome of all this 'to-ing' and 'fro-ing' is that the positive ions cluster around the cathode and the anode then dissolves.

Now, on a car's body, the metal surface, covered with water, results in anodic and cathodic action occurring in the same way, the area of bodywork beneath the water being starved of oxygen becoming anodic, while the area not so deprived becomes cathodic. Consequently corrosion sets up in the anodic area and when the water is polluted by road dirts and acid, the conductivity is increased and rusting accelerated.

With all these horrors raging on, it is obviously vitally important to keep an eye open for the first signs of rust. It usually takes the form of tell-tale bubbling under the paint. The most likely areas to suffer in this way are the sills, the bottom of the floor pan, any gaps in welded joints or seams, the headlight surrounds and the top and sides of the wings adjoining the front doors. This last named area applies specifically to post-1945 cars. These are all fairly noticeable being on top of the car, but there can be even worse things going on down below. Pay attention to the anchorage points relating to suspension, brakes and steering. The way to test these areas is to prod around with the large screwdriver we encountered in Chapter One. If the metal is sound, you will not damage it, but if it is not, you cannot make the trouble much worse, just find out how bad it is, and get there before the DOE tester!

However, it is possible to arrest the spread of rust, but first a few thoughts on rust inhibitors would be appropriate. There is no chemical process which will turn rust back into sound metal, short of the smelting furnace. Rust inhibitors work by changing the rust into a chemical compound, which no longer attacks the metal, but they cannot put *strength* back into the steel. Most rust inhibitors use phosphoric acid as a base, though some use hydrochloric acid as well, to speed up the process. Although they work faster, these hydrochloric based inhibitors have to be neutralised with water, if not, once they have finished with the rust they start on the sound metal. There are a number of other variations on the theme, using tannic acid, but the phosphoric type have the advantage of not requiring neutralising, and are also cheaper, which is important.

In addition, there are paints which have a rust killing action, and these also contain phosphoric acid. The acid converts the rust, but then the paint takes over, sealing the metal from further attack. Other paints contain a finely powdered zinc dust, and providing there is enough zinc present, the results can be quite impressive. If water gets in, the zinc and iron start off the old battery business again, with the body as the cathode and the zinc as the anode. But the difference is that the zinc corrodes and the body does not, which is why paints such as these are sometimes called sacrificial anode paints. When zinc corrodes to zinc oxide, it does not bubble and swell like iron oxide, but stays the same size and clogs up the paint pores and stops further water getting at the body.

Clean the area to be proofed as well as you can, removing as much loose rust as possible, as well as eliminating all traces of grease or oil. Then you can apply the rust inhibitor. Wait for the prescribed time and then apply primer, followed by a colour coat if the area under renovation is an exposed section of body.

You can deal with small holes in the bodywork yourself, though the only really satisfactory way is to have them repaired professionally by an expert who can use body solder. Unfortunately, finding such an expert can be difficult these days. So I will deal with the alternative, which you can carry out in your own workshop. If you are not going to completely respray the car then protect the area immediately around the damage with masking tape. About 10in. around the corrosion is about average. Then clean off the paintwork with the aid of an electric drill and wire brush, following up with 120 grit sandpaper. Then hammer the damaged area until it is well below the level of the body contour. Mix up a paste using one of the many filler kits on the market and apply, reinforcing it, either with perforated zinc, or glass fibre matting. For best results use a plastic spatula, smoothing the paste until it is proud of the surrounding bodywork. You will find that with most kits the paste takes about 20 minutes to 'go off'. Once this has happened, rub down with a coarse 80 grade sandpaper, though for final shaping use a 320 grit wet and dry paper. If any blemishes are apparent, repeat the application. Any indentations can be felt by rubbing your fingers over the surface. Wash the repair and surrounding area with lukewarm water and allow it to dry. Then apply a priming coat, overspraying by about 3in. onto the surrounding bodywork. Apply 400 grade wet and dry paper to this surface, following with undercoat and top coat.

Dealing with a dent

One of the more likely failings you will have to deal with is a common dent. Now this may involve some panel beating, and I will be the first to admit that it is a lot easier to write about than to do. I have watched expert panel beaters at work and it looks simplicity itself until you are handed the hammer and dolly and told to get on with it. The basic panel beating kit should include a selection of planishing spoons, a body hammer, a variety of dollies and a body file (which is adjustable).

The dented surface is first roughly knocked out using the hammer and dolly block. The correct dolly should weigh about three times as much as the hammer, and should be about the same curvature of the body which is to be straightened. The dolly is positioned behind the panel which is then struck with the hammer. The first difficulty the amateur will experience is to ensure that he is actually hitting the concealed dolly, but the task is made slightly easier by the fact

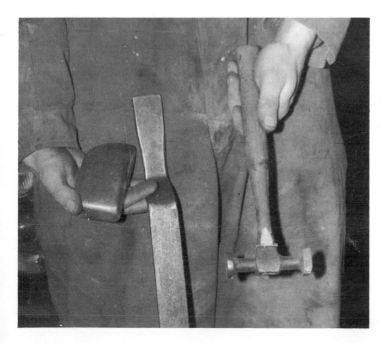

The panel beaters tools: dolly, flipper and hammer

193

that the hammer has a broad face which distributes the blow over a wide area. But do not necessarily think of the dolly as an anvil, for there are instances where you want to raise the metal, whether it is hit directly by the hammer, or by an adjacent blow. Another rather distracting habit the first timer will experience is the business of the dolly bouncing back after being struck by the hammer through the panel. Although it is likely to bounce slightly, it is the hammer that should rebound from the repeated blows to the surface of the metal. Striking the dolly directly with the hammer is known as the 'hammer on' technique, which is designed to raise the lowest points of the metal, the pressure on the dolly being progressively increased to raise the surface. With the 'hammer off' procedure, the dolly is positioned adjacent to the hammer, rather than immediately in front of it. This, naturally enough, has the effect of forcing the high spots down because they are unsupported. This transfers the blow from the hammer to the dolly and if skilfully applied, the pressure from the dolly can force the low spots up. Thus you vary the pressure with your left or right hand, depending on which highs and lows you want to deal with. When applying this technique you should always hammer the high adjacent to the low, never the other way around.

The next stage is to finish off with the spooning. The spoon, or flipper, is often made from an old file, bent so that the convex side can be used on the body. But the first thing to do, after you have finished with the hammer and dolly, is to go over the surface with a body file, set to the correct curvature to the body part under repair. The serrations on the file will indicate the high spots, producing bright scratched areas, but the file must be regarded as a guide only, do not try and file the highs off with it! Taking up the dolly again, place it behind the panel and hammer away at the surface with the spoon at the low spots revealed by the file. This should have the effect of raising the low spots to the level of the highs. Take up the body file again, indicating new contours (in theory) and fewer and smaller hollows. Then it is back to the spoon until no more low spots remain. Again, it is far better to feel for these lows than rely on your eyes. Then fill, prime and apply undercoat and top coat in the usual way.

As can be gathered, panel beating is not one of those skills that can be picked up in five minutes. It takes a lot of time, patience and skill to produce really satisfactory results, but I trust that the aforementioned will suffice as a guide. Fortunately there is another way of removing an awkward or small depression. Find what appears to be its deepest part and drill a small hole suitable for a self tapping screw. Screw it in, and then with the aid of a pair of grips, pull the panel out. Sometimes it will just pop back into place, but if it is particularly stubborn, then a slide hammer may be the only answer. It is then a matter of filling the hole and the small depression which may remain.

Having attempted to keep the rust at bay, what can you do on a more long term basis? Most of the larger commercial organisations are geared for current everyday models, although some will go over an 'old' car with their rust proofing process, which is nonetheless designed for monocoque body shells. An alternative is to do the job yourself, using a product such as Waxoyl by Finnigans Ltd., of Prudhoe, Northumberland.

Welding

When considering the state of your car's bodywork your welding abilities are an important aspect. You can save yourself money if you undertake the work yourself but make no mistake: it does take time to master and it's certainly not worth investing in the necessary equipment if you're only going to do one job. If you're really keen on acquiring a welding skill then why not attend local evening classes that specialize in the subject? There it is possible that you'll meet some fellow enthusiasts and you might all club together and purchase the necessary tackle.

With amateur welding there are a number of options of which I'll be mentioning three here: oxy-acetylene, arc and MiG. There are pluses and minuses to all systems and you should always be aware that your principal enemy, when it comes to welding, is heat and the distortion that can result from it. First I'll have a look at oxy-acetylene welding, or gas welding as it is more familiarly known. Before proceeding any further however, it is vital to underline the importance of proper safety precautions when using any welding equipment. First, you should thoroughly read the instructions supplied with the unit and make yourself aware of the all important safety precautions that are

Once the trim of this Vanden Plas bodied 3-litre Bentley had been removed, the wooden framework was readily apparent

Another part of the same car. Note the re-inforcing irons. Most large coachbuilding establishments included a forge to make up these simple brackets. They are therefore straightforward to reproduce

Close up of the work involved in building a replica body frame. This Bentley body was built by North Stables Coachbuilding of Milton, Abingdon, Berkshire

195

essential adjuncts to the welding process. Fire is, of course, a hazard and you should ensure that there is no inflammable material in the immediate work area. If fire should engulf the cylinders you have the makings of a bomb so a fire extinguisher, filled with foam, should be to hand. You will also need goggles that conform to the Protection of Eyes Regulations 1974. Seek advice from your local distributor for the correct variety for the type of work you are undertaking.

The equipment consists of two cylinders, one painted black, containing oxygen, while the acetylene one is painted maroon. For safety reasons the hoses are coloured red for acetylene and blue for oxygen and so that there is no risk of confusion they are left and right hand threaded. To begin, turn off the oxygen and then ignite the acetylene with a spark lighter so that it burns a yellow, smokey flame. It is then a matter of slowly turning down the acetylene valve until the smoke almost disappears. Once you've got this far you turn the oxygen valve up until a cone appears in the centre of the flame. Now turn the oxygen down until there is a faint haze around the cone which indicates that equal amounts of oxygen and acetylene are being burnt; this is called a neutralising flame. However, there should be a slight acetylene haze in the centre of the cone as there is a tendency for the flame to oxidize as the work progresses, to the detriment of the weld. In certain instances an oxidizing flame is required and this applies to brass and bronze welding. To obtain this the acetylene content is reduced and the flame pales and shortens.

If you're welding for the first time then allow plenty of time for trial runs with pieces of scrap metal. It's vital that the metal you're about to weld is free of dirt, paint, oil and grease. The absence of the latter is important as it is highly combustible. When you apply the torch to the metal the cone should be around 1/8 inch from the surface which should produce just about the right amount of heat and will prevent backfiring which can take you by surprise, particularly if you're new to the welding business. The torch should be around 45 degrees to the metal but if the angle is too acute then you'll find that the metal won't get hot enough and the weld won't 'take root'. If, on the other hand, the weld is held at right angles to the joint, you'll get plenty of penetration but the flow of the weld is lessened and you'll run the risk of burning through the metal.

You'll be able to see the cone through the goggles and it won't take long for the metal to become molten. Then move the blowpipe in a leftward direction and you'll find that the metal is becoming molten just in front of the flame, though keep the torch on the move or you'll burn right through the metal. Once you've got used to handling the blow pipe you can take up a welding rod. On the assumption that you're right handed, you should use the torch in the right hand and the rod in your left. The aim is to place the rod just ahead of the weld pool but it shouldn't touch the metal. The rod will provide the weld and the length of time that it, the flame and pool are together will much depend on the amount of weld required by the joint.

If you should want to weld metal over $\frac{3}{16}$ inch thick you should adopt the rightward welding process. If you are concerned with metal from $\frac{3}{16}$ to $\frac{5}{16}$ inches thick then the edges should be bevelled at an angle of 30 degrees. This is carried out with the weld begun at the left and then progressing towards the right and the flame preceding the filler rod in the direction of travel. You should move the rod in a circular motion as the torch is moved along the seam. You'll find that this method is rather faster than the leftward method described earlier and also uses less gas. This is because the V angle is smaller. Also, you use less rod and distortion is kept to a minimum.

There's no doubt that your main enemy is distortion though this can, to some degree, be prevented by tack welding. You start by making a spot weld at the end of the joint and then about every $\frac{3}{4}$ to 1 inch along its length. If the joint is likely to be exposed, you may like to tidy up the tack with a hammer and dolly. With this part of the job completed, you can press on with the welding proper. You'd be well advised to adopt this approach, particularly if you're new to the welding business. But you will have to realise that there is likely to be some element of distortion with relatively flat panels. Another difficulty that you might experience is that you successfully attach the welding rod to the base metal which is certainly not the general idea! This is usually caused by the rod not being sufficiently hot when it's brought into contact with the puddle of weld.

Not only can welding be carried out with gas welding equipment but so can brazing. In truth this is a form of soldering and although not as strong as a fusion weld it does have the advantage of employing lower temperatures so there is considerably less distortion. You'll require a neutral flame, the exception being when brass is bronze-welded where a slight oxidizing flame is required.

With brazing you can also join together different metals, such as steel and brass. But you should recognise that a disadvantage of the system is that the strength of the joint is somewhat lower than the metals that are being joined. It's worth noting that it can also be used for filling; badly scored bumper over-riders are a good instance. When you're brazing, it's very important, as with welding, that the surface of the metal is perfectly clean and you should grind or wire brush the appropriate area. Although the filler rods that you use are called bronze, in fact they're made of copper, tin and zinc alloy and are used in conjunction with a flux. This cleans the weld area and prevents the formation of oxides and is introduced to the weld by heating the filler rod and then dipping it in the powder.

As there are lower temperatures involved, the torch is used in a rather different way and it's important that the cone of the flame doesn't touch the brazing rod. If, by chance, this does happen then the rod will burn too quickly and a porous, weak joint will result.

With brazing, it's important to pre-heat the metal until it glows a dull red. You then introduce the braze rod to the pre-heated surface. The rod will melt instantly and you can tin the surface with a thin layer of metal prior to building it up with braze using the rod suitably coated with flux. Brazing is well suited to attaching replacement body panels to the car's structure where you're working with relatively thin panels.

So much for the basic principles of gas welding. So what are the advantages of the alternative arc welding process? There are advantages and disadvantages over the system just described. Most significantly it employs less heat which means less distortion and it is quicker to apply but is probably more difficult for the amateur to master. Arc, like gas welding, is a fusion process with the joint being melted with new metal from an electrode which is fused into the joint. The heat comes, not from gas but an electrical arc which is regulated by a transformer and is created when an electric current flows across the gap between the welding rod and the metal being welded which is attached to an earth connection. When you come to strike an arc with the rod there is an intense electrical discharge. The welds are rather narrower than those required for gas welding.

Like the former system, safety is a vital prerequisite and you should ensure that there is no fire risk. Don't forget (and this also applies to gas welding) if you're working around the rear of the car, to drain and remove the petrol tank otherwise you run the risk of an explosion. In addition a mask that is heat resistant and will also protect your eyes, is essential before you start welding. You look through a special lens designed to protect your eyes which is covered with clear glass so that it doesn't get damaged by weld spatter. On the other hand you could wear a protective helmet and this means that at least you've got both hands free. You will also find this protection useful when you come to clean up the weld with a grinder as there are plenty of sparks generated. Don't overlook the fact that the arc will damage unprotected eyes, so don't let people watch while you're at work unless they, too, have some sort of protection. This also applies to family pets such as cats and dogs so make sure that your workshop doors are properly secured. Your skin can also get burnt by ultra violet light so don't weld with bare arms.

Practise using scrap metal. Bring the welding rod into contact with the metal you're intending to weld. The first skill you've got to master is to strike an arc and if you're having a go for the first time, you'll probably scratch the rod on the surface and then raise it, about $\frac{1}{16}$ to 1/8 inch, to produce the desired effect. The correct method is to strike the metal with the top of the rod so that the rod bounces and forms an arc. The important thing is to strike the metal as quickly as possible so that it remains in contact with the metal for the minimum of time. Should you make contact without the striking motion then the rod will stick to the metal and you can end up with a direct short circuit. If this should occur, turn off the transformer immediately and remove the rod by moving it from side to side, making sure that you don't damage the coating of flux.

The whole business of striking an arc is a difficult exercise and may take some time to master. Should you experience difficulties, then it's possible that the earth connection is loose or you may be using the incorrect current for the rod that you're using. You can gauge the correct level for striking the arc by the sound produced. Reduce the gap until you can hear an intermittent spluttering sound. Then progressively raise the rod until the sound disappears. Between these two extremes you'll find a regular crackling sound and that's the one you are aiming to achieve.

Once you have got to grips with striking the arc you can then push ahead to the next stage and produce a weld bead. You need two actions to produce this: the properly mastered downward movement as the rod length diminishes followed by a second one in the direction of the weld travel. Needless to say there are inevitable pitfalls to this; for instance, if you move the rod too slowly, slag will build up ahead of the weld puddle.

Your aim is to produce a weld that is of uniform size and penetrates the metal to an equal depth. This, if you're a beginner, is difficult to maintain. Once you've produced some beads you can go ahead and move the welding rod from side to side which will tell you whether you've the correct current setting. If you've got a thin bead with very little penetration then the current is set too low. In addition there'll be plenty of spluttering and crackling. If, conversely, the current is set too high, the welding rod will become red hot prior to use and will burn away very quickly. You'll also get too thin a bead but penetration will be slightly better.

Like the gas welding process, your main enemy is distortion and if you want to keep it to a minimum you should use tack welds and also apply supports that can subsequently be removed. You can also control distortion by welding on opposing sides of the metal if this is feasible remembering that it's important that not too many welds are concentrated in one place.

You can also braze with an arc welding set. This is achieved by the use of a carbon arc kit which consists of a handle which holds two carbon rods that are insulatd from one another and are connected to the earth clamp and the electrode. As with gas welding, brazing is very similar to soldering. The two rods are brought together and on separation an arc forms between them. The arc's intensity varies with the size of the gap and the process also sounds different from welding with a buzz rather than a crackle being produced. The torch is applied to the metal which pre-heats it and filler rod is then applied to the area to be welded. Once it has made contact, the rod melts, the result being a strong, brazed joint.

So much for the rudiments of arc welding. There is, however, one further device that provides the dual advantages of minimum distortion and straightforward operation and that is the MiG welder. The equipment, unfortunately, is expensive but it is just the sort of device that could be purchased by a group of restoration enthusiasts and, provided it has plenty of use, will earn its keep. The device is, in fact, an electric arc welder but doesn't present its shortcomings and is relatively easy to use. The reason is that argon, an inert gas, or sometimes carbon dioxide, is used to shield the weld from the air. In consequence the weld is kept cool and oxidization is prevented. The gun contains not only the gas but a feed of welding wire which emerges when the trigger is pulled. You can also place the gun in position prior to lowering the face mask and, of course, you won't need to strike an arc as with conventional electric welding. The process is a single handed operation; yet another plus.

Fitting panels

There has, in recent years, been a growth in the amount of replica body panels available for classic cars though inevitably the more expensive sporting end of the market tends to come off best. Therefore if you are a Jaguar, Austin Healey or MG owner you'll probably find a panel to fit most needs. If, on the other hand, you have the opportunity to obtain a manufacturer's panel, and they still turn up from time to time, then you'd obviously be better advised to fit that. Incidentally, BL still manufacture some body panels for the Morris Minor which represents a definite plus for the ownership of this well-mannered saloon. With any post-war car, should the make still be in production or only recently out of production, it's well worth asking at your local agent whether a particular body panel is still available. You may be in for a pleasant surprise.

The Minor, like the MGB and Volkswagen Beetle, has bolt on panels which is a definite plus for the DIY enthusiasts providing that you recognise that there will be some welding and cutting to do. Unless you're particularly proficient in these skills you'd be well advised to leave the job to a professional restorer allowing about the same amount of money for the cost of fitting as you did for the panel itself. However, if you've got to grips with the welding process, as described earlier, this is a perfect opportunity to put theory into practice.

Your first course of action is to establish where the various attachment points are and you should place the new panel alongside the old as a guide. With a front wing you should pay special attention to the vicinity of the scuttle to check where it attaches as well as the area of the radiator grille. Once this is established, the old wing should be removed, and it's best to tackle it at the most difficult point: namely at the scuttle where the wing joins the sill. The joint itself may be all too obvious or it could be concealed by leading. You'll probably find that you have to burn the paint off to find the joint and you can use the replica as a guide. Check that there aren't any petrol pipes nearby and the same goes for any wiring or soundproofing material that might ignite. You might find that the joints are leaded and you can melt these with a blow lamp though you might care to collect the residue in a drip tray or similar receptacle.

Once the leading has been removed you can press ahead and remove the wing. There are a number of ways in which to carry out the job, either with heavy duty cutters or, ideally, an electrically driven power wheel. The latter is probably the most satisfactory method of removal but you'll need a pair of goggles to protect your eyes from the sparks and also cover any nearby glass as the surface can be damaged. The wing should be removed a couple of inches from the weld line and on a front wing you may well find that there is a closure plate behind the wheel arch. If there is such a plate then this will have to be removed first.

Unless they're bolted into position, most wings are spot welded to the body structure. You can drill these out; a $\frac{3}{16}$ or $\frac{1}{4}$ inch drill should do the trick. Inevitably there will be some chiselling to do and you have to take care to ensure that the lip left on the car isn't buckled in the process. There will also be some wing support brackets to be considered. You have the choice of either detaching them at the wing end or leaving them on the body.

With the old wing removed you should then go along the mounting flange with a hammer and dolly and remove any high spots there might be left along with any old spot welds. Fitting the new wing can be tricky, particularly as its positioning must line up with its opposite number on the other side of the car. It isn't a bad idea to first tack weld the panel into position to try and get it correctly located. If it isn't correct, then it's reasonably easy to remove it and try again. Having got the alignment just about right (I warn you it's a lot harder to do than to write) you can then weld the wing into position. If you reckon that the original had spot welds placed at around $\frac{1}{2}$ inch intervals then $\frac{1}{2}$ inch long welds should be able to cope. Yet another method is plug brazing where you drill $\frac{1}{4}$ to 3/8 inch holes, clamp the two flanges together and these are then filled with braze.

A further thought. If you haven't got access to welding equipment you can save yourself some money by going ahead attaching and fitting the wing using our old friend the self tapping screw, then taking the job to a welding specialist to be finished off for you.

This leaves you with the various other joints to be filled and these can be leaded. You'll find that particular process described on page xx. On the other hand you might find that if yours is a relatively modern car it might benefit from the use of an epoxy putty rather than lead as it must flex with the bodywork. With the wing in position it is then a matter of re-spraying, as set down later in this Chapter. When you come to fit rear wings, which in most instances are rather more straightforward, you'll find that you have to remove the car's petrol tank in view of the proximity of the welding torch.

The body components which are most likely to rust and can dangerously weaken the structure of your car are the sills. These are probably the most readily obtainable replacement body part as they're about the easiest to replicate. Most sills are to a greater or lesser extent structural though their role is far more significant on those cars that don't have a chassis frame than those that do. If your car comes into the former category then it's essential that the car is properly supported when you remove the old sills. You'll need some angle iron or pieces of stout timber to take the place of the missing reinforcements and these should be positioned in the front boxed or angled sections and at the vehicle's rear. To make sure that they're doing their respective jobs, use a couple of jacks underneath the supports so they're well positioned against the body.

The old sills can now be removed and the outers can be detached by hacksawing after carefully checking the length of the replacements. Pay particular attention on a four door car to how the door pillar is attached to the sill, particularly if you are unable to get a replacement. It is possible that the base might have rusted badly and if this is the case the only answer is to make a new section and weld it in. With the outers well out of the way you'll be able to see the state of the inner sills. If they're intact so much the better but they probably won't be and it's likely that the top

199

Typical of the sort of problem that can occur
with sills. The outer one is obviously in a bad
state and the same will probably apply to the
inner

And so it has. Here rust has attacked the inner
sill, which is serious, particularly on this MGB,
as it provides essential reinforcement on an
open car

Don't be tempted to fit a cover sill which only has the effect of papering over the damage, as this 'sandwich' reveals. This example was removed from a scrap car by John Hill's MGB Centre of Redditch, Worcs

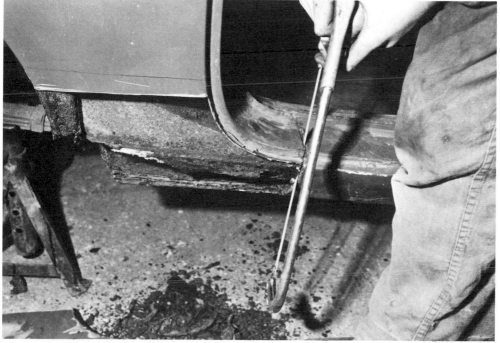

Remove the old sill; hacksaw between the top of the sill and bottom of the door pillar

Chisel along the top of the sill from pillar to
pillar. You'll also need to drill out the spot
welds

Having removed the remainder of the sill from
the front door pillar, it can be folded forwards
and down and cut along its bottom edge

In goes a new full sill section, John Hill
undertaking the work. It is first tack welded into
position and then carefully checked for
alignment prior to final securing

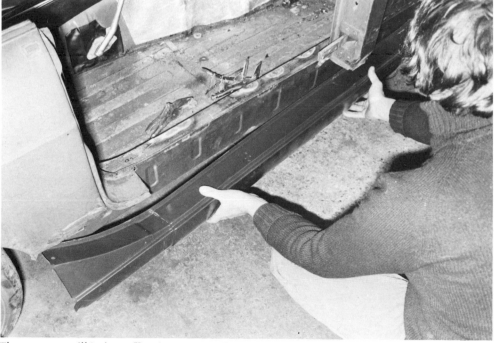

The new outer sill is then offered up. It is vitally
important that it lines up with the door before
being permanently secured

203

The new sill in position. Note how the door pillar flange is fitted to the top of the sill. The forward part of the sill is covered by the front wing

Removing the old door skin. A strong oxidising flame will produce a neat cut which can then be cleaned up with an angle grinder

This is the old door skin, along with the new.
On a popular classic, like the MGB, availability
of new skins is a big plus. A new base panel is
also offered in this kit by John Hill

Attaching the new skin to the frame. The edges
of the skin should be tapped a few degrees
inwards all the way round

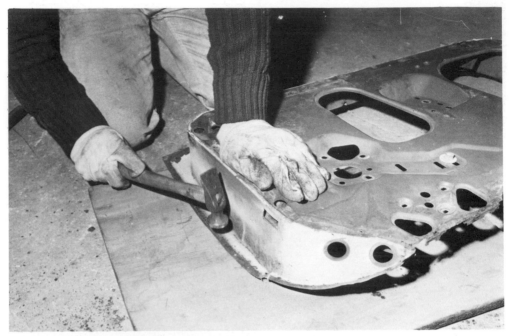

Then start again and fold the flange over with a
hammer a little at a time. If this isn't done
evenly the metal will stretch and you'll end up
with a kink on the face of the door

To attain a surface that is free of hammer marks
go around the flange with a piece of wood. Note
that the door has been angled to ensure that the
face of the door is protected by a board
underneath

Removing a front wing. On the MGB the job is a straightforward one where the securing bolts aren't in direct contact with road mud. Despite this snag this type of wing is a lot easier to remove than the welded on variety

Ensuring that you don't damage the surrounding bodywork, in particular the leading edge of the door, lift the wing free. When you're attaching the new wing, fit all the bolts loosely, prior to tightening

face will have rusted. If this is the case, it's advisable to fit the new top face of the outer sill prior to removing the inner. Then go ahead and remove the inners and tack weld the new ones in position, checking that the doors still open and close correctly. If not, make the necessary adjustments and then weld the inner in place having clamped it in position to prevent distortion. With the inners in place again check how well the doors fit and then carry out a similar welding operation on the outers.

The doors themselves can also rust badly, the trouble usually being the result of the drain holes having become blocked. This can be rectified either by repairing with plastic filler or welding in a new door bottom section though it can be difficult for the amateur to achieve acceptable results. Yet another alternative and this only applies to the more popular classics, is to fit a replacement door skin. First remove the door from the car. This in itself can be a demanding job and you might find it necessary to use a brace fitted with the appropriate screwdriver head if the screws prove stubborn, or even better use an impact screwdriver. The first stage is to remove the old skin from its frame. This can usually be achieved by grinding around the edges of the door though this might not be as easy as it sounds as there might be some tricky spot and seam welds to cope with. You might also find that the frame's bottom plate has rusted badly and might require replacement. With the skin off the frame this is a good opportunity to use a rust inhibitor on it and apply a zinc based paint.

The next bit is rather tricky. You place the new skin on a smooth surface and then place the frame inside, tapping the skin's edges around it. Here you've got to support the door's outer face on a piece of wood, covered with leather, or similar, to prevent it from marking the panel. Then, doing a little at a time, gradually work your way around the edge, tapping the lip over. You'll find some problems at the corners, and you'll have to hacksaw the joints to make a mitre. Incidentally, make sure that you don't hammer too hard as before you know where you are you'll have damaged the outside of the door. For the same reasons you shouldn't use pliers or a Mole wrench to crimp the edges into place. Once this has been completed you can either weld or braze the lip onto the frame, following the pattern of the original.

I should stress, however, that cars vary enormously as far as their body structures are concerned and these wing and sill fitments should be regarded as guidelines only. Check with your one make car club, or a fellow enthusiast, who has undertaken similar work, before taking the plunge.

Door problems

One of the bodywork problems that you may experience on a pre-war car is that of the door hinges wearing, which can result in the doors dropping. To check whether this is happening, half open the door, position your hand underneath it, and gently lift. You should be able to feel, and see, any movement in the hinges, the bottom one usually being the worst affected. If this is the case, you will need a new hinge pin, but it is possible to fit it without going through the drama of removing the hinge.

To do this, first slacken off the screws on the door side about half a turn. Then shut the door and carefully punch out the pin with a drift which is a smaller diameter than the pin itself. Once this has been done, you will be in a position to fit an oversized pin. To get a really good fit, the holes in the brass should be reamered out. To make sure that the hinge is correctly aligned for this part of the operation, insert the old pin through the bottom of the hinge until it engages with the hole at the top. Once the reamer has passed through the first hole it will force the old pin down, and this will ensure that the holes are in line. Then carefully knock in the new pin, having greased it beforehand. Tighten up the screws that you loosened off, and check the hinges for play once again. If there is still some movement in the door, then repeat the operation on the top hinge.

Building your own body

Of course, you may not have any body at all, for it is by not means uncommon for pre-war cars to be acquired in chassis form, or to have gained at some stage in their lives a completely unsuitable body that must be removed if a complete restoration is to be achieved. If you require a new body one answer is to farm the job out to a specialist, but it is possible to do some of the work yourself. This, however, only applies to those cars with bodywork constructed with the time-honoured ash framing covered with aluminium or steel cladding. I must stress, though, that the construction of this framework should only be undertaken if the reader has clearly defined abilities in the field of carpentry or has dabbled, for example, in the do-it-yourself wooden boat-building field. But while a fair amount of people can claim some proficiency with a hammer and chisel, the tricky business of panel beating and welding is outside the scope of most of us and cladding your first effort in body construction is hardly the best area for experimentation. So if you do decide to build your own ash frame, you will save a lot of time and trouble if you find a local panel beater to carry out the 'skinning'. You should consider the following guidelines in conjunction with David Cooksey's excellent drawing.

Finding a comparable body   Once you have decided to take the plunge, the first thing to do is to find another car of the same model, and year, as your own, fitted with the type of body you want to reproduce. If you have a particularly rare vehicle then try, at least, to find a car of suitable size and age, and use this as a pattern. Take as many measurements as possible, but the most important ones are:

The width of the windscreen
The width of the body in front of the door tread plates
The distance from the bulkhead to the windscreen
The distance from the bulkhead to the top and then the bottom of the back of the body
The height of the rear wheel arch to the higheset point of the wing (usually on the vertical centre-line of the axle)

   Take great care to double check these measurements, as one miscalculation can throw out the whole look of the body. Then take as many photographs as possible from every angle, not forgetting interior ones with the doors opened and closed, as well as the positioning of the floorboards. Another vital dimension is the thickness of the doors, as more often than not this dictates the thickness of wood used throughout the body.

Wooden body frames everywhere, again at North Stables

Buying the timber   Ash predominates in car bodies, being light in weight, hard and durable. For this reason it used to be used for aircraft fuselages (along with spruce, which predominated) and far earlier for felloes (one of the sections on the rim of a cart wheel).

Unfortunately, one of the difficulties of buying ash nowadays is to obtain really well seasoned timber. The natural process of seasoning in the open requires about a year for every inch of thickness of wood, so it is hardly surprisingly that nowadays most wood is kiln dried; timber up to three inches thick takes only about three weeks to season in a forced draught kiln. Regrettably, this artificial process tends to be more satisfactory for soft woods than hard ones, so be prepared for so-called seasoned wood to feel damp when you cut it; you will be able to tell by the resistance to your saw blade. As for the size of wood, remember that the thickness will generally be narrower than the width, so 1.25 to 1.5in. thickness will be required. You will need considerably less than this if you decide to laminate the wood.

Obviously, the actual dimensions will vary from car to car. In addition to ash, you may require oak for the bottom side frames as this has greater resistance to water, an important advantage in view of their proximity to the road. Plywood was used in increasing quantities in the 'thirties, so if you are contemplating the restoration of a car of this age, and after, you will need some. Marine ply is obviously the more desirable variety, but if you cannot run to that, exterior quality plywood will not de-laminate and is obtainable in a wide variety of thicknesses. It can also be used for the floorboards. Vintage cars favoured 0.75in. boards, while 0.375in. appeared from the 'thirties onwards.

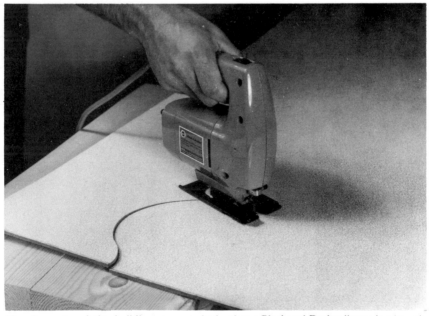

If you're contemplating building your own body, then a Black and Decker jigsaw is a 'must'

The body itself   As I mentioned in Chapter Two, it is advisable to build the body before restoring the chassis. But prior to starting work on the body proper, there are some important precautions to take as far as the chassis is concerned. First check that the axles are parallel with each other, so that when you take a measurement from one side, it will be the same as the other. It is quite likely that the springs have worn unevenly, the offside, for instance may be softer than the nearside, so allow for this. Remove the front wheels, mounting the front of the chassis on axle stands, but leave the rear wheels *on*. Then check the main side members with a spirit level for equality. This is important, because a channel section chassis can easily twist out of true. If the chassis is bent, or badly twisted, then it will have to be straightened. When this has been done, clean off any loose rust and you are ready to begin work on the body proper. But if the gearbox is fitted with a right hand gearchange, now is the time to position it.

There are some really vital tools that you will need; first and foremost is a Black and Decker Jigsaw. You can cut practically all the timber with it. You will need an electric drill as well, though a word about drilling ash may be relevant. When you come to make holes in this wood, you will have to drill the whole depth of the screw. You will also need two bits, one for the shank and the other for the thread. The screws themselves should be steel or if you are feeling affluent, stainless steel.

Before launching into the business of actually constructing the body, it is not a bad idea to mock up the rough outline of the intended shape with pieces of hardboard and oddments of wood. But do this with the radiator in position. This is because practically all coachwork tends to slope gently downwards from the windscreen to the radiator, therefore the height and positioning of the bulkhead is particularly important, otherwise the car will look as though it is going up hill all the time!

Now a word about lamination. This method of building up layers of wood to a required shape is particularly useful when you are faced with the problem of using timber which is not particularly well seasoned. You can laminate straights as well as curves, incidentally. I will give you an example of the former instance. On many bodies, the main chassis runners have a rabbet on the inside edge to receive the floorboards. It is much more satisfactory to laminate, in this particular instance than rely on a batten.

Here is how to do it. The straights obviously present no great problems, the sections being glued and clamped together. But if you want to reproduce a curve, then you will have to make up a simple jig. Ascertain the curve you require and then take a piece of chipboard, or the like, and screw, or nail, two rows of blocks just a bit wider than the shape you want. You can confirm the accuracy of the jig by testing it with a cardboard template. Then make up a series of small wedges and put them aside. Do not forget to place a piece of newspaper between the blocks otherwise you will effectively stick the laminate to the baseboard! Use rough cut, rather than planed ash, as the serrations will provide a good key and do not use less than 0.25in. thick laminates. Liberally coat the mating surfaces with Cascamite glue, or similar, and place the layers of wood in the jig, knocking the wedges you previously made up between the laminates and the locating blocks, together with strategically placed G clamps. This process can be effectively used to produce the rear wheel arches and parts of the door frame.

The only other thing you will have to consider before you start work is the metalwork which is used in building a body frame. These parts are usually very simple to reproduce, being made of mild steel, and are often found reinforcing the hinge and slam pillars and attached to the heelboard and rear wheel arch. And again metal is sometimes substituted for the wooden bottom side rails. Now for the woodwork. Most of the joints are extremely simple half lap fittings, but do not worry if they are not too accurately cut as this will permit a degree of desirable flexibility. The body should first be screwed together, then taken to pieces and glued, and then finally screwed again. The things to avoid when building a body are, quite simply, flats. For even the most angular looking body has gentle and almost imperceptible curves, and any straightness, in the mechanical sense of the word, will offend the eye.

The bulkhead mountings are a priority fixture, also the two scuttle pillars which may support the door. Then on go the main body runners, which can be either metal or wood. In the Vintage era they were often bolted directly to the chassis, though in the 'thirties and subsequently, you will be far more likely to find that they are mounted on outward facing brackets at right angles to the chassis. It is customary to sandwich a piece of rubber, about 0.125in. thick, between the bracket and the runner to absorb the worst road shocks and vibrations. The floor, which is usually plywood, should put in an early appearance. Next, the heelboard and flap (again of plywood) which covers the rear axle, is fitted, followed by the bottom back rail. Now the hinge pillars can be positioned, followed by the wheel arches. Do not be afraid to make the verticals longer than you require. Far better than making them too short! It is a good idea to strengthen these unsupported posts with temporary cross bracing to prevent them moving out of true. The next stage is to fit the back pillars (there are usually three), the centre one often being a thick piece of 0.5in. plywood being fitted *after* the top rail. Now you can fit the top back rail, and it is vitally important that this is parallel with the bottom one, as this will dictate the equality of the rest of the body. Do

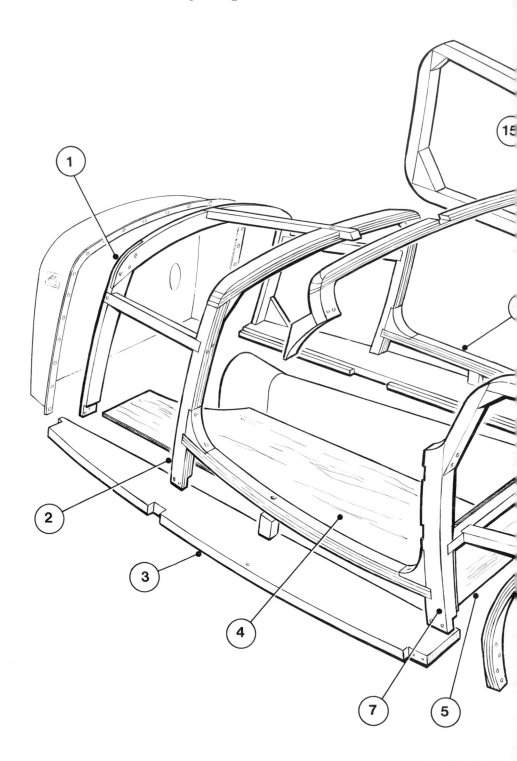

The principal parts of a typical body of the nineteen thirties. *Key* 1, bulkhead mounting; 2, scuttle pillar (L);
3, main body runner; 4, floor; 5, heelboard; 6, bottom back rail and flap; 7 and 14, hinge pillars; 8, rear
wheel arch (L); 9, back pillar; 10, top back rail; 11, centre rear pillar; 12, wheel arch block; 13, top side rails;
15, scuttle cross rail (L); 16, door; 17, rocker rail (L). L=laminations

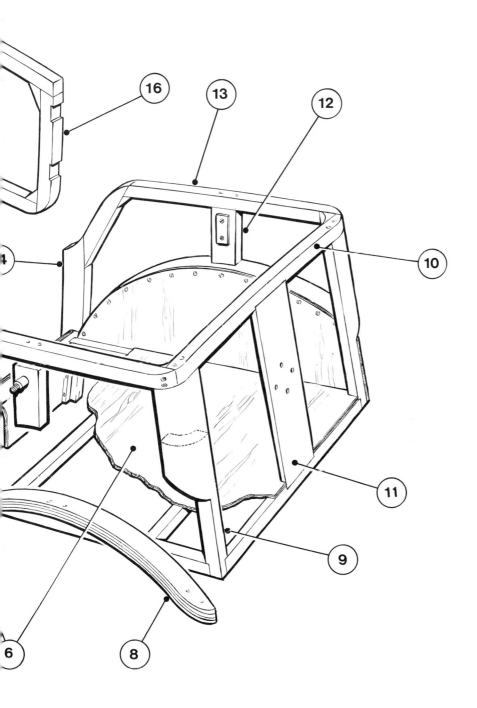

not worry if you have to use the occasional piece of packing here and there. It is amazing the way that items like folded up cigarette packets often turn up, squeezed into crannies as a spacing medium in old bodies!

Fit any additional verticals that are required, and then on can go the top side rails. The design of the doors, however, has a bearing on the rail's length. On Vintage, or early 'thirties cars, the tops of the doors were purely a continuation of these rails. However, as the post-Vintage years progressed, the doors became entities in their own right, being more cutaway in design. So if the body you are building is of the earlier type, then continue the top rail all the way to the bulkhead, and part of it will be used as the top of the door, though if you have a staggered joint between the edge of the body and door, it will have to be made of two pieces. But in later designs, the side rails will be quite short, with an elbow pillar stepping down to the hinge pillar. Whatever the method of design, one of the basic golden (or should it be wooden?) rules should be closely observed.

This is: do not build the body and make the doors afterwards, and then try and fit the two together. Build the doors and doorframes together as an entity and part of the body.

Make up the door frames, temporarily securing them to their respective hinge, shut and rocker rail (the last named sits at the bottom of the door) and sandwiching a piece of packing between the doors and their surrounds, allowing a minimum of 0.185in. for small bodies and 0.25in. clearance for larger ones. This gap is a very necessary one, and will soon close up once the metal cladding is attached to the frame. Having ascertained this clearance, take the door frame to pieces and glue and screw it, replacing it in the door surround, so that it follows the right shape. If you do make a mistake when making the door frame, it will most likely be when you come to reproduce the correct angles, so you may have to make up wedges to counteract this shortcoming, by taking the joint apart and packing it out. And if the door has a rabbet in it, then you can laminate. Make up a second piece overlapping the correct amount. Far better to *add* pieces to the body than weaken it by removing bits. Once the doors are dry, attach the door hinges, using countersunk bolts and nuts, rather than wood screws. Remember that door hinges usually have five lugs, the flap with the three lug side is attached to the body, with the two lug piece going on the door itself.

As I mentioned earlier, many bodies built in the 'thirties used a certain amount of plywood and this was usually found around the rear end. On some MG bodies, for example, the plywood was covered with aluminium; now is the time to fit the 'wood.

After gluing, the frame can be finally shaped using a spoke shave, a Surform file and chisel, finishing off with sand paper. And jolly hard work it is too! When you have finished the job, do not forget to give the whole body a good going over with Cuprinol, to keep the dreaded woodworm at bay, for the timber may already be infested.

How replica front wings are manufactured by Marsh Development Ltd., of Guildford, Surrey

Marsh Developments also produces complete Morris Eight running boards

Replica bodywork: some still to be done to the rear panel of an AC Ace on its wooden former at Classic Auto's workshop at King's Langley, Buckinghamshire

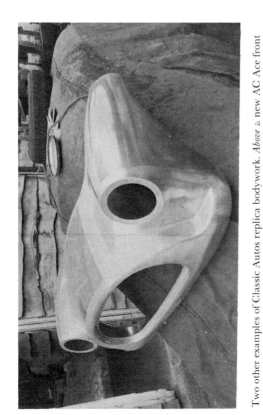

Two other examples of Classic Autos replica bodywork. *Above* a new AC Ace front end and *below* a Healey rear wing

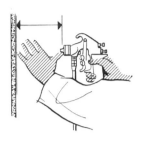

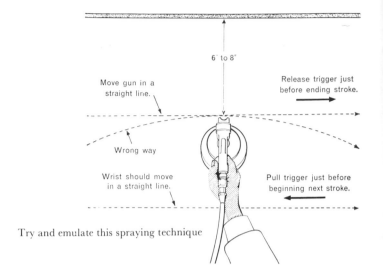

The spray gun should be held at right angles to the surface being painted, the distance between the surface and face of the air cap must be 6 to 8 inches (150 to 200mm), or a hand span, as a quick check

Try and emulate this spraying technique

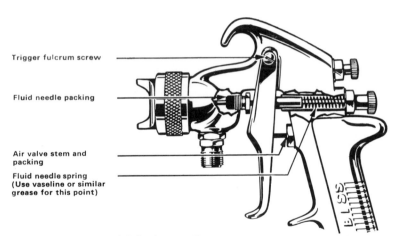

Trigger fulcrum screw

Fluid needle packing

Air valve stem and packing

Fluid needle spring (Use vaseline or similar grease for this point)

The parts that require lubrication on a DeVilbiss spray gun

The spraying order for a typical saloon body. 7 is the front nearside door

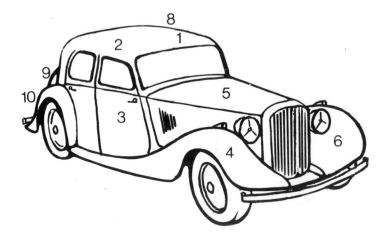

The frame is now all set for cladding. This is usually carried out in SCl (standing for Soft Commercial) 18 gauge aluminium, and as I warned at the beginning of this section, the job does tend to be something of a specialist business. As far as the wings are concerned, if the car is a popular one, you may be lucky to get hold of some spares and have them restored. If not, they will have to be made at the same time as the body. I have seen some Ford Transit back wings which were cut down the centre and suitably narrowed to provide rear wings on a Bullnose Morris; there is some food for thought! When you get the body and wings back from your local panel beater, you can think about what is involved in spraying, which is the subject I am going to consider next.

Spray guns and how to use them

Spraying equipment is fairly expensive, so you either hire it, or borrow a gun and compressor from a wealthy friend! For it is hardly worth going to the lengths of buying a complete spraying outfit, if you have decided that your first restoration is going to be your last one. But if you get really keen, then the investment may well be worthwhile.

First some thoughts on spray guns. I would be inclined to avoid the gravity fed type, which has a plastic cup mounted on the top. The bulky reservoir can interfere with visibility and it is quite easy to spill paint out of the bleed hole at the top. No, you are far better off with a suction feed gun. For apart from anything else, its quart container usually holds enough to give the average size car one coat of paint. It is operated by a stream of compressed air which siphons paint from the container which is attached to the spray head under the gun, and so out from the nozzle.

The compressed air is, naturally enough, supplied by a compressor, and if you hire one, remember that you should expect an output of around 4 cubic feet per minute, per horsepower, from an electric motor attached to a piston type compressor. About 10 cubic feet per minute is usually demanded by the average spray gun, so the compressor should, at least, have a three horsepower motor. As most spraying is done between 40 and 70psi, maximum pressure need not exceed 100 psi.

Car spraying is usually carried out with the horns of the spray gun in a vertical position, which results in a vertical spray. Before starting work on the car, it is very important to get the correct air/paint mix. Having filled the gun's reservoir with paint and thinner (usually at a 1 : 1 ratio) find a spare piece of garage wall for spraying a test pattern. The spread adjuster valve in the gun is opened as far as it will go, and the fluid adjusting screw is turned anti-clockwise until the first thread is visible. You are now ready to spray a test pattern. You do this by holding the gun steady, momentarily triggering the lever on and off, holding the gun about 6 to 8in. from the surface you have selected for the test. As a guide, a gun requiring 55psi will produce a pattern about 10in. wide. Next you should spray an area to check the speed of the operation. Should the pattern appear starved of paint, the fluid adjusting screw should be opened wider which will allow more paint through. But if atomisation is too fine, which will show itself by excessive overspray, or a dry spray, the air pressure should be reduced while keeping the fluid adjustment wide open. If, at the other extreme, atomisation is too coarse, which manifests itself by producing a speckled effect, or a dimpled finish, then the air pressure should be increased or the material flow cut down. But if, when the spreader valve and fluid screw are wide open and the spray pattern turns out to be too narrow, then the fluid flow can be increased by raising the air pressure or by further thinning the paint. Yet another variation to achieve a wetter coat is to turn the spreader valve to narrow the spray pattern, followed by a slight increase in air pressure.

To achieve the best results from a spray gun, four principle rules must be adopted:

(1) Keep the gun six to eight inches from the surface to be sprayed. The air cap, which is the most prominent part of the gun is designed to harness the air energy being delivered at this particular distance. If you get too close, the coating will be very wet and non-uniform, but if you are too far away the result will be a sandy and uneven coat of paint.

(2) It is vitally important to ensure that the gun is stroked at the right angle across the surface to be sprayed. Pointing the gun up (arcing) or down (angling) will produce an uneven spray. Normally spraying is carried out in a horizontal direction to the object being sprayed. If for some reason a vertical stroke is preferred, then the air cap can be rotated 90 degrees, which will produce

Bare metal body stopper being applied

Careful masking is essential for a good spraying job

The gun should be moving continuously, being 'triggered' at the end of each stroke

Application of a polishing mop is one of the last stages of the operation

a horizontal spray pattern and permit vertical spraying.

(3)   When the gun is being moved backwards and forwards across the car, overlap the spray coats by a good 50 per cent.

(4)   Before starting the next painting stroke, the gun should be 'triggered'. You do this by releasing the trigger, so that the flow of paint will be momentarily stopped while moving the gun to position for the return stroke. In other words, the gun must be mobile *before* the trigger is pulled and kept moving *after* the trigger finger has been relaxed.

It is also important that you position yourself correctly, placing yourself 'left of centre' from the item being sprayed. Of course, to get the best possible results from your gun, it is vital that it is correctly cleaned and lubricated. The foregoing instructions apply to the suction feed type of gun only. First loosen the air cap from the gun, and while the fluid tube is still in the cup, unscrew the cap about two or three turns. Then holding a cloth over the cap, pull the trigger. In this way, air is diverted into the fluid passages, forcing the paint back into the cup. Then empty the gun and replace the paint with a cleaning solvent, and spray it through the gun to flush out the passages. Then remove the air cap, emersing it in cleaning solvent and dry it by blowing it off with compressed air. Should the small holes in the cap become clogged, soak the cap in solvent. If you have to clean out these holes, use a match stick, broom bristle or orange stick, never a metal prong, as this can enlarge the holes and consequently affect the spray pattern. Replace the aircap on the gun. After cleaning, place a drop of oil on the fluid needle packing, the air valve packing and bearing screw. Occasionally, remove the needle packing and soften it in oil, while the fluid needle spring should be coated in Vaseline. Check the instructions supplied with your particular gun though.

There are, unfortunately, a number of maladies which can plague a spray gun, many associated with poor cleaning and maintenance. These will manifest themselves during the test spray, the shape of the pattern indicating where to look for the obstruction. It can be distorted in a number of ways: top, bottom or side heavy. The position of the obstruction can be ascertained by rotating the air cup half a turn and spraying again. If the defect is inverted, then you can deduce that the obstruction is in the air cap itself. But if it remains constant, then you will know that the trouble lies in the fluid tip. While it is easy enough to clean the cap, the defective pattern can be rectified by cleaning up the fluid tip with 600 grade wet and dry paper or removing the dried paint which often builds up just inside the opening.

One of the most familiar shortcomings in spray painting is the appearance of the dreaded orange peel, so called, strangely enough, because the finish takes on the appearance and texture of orange peel. This can be caused by a variety of shortcomings. It can be the result of using the wrong thinner, air pressure either too low or too high, the gun being held too far from or too close to the work, paint not sufficiently mixed, a draught at the spraying premises, an improperly prepared surface and too low humidity (synthetics only). So take your choice!

The other most likely failing is streaks appearing on the finished surface. This can be caused by tilting the gun so that one side of the spray pattern hits the surface in greater quantities than the other, the air cap or fluid tip having become dirty or burred resulting in a top heavy pattern, or the spray patterns not being properly overlapped.

Which type of paint?   You should now ascertain which type of paint was used on your car. If it is a Vintage car, then the chances are that coachpaint was used up until about 1925, when cellulose took over. You can therefore reckon that most massed produced British cars made before about 1949 had a cellulose finish, from then on synthetics predominated. However, high quality specialist cars continued to be finished in cellulose. The best way of finding out which type of paint was used on your post-war car is to find an unobtrusive area of bodywork and rub it with a rag dipped in cellulose thinners. If cellulose paint was used on the car, then the rag will be colour stained. If it is not then synthetics were used.

Now what sort of paint should you use on your car? There are pros and cons for both types. Cellulose is faster drying than synthetic paints, and can be successfully used for 'touching up' repairs, as well as for a complete respray. On the other hand, a synthetic finish is excellent for building up body imperfections, it is easy to work during the all important flatting operation, but does not lend itself so well to touching up.

On balance, I would be inclined to opt for a cellulose finish if you intend stripping the bodywork down to bare metal and doing the work yourself. This is because although modern synthetics offer advantages to professionals, their slow drying times make them less suitable for the amateur who lacks proper premises to prevent excessive dirt and dust settling on the film when it is still wet. By contrast, cellulose paints (such as ICI Belco) offer an advantage in being quick drying and any minor blemishes can be polished out when hard. (Older vehicles may respond to a Dulux Coach finish, however. Check with your spares registrar.)

Time for plating

Now is the time to remove the various components from the bodywork to have them replated. Nickel plate was practically universal up to about 1929. Remember that there are two types of nickel plate; a bright finish, and the Nivo process which produces a matt surface. Most under-bonnet nickel plate was of the latter variety, and these variations can be reproduced by Murrivans Ltd., of West Croydon, Surrey. Chrome took over at the end of the 'twenties and has been with us ever since.

But if metal parts do require restoration (such as a split or dented radiator grill) have them repaired *before* the plating is carried out as most platers do not have the facilities for this type of work. The plating business, on the whole, is a very straightforward affair, but there are exceptions to any rules and in this particular case the fly in the ointment is the Imperial Smelting Corporation's Mazak die castings. Mazak (which stands for Magnesium, Aluminium, Zinc and Kopper [sic!], the latter metal was rarely used after the war) is extensively used for door handles, radiator grills, plinths and decorative strips. The trouble is that it is extremely difficult to plate. Because it is so porous, it retains the sulphuric acid which is used for stripping the old plating off and inevitably the new coating of chrome soon succumbs. A tricky problem this and some one make car clubs are going to the rather elaborate lengths of having the Mazak parts recast in gunmetal or bronze. Perhaps the only other alternative is to seek out a duplicate part that is in better condition to the one fitted to your car.

The problems associated with plating Mazak. This Wolseley radiator cap has suffered badly from pitting. The only answer is probably to have it re-cast in another metal or to seek out a better example

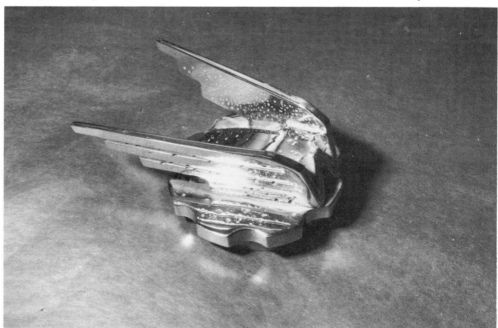

The respray

Having removed all the parts for chroming (the bumpers can take ages, incidentally), take off the wings if they are removable and cover the wheels with old sheets to prevent the overspray discolouring the tyres. If you are out to achieve the very best results, it is essential to strip all the old paint off the car. You can use any of the proprietary strippers; I have experienced good results with Nitromors. Apply the stripper with an old brush. The paint should bubble up in a few minutes and can then be removed with a scraper. Do not be tempted to use a blow lamp, for the flame can buckle the panels and may catch the interior trim on fire. You may experience a little difficulty in removing the paint from the crevices, but this can usually be done by applying the stripper soaked in wire wool. If the car has been subjected to more than one respray, a second application of stripper may be necessary. To speed up the process, score the surface of the paint. Once the body has been stripped down to bare metal, any outstanding repairs should be carried out.

To ensure that the fresh paint adheres to the bare metal, it is a good idea to thoroughly clean the surface before going any further. Apply Deoxidine 125 (and all the following instructions apply specifically to ICI products that are available throughout the country), for although bare metal appears clean and bright, it may carry contaminates which can attack the paint and impair its adhesion and durability. Deoxidine is designed for use on both steel and aluminium and in the former instance removes rust, and traces of oil and grease, and even the corrosive elements present on your hands! It also etches the metal. Therefore mix one part of Deoxidine with two parts of water in a polythene or rubber bucket and apply it to the bodywork with a long-handled brush. Brush well in, paying particular attention to any badly rusted areas, then thoroughly rinse off the surface before it dries, with cold water, ideally with a hose. But if it does not dry, then apply some more Deoxidine and rinse off again. After this, dry the metal as quickly as possible, using a clean dry cloth, sponge or leather, paying particular attention to any seams or crevices. (Deoxidine will attack zinc or galvanised surfaces though. A special etching primer P565-5002 is available for use with such finishes.)

After this cleaning has taken place, it is vital that aluminium and aluminium alloy surfaces are treated with an etching primer, which steel surfaces will also benefit from. The ICI Etching Primer is activated by mixing it with equal amounts of Activator P273-5021, allowing the mixture to stand for 10 minutes.

The etching primer may require thinning, so add Thinner 851-396, which is recommended for use with spray cap BS B4 on the gun, but never add more Activator. Spray a thin uniform coat, rather than a thick heavy one, as this may affect the adhesion of subsequent coats. This primer is water sensitive, so undercoat should be applied as soon as possible; air drying for 15 minutes is quite sufficient.

As this is then sprayed on it is probably an appropriate moment to consider the correct spraying sequence, which should be carried out after masking.

When spraying, aim for continuity to minimise dry overlap joints. Difficult areas such as door shut channels, boot and bonnet edges should be sprayed first as any dust, or any other materials which have lodged there, will be laid and prevented from spoiling the surface finish. The diagram shows the correct order of spraying. And now for the flatting!

Flatting is probably the most boring, but most important part of respraying. What appears to be the smoothest of finishes, on close inspection will be found to be a mass if irregularities and adding further coats of paint purely accentuates them. So it is important to flat off the peaks to the level of the filled troughs. This is achieved by rubbing the paint with wet or dry abrasive paper which is lubricated with water and to which a little soap is sometimes added. The best results are achieved with hand flatting and this is aided by the use of a rubber, or felt, rubbing block to which the paper is attached. Each coat (with the exception of the top one should be flatted), 360/400 grade being used on the primers, while 400/500 grade should be reserved for the final primer-surfacer. 600 grade should be used for colour coats, but if you want a really outstanding finish, 800/1200 can be applied.

If you do not want to go the whole hog and remove all the paint from the car, clean the paintwork with Body Kleen 901 which is usually diluted to one part of solution to four of water,

The finished product. This 1961 MGA served the author as everyday transport for over three years

but if you are having to remove a good helping of oil and grease, then step up the concentration to one to one, rinse off with cold water and wipe over the surface with a rag soaked in white spirit or cleaning petrol.

Should you want to remove any traces of silicone polish, go over the surface with the aforementioned Body Kleen then wet flat with 400 grade paper (or 500 or 600 grade if applying colour direct) using nine parts of water mixed with one of Body Kleen. If there is any polish left, it can cause cratering of the finished surface, so do the job thoroughly.

If you are intending to spray on top of red or maroon, apply a coat of Belco B.1 Sealer Black PO82-28 (thinned 1:1 with Belco Fast Thinner 851-396) to the surface after it has been prepared for painting, allowing it to air dry for 30 minutes. But do *not* flat this sealer coat. Apply at least two coats of undercoat before the top coats. When flatting the undercoats, make sure that you do not rub through to the sealer. If you do, then spot in with B.1 Sealer and cellulose primer filler, before continuing with the process.

Having dealt with all these variations, we can now continue with the respray! Apply Hi-Build Filler Beige PO84-678 thinned with equal quantities of Belco Fast Thinner 851-396. Let dry for 10 to 15 minutes between coats and for 30 minutes before wet flatting with 400 grade paper (this is particularly good for heavily scored bodies). Apply three coats of this undercoat.

Any indentations can be filled with ICI Stopper PO83. Knife in thin layers over the first coat of cellulose primer or primer filler and it can be applied to bare metal if it is well scuffed beforehand. The amount of stopper applied will obviously vary considerably, but if you have cause to apply more than one layer, let each application dry for 15 to 20 minutes and the final layer an hour, to an hour and a half, before wet flatting with 320 grade paper. Any bare metal revealed can be touched in with cellulose primer filler. Now for the colour coats.

There should be at least three of these. Use Belco Car Finish 1:1 with Thinner 851-804. For best results apply the first two top coats in one day, leave to dry overnight and then wet flat before applying the final coat. After drying, use ICI 2B Rubbing Compound P562-32, either with a clean cloth or a clean lambswool mop. Complete with polishing with ICI Car Polish No. 7.

Once the paint has dried, refit the wings (if you have detached them) using new piping. This is obtainable from Edgware Motor Acessories of Edgware, Middlesex who can also supply many of the rubber extrusion found on elderley motor cars, such as those used on the boot, bonnet and door surrounds. Replacing the replated body parts should complete your exterior renovation and if you have done the job well it should be the most visually satisfying part of the entire restoration process.

Notes on development

1919 – 1929   At the beginning of the 'twenties, the four-seater tourer, constructed by cladding an ash frame with aluminium or steel sheet and being built largely by hand, dominated the motoring scene. Yet by the end of the decade, the saloon was pre-eminent, its pressed steel panels being produced on large and expensive machines. A production revolution had taken place within this ten-year span.

Like so many innovations in automobile manufacture, the mass produced pressed steel body hailed from America. Edward Gowan Budd had worked for the American Pulley Company of Philadelphia which produced pulleys from stamped steel sheet, rather than the more traditional cast iron or wood. This had been in 1899, but three years later he joined the Hale and Kilburn Manufacturing Company, who were pioneers in the use of steel pressings in the manufacture of railway rolling stock. Extending the process to the new, and rapidly expanding, motor industry no doubt appeared as a logical progression to Budd and in 1912 he set up on his own to win manufacturers over to the pressed steel body which, above all, could be produced with unskilled labour. The following year, the Dodge brothers approached Budd with a contract for steel body-work, and by 1916, no less than 70,000 had been built. Although these were tourers, the all-steel saloon was just around the corner and this went into production in 1919 and was no doubt a contributory factor in Dodge selling his millionth car in 1923.

Other manufacturers soon followed suit and two years later, William Morris, who kept a watchful eye on American technological progress visited Budd's factory, the outcome of which was the establishment in Britain of the Pressed Steel Company at Cowley in 1926, the plant going into production the following year. The new process meant that wood could largely be eliminated in a structural sense which meant that high temperature baking processes could be introduced and with the fire risk eliminated, welding began to usurp the traditional nut and bolt.

Apart from the manufacturing advantages, the new process was destined to have a profound effect on styling, for the elimination of the ash frame meant that designers were no longer constrained by angularity, which was the hallmark of most mass produced bodywork of the 'twenties.

A short-lived variation in body construction attained popularity at the end of the decade. The fabric body had been invented by the Frenchman, Charles Weymann in 1922, one of the more obvious features being the introduction of a padded fabric, in place of metal, as a cladding for the traditional ash frame. The result was an elegant, light body, but one which quickly began to look shabby if it was not regularly cared for, so the style made little impression in the 'thirties.

Before the First World War, cars were hand finished with coachpaint which was made from a mixture of linseed oil and appropriately coloured dyes. The gloss was provided by varnish, again made from linseed oils boiled up with natural gums and resins; in short, a slow and laborious process, which lingered on until about 1925. It was replaced by sprayed cellulose enamel, one of the early advocates of the new process being Sir Herbert Austin who used the Frederick Crane Chemical Company's cellulose, Cranco. Naturally the adoption of cellulose considerably speeded up the manufacturing process, which was accelerated by the introduction of pressed steel bodywork, as the surface of the metal required far less preparation than the coachbuilt variety.

Brightwork for most cars tended to be nickel silver, or brass fittings plated with nickel. (Nickel was so called because in the past the metalsmith's ability to transform a grubby piece of ore into a bright and shining metal was associated with Old Nick himself, and the name stuck.) One of the metal's disadvantages, however, was that it required regular polishing to maintain a shine, so around 1929 many manufacturers introduced a layer of chromium plate on top of the nickel, it then requiring the minimum of attention. Chromium plated bumpers were also introduced at the same time.

Thus nickel, with its soft restrained finish, a truly Edwardian inheritance, made way for the brash chrome of the 'twenties, which together with the elimination of the coachbuilt body, as far as large manufacturers were concerned, demonstrably marked the end of the Vintage era.

1930 – 1940   The 'thirties saw the increasing predominance of the small, pressed steel saloon, with windscreens and radiators being inclined from the vertical to appeal to the 'streamlined' fashion of the day. Styling for the vast majority of mass produced cars evolved slowly, being an

223

inheritance of the angular body shapes of the 'twenties, though Morris, for one, cribbed the more up to date lines of the Ford model Y for his famous Eight of 1935, destined to become the best selling model of the decade. During the 'thirties, luggage boots became increasingly popular (though the Riley Nine had one back in 1926), while at the front of the car, a chromed radiator shell made way for a painted one on the cheaper models, the core being relegated further into the engine compartment. Morris again pointed the way in Britain, in 1939, by fairing the headlamps into the front wings on his series E Eight. The handsome plated lamp shells were thereafter destined for obscurity.

The sporting two seater of the 'thirties was a far handsomer affair, the relatively small production runs, in the main, making the introduction of pressed steel bodywork uneconomic, so the traditional coachbuilding processes were maintained. Inspiration for much of the styling sprang from the exquisite Zagato and Touring bodied Alfa-Romeos and although few British two seaters could match the performance of the twin overhead camshaft cars from Milan, the looks cost little to reproduce. . . .

1945 – 1960 Although the immediate post-war period saw the continuation of many pre-war designs, the new generation of mass produced four-seaters reflected a high degree of American inspired styling. An important factor of this design philosophy was Gordon Buehrig's 810 Cord of 1935, which, despite a short lived production life, had a considerable influence on car styling throughout the world. The Cord, with its strong emphasis on horizontals, aided by the use of front wheel drive, finally removed the last vestiges of a radiator shell from the front of the car, though its outline was suggested by the blunt nose of the bonnet. Then there were the headlamps which retracted into the front wings, concealed door hinges and the elimination of running boards all of which pointed to the shape of things to come.

The sporting end of the market, clearly remained wedded to the Old World, the lines of the special Touring bodied 328 BMWs of 1940 cropping up again and again, while the full width bodywork of the post-war Ferrari 166 were also readily apparent.

New production processes were introduced with the universal adoption of monocoque construction for high production, low cost cars (as recounted in the Notes at the end of Chapter Two) and from around 1949 synthetics started replacing cellulose finishes at the lower end of the market. Synthetics had been introduced in this country from 1927 when Dr. H. Houston Morgan, returned from America with some new synthetic resins. Although the new paint took longer to dry than the cellulose finish, it did not need the same time consuming polishing at the end of the spraying process required by the older material.

Split windscreens were found on many cars of the 'forties and 'fifties though the Jowett Javelin and Humber Hawk of the late 'forties are early examples of cars with curved screens Another departure came in 1956 when that year's Vauxhall Victor was the first British car with a wrap around screen. Triplex, had been making safety glass since 1914 when Reginald Delpech acquired the English patents for a French invention for a three ply laminated glass, which had been in production in Paris since 1911. During the 'twenties, Triplex was offered as an 'extra', but in 1928, Hillman were the first manufacturer to offer Triplex laminated safety glass as standard equipment. From 1932 all new cars had to be fitted with safety glass by law, while second hand ones were given until 1937 to be converted. Although Triplex anticipated the post-war 'wrap around' look by making curved safety glass windscreens for the cabs of provincial trams in the 'thirties, it was not until the mid-'fifties that they became a mass production reality. It is also worth noting that laminated rear screens fitted with heating wires were available on Rolls-Royces back in 1948.

Monocoque construction added another nail in the coffin of the open car, as special reinforcement was necessary to cope with the absence of the strengthening roof. The almost complete dominance by the saloon was in stark contrast to the days of the early 'twenties when the tourer ruled the roost.

1960 – 1970 But for a gradual change in styling from the 'curved' of the early post-war years to the 'razor-edged' of the late 1960s, little changed in body construction other than the refining of the monocoque technique, and the obvious thinning-down in the material used. By the end of the decade interest had begun to develop in better rust prevention finishes, and the use of plastic trim externally was becoming more prevalent.

Chapter Eight

Interior renovation, doors and instruments

A driver with a very long back will not enjoy his journeys if the back of his seat is too low; and, if his legs are too long for the maximum adjustment of the driving seat, his ankles and knees will become very cramped on all long rides. Similarly, a woman whose measurement from knee to ankle is short, will always be uncomfortable if the rear seat cushion has a high front and steep backward tilt. Some cheap upholstery is very hard. These small matters should always be tested by trying the various seats very carefully before placing an order **The Autocar Handbook (1926)**

When you come to consider restoring the interior of your car, there is often a tremendous temptation to pull everything out, throw away the bits which appear to be worn or mouldy, and begin again from scratch. Well, to start with, there is an important rule that you must observe, and it is this: do not throw anything away until the restoration is complete and only then when you have satisfied yourself that a fellow enthusiast may not be able to make use of the relics. There are two reasons for adopting this course of action. Firstly, the pieces, however damaged, can serve as a pattern for the new parts. This applies to pieces of seat, head lining and carpeting. The second reason is that the worn out fragments of fabric and leather may still be sufficiently complete to indicate their method of construction and you should ensure that the new material, as well as being as close to the original as possible in appearance, is also stitched or stuck in the same way. If you want to discover how the old part was put together, take it to pieces and find out.

This, of course, only applies if the interior is damp, tatty and scruffy. You would be far better advised to retain as much of the original finish as you possibly can, but with an open car which has been left out in the open, or in a leaky shed, there often is not much to salvage.

I do not think that it is an exaggeration to say that trimming is one of the trickiest aspects of restoring a car because you have to work really hard to get a professional finish. If you have a flair for this type of work then go ahead, but there is nothing worse than making an excellent job of the car's mechanics and bodywork and then spoiling the whole effect with an amateurish interior. This does not mean that there are not some areas that the amateur can cope with. Most of us can deal with making new carpets, recovering door panels and if you can count on the asssistance of a wife or girl friend, plus her sewing machine, the tricky business of fitting a new head lining. Re-upholstering is another kettle of fish altogether and without access to an industrial sewing maching to say nothing of plenty of skill, I would advise against undertaking it, unless you have some experience in this quarter. But there is nothing to stop you taking on some careful patching, but I would be inclined to draw the line there. The same goes for making a new hood. I have seen some ghastly amateur efforts, and nothing can be guaranteed more to detract from the lines of a tourer than an ill-fitting, sagging, and bulging hood which looks rather like an unmade bed.

Having decided what you can and cannot do, go ahead and strip out the car's interior. Start with the seats, following with wood or plastic door fillets (do not forget to mark them accordingly), door and window handles, door panels, pillar fillets, draught excluder, headlining and carpeting. Well, that is the order, but now let us look at some of the more important items individually.

Seat repairs and renovation

The vast majority of seats and squabs are made up on a wooden millboard base, on which is mounted the spring case. This is covered with a hessian or calico envelope, then an overlay of wadding or sponge rubber. There is another calico envelope and finally the leather, or leathercloth covering. Obviously the condition of the upholstery does vary according to the age and quality of the car as well as the sort of life it has led.

When upholstery sags, the trouble may be due to the filling or underlay having rucked up or disintegrated. This can be sometimes remedied by fitting new wadding. But a broken spring case can present quite a problem. You can obtain a second hand case from a breakers yard (those fitted in the back seat of a Morris Minor estate car can serve the purpose well), or replace with Dunlopillo. Cut the rubber with a hacksaw, and if you have to attach an extra piece of it to achieve the right shape, use the correct Dunlop adhesive.

Pleated upholstery is a lot easier to repair than the non-pleated variety. One of the most common failings is when the threading gives way between the pleats. With the use of a device called a Circular Needle (actually it is semi-circular), you may be able to carry out the repair without disturbing the rest of the upholstery. You should use a strong waxed, or linen thread. If just one pleat is badly torn you may be able to fit a new one.

Should the upholstery be nothing more than shabby, snip a small sample from an unobtrusive area and send it off to Connolly Brothers (Curriers) Ltd., of London NW1, as they no doubt supplied it to the manufacturer in the first place. They will be able to provide a small supply of the original coloured lacquer used when the leather in your car was first produced. It is sold in half litre quantities and a car the size of a post-war Rolls-Royce would require about three and a half litres. First, thoroughly clean the interior with glycerine soap. A small brush can be used for any dirt that may 'have become ingrained. Then while the leather is still damp apply a coat of Connolly's Hide Food. This should have the effect of returning the leather to its original suppleness by feeding and nourishing the fibres, but the results obviously depend to a great degree, on the sort of treatment the upholstery has enjoyed in the past. Wait for 24 hours, and then clean off the surplus hide food that may remain. You are now ready to apply the coloured lacquer. After checking that the leather is quite dry, stir the lacquer well before using and pour a quantity into a shallow container and dipping a swab of stockinette into the lacquer, apply it evenly, and sparingly, to the leather. If necessary a further coat can be sprayed on to give a more even finish. Make sure that you carry out this particular work in warm and dry premises, which sounds more like the house than the garage. . . .

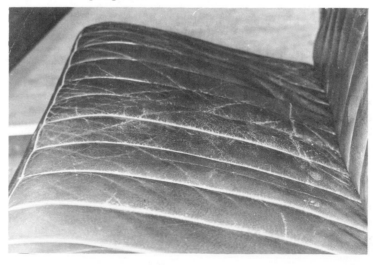

It is quite possible to improve this upholstery by the use of Connolly's Hide Food and their special lacquer

Original upholstery being removed from a Vanden Plas bodied Bentley

A replica Vanden Plas bodied Bentley being retrimmed by North Stables Coachbuilding

These instruments were renovated by John Marks of Vintage Restorations of Tunbridge Wells, Kent

Oily stains can be removed by using the rubber solution from a cycle puncture repair kit. Squeeze a layer over the mark and let it dry for 24 hours. Then roll off, and the chances are that it has absorbed some, if not all, of the oil. But if the stain has penetrated the wadding underneath, then there is little that can be done. Should you find that the upholstery is suffering from mildew, use a five per cent solution of Mystox in white spirit (the former being available from Picreator Enterprises Ltd., of London NW4). Its protective layer will also prevent further attack.

For waterproof finishes such as Vaumol, wash the leather thoroughly with warm water and pure non-caustic (Glycerine) soap or with Connolly's concentrated cleaner. If the latter is used, then make up a solution of one part of cleaner to 12 parts of water. It is important that the cleaner is not used in its concentrated form. Then immerse a soft cloth in the solution, wring out the cloth, and lightly rub the surface to be cleaned. Repeat the operation removing any traces of the cleaner with a fresh cloth, damped with warm water. Then dry well with a damp cloth.

A nail or small brush, which is not too hard, should be used to remove dirt that may have become ingrained in the top or corners of the seat. Do this in conjunction with soap and water, but caustic and detergent soaps should be avoided. Also do not be tempted to use cleaners which appear to remove dirt very quickly, as this may damage the finish of the leather.

If you are just contemplating routine maintenance, clean the leather about every four months in the aforementioned soap and warm water, applying Connolly's Hide Food twice a year.

Re-covering the door panels

The panels are secured to the doors, either by self-tapping screws and cup washers, or by spring clips. You will probably have to remove the garnish rail at the top of the door before you can take the panel off, and then there is the business of removing the door handles.

With the cross pin type, the escutcheon should be pressed inwards until the retaining pin, which passes through the handle shank and shaft, is exposed. The pin should then be pushed out. Another variation is the spring loaded cross pin type. With this sort, the handle is retained by a spring loaded cross pin, which is tensioned by a coil spring fitted in the handle shaft. The end of the spring is retained by a blade which is attached to the outside of the shaft. To remove the pin, the escutcheon is pressed inwards until the projecting pin is exposed and it can be pushed into the handle shaft. The handle can then be removed. There is a further, and rarer, type where the handle is secured underneath by a small grubscrew. Also, before the door trim can be taken off, the escutcheon, which is also held in place by two screws must also be removed. Then there is the clip-on variety comprising of a hair pin type spring in the handle shank, which engages with an appropriate groove in the shaft. To release the handle, a flat piece of metal should be pressed upwards between the handle and its packing washer, sufficient to disengage the spring.

The panels themselves will be made of plywood or board. If they are damaged (sometimes the bottom edge has suffered rot as a result of blocked drain holes), it is not a bad idea to make new ones from plywood, about two or three millimetres thick, using the old board as a pattern. The most straightforward type of panel to reproduce is the sort without a pocket. The panel will also have a much more professional finish if it is beaded properly around the edge, though this applies more to the older type of car. You can use plastic clothes-line covered with leather, or leather cloth, to reproduce this beading, or alternatively rather grand brass beading is fine if you can track any of it down. Whatever you decide on, this should be positioned prior to the replacement of the panel.

When you come to cover the panel, there should be a thin layer of cotton wadding between the leather or leather cloth, but again, this is probably more applicable to older cars than to more recent ones. The thing to remember is to stick the wadding to the panel, *not* the covering. Having made certain that your new panel is the correct size, so it will not prevent you from shutting the car's door, apply the material, sticking it down on the *back* of the panel with Copydex. You may need to use temporary tacks to stretch the material, but these should not feature on the finished product.

Things are made a little more complicated if a door pocket is fitted, for the sides of the panel should not be stuck down in the first instance. Make up the new pocket, having taken the old one to pieces to serve as a pattern, not forgetting to position a strong piece of elastic in the top. It can

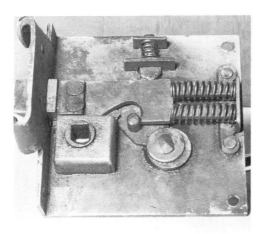

Crude, but effective, a simple slam lock from a car of the mid 'thirties

Door panels are usually located by spring clips or screws

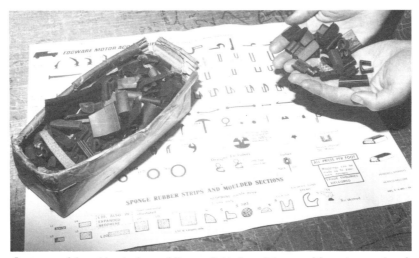

Just some of the rubber body moulding available from Edgeware Motor Accessories of Edgeware, Middlesex

When a fault develops with a window winder, it is usually associated with the spring or cog which meshes with the quadrant (*foreground*)

A restored Morris Eight door panel, just the type of job that can be tackled by the amateur

then be tacked into position, but to avoid the points of the tacks piercing the covering of the panel, place a metal rule between the leather cloth and plywood and hammer the tacks on to the rule. This should produce a riveting effect and the tacks should not pierce the outer skin. The rule can then be removed and the sides of the covering stuck into position. Do not yet make any holes in the material for the door and window handles (though you have obviously made them in the plywood), but when the time comes to position the panel, place it adjacent to the door and tap both shafts with a hammer so that they make their own holes.

After you have finished working on the door panels, you may care to turn your attention to the locks on the door, particularly if they have been giving trouble, resulting in the door not closing properly. If you are missing a door key, and can find out the number, then replacement is no problem, but if you have an old lock, then this will have to be taken off the car and given to a competent locksmith, who will then make a new key. J. D. Beardmore and Co., of London W1 can do this for you. However, I will now consider some of the securing mechanisms that you can expect to find lurking in the door when the panel is removed.

During the pre-war era, the slam lock predominated, but partly due to the requirements of the unitary body construction, it was augmented by the rotary cam and rotary lock, both of which provided vertical and horizontal restraint. Now let us look at these terms in a little more detail. The slam lock relates to the basic form of lock which relies on a spring loaded sliding bolt to keep the door in a closed position. A familiar feature of this design is the striker which is positioned on the door pillar and is stepped to provide an intermediate 'first safety' and fully closed position. A separate metal dovetail provides vertical door restraint.

With the rotary cam lock you can easily recognise the specially shaped latch. When the door closes, it rotates downwards, and outwards, by a striker stud on the door pillar and in doing so brings an inner cam into play and a two position pawl mechanism. This has the effect of retaining the door in an intermediate 'first safety', or fully closed position. At the same time, the top of the latch comes into contact with a spring loaded sliding wedge mounted on the door pillar.

The rotary lock works on the same principle as the rotary cam lock. The main difference, however, is that the rotor operating on a striking rack is used to operate the two position pawl mechanism. This can act directly, or in conjunction with, (depending on the version) an internal rachet.

In the cases of the rotary cam and rotor operated mechanism, the lock, or striker, includes an integral dovetail fitted with a sliding spring loaded wedge. This results in the door being restrained both horizontally and vertically by the relative position of the striker on the door pillar. It is for this reason that the plate is mounted on a captive plate inside the pillar so that when the retaining screws are slackened off, the whole assembly may be moved to a new position. This is usually only necessary when a new lock is fitted or when the original has to be removed for repair. The important point to remember when adjusting the striker is that it must be retained at right angles to the door hinges plane. And the only way to do this is by trial and error which is established by checking the door's closing action and its position in relation to the rest of the bodywork, when closed. But do not slam the door when making these adjustments, as the hinges, striker and lock may be strained as a result. If the striker is wrongly placed it can produce one, or a combination, of the symptoms shown in the table below.

Door faults	Striker plate adjustments
1 Shut edge of door is below body profile when closed.	Striker parallel to hinge line, but set too far in.
2 Shut edge of door proud of body profile when closed, probably rattles.	Striker set too far out.
3 Shut face of door drops when closed. Top, bottom and side lines uneven.	Striker set too low. (Slam locks, separate dovetails set too low.)
4 Shut face of door rises when closed. Top, bottom and side lines uneven.	Striker set too high. (Slam locks, separate dovetails set too high.)
5 Door fits properly, but rattles. Can be lifted when shut indicating clearance between wedge and latch (or rotor).	Top of striker inclined to car interior. (Slam locks, adjust or replace dovetails.)
6 (Rotary cam and rotary locks only.) Door closing action is hard. Continual slipping to 'first safety' position. Wedge forced back against housing.	Top of striker inclined to outside of car.
7 (Slam locks only.) Door continually slipping to 'first safety' position.	Remote control out of position or badly placed striker allowing bolt to be moved back by vibration. Set striker at angle to approach of bolt so that only its inside edge is in contact with the bolt.
8 (Rotary cam and rotary locks only.) Jerky closing and stiff opening.	Striker stud not 'pointing' at hinge pivot.

After you have replaced the panel, do not forget to fit new draught excluder which is available from Edgware Motor Accessories of Edgware, Middlesex.

Fitting a new head lining

You may be lucky, the lining may simply be dirty, and providing the cloth is in sound condition, it can usually be cleaned with a good quality carpet cleaner. A tear can sometimes be dealt with by sticking a suitably shaped card coated with adhesive, through the hole, pressing the torn edges on to it. Another alternative is to repair nicks with a needle and thread. Here the circular needle, which you may have used on the upholstery, can provide sterling service. If none of these alternatives apply, then the only answer is to replace the old head lining with new.

When you remove the old lining, take great care that you do not tear the material, as you will require it for a pattern. The lining will probably be secured to the roof by strips of cloth called lists which are, in the case of older cars, tacked on to wooden roof rails, or on more recent ones, a metal bar is pushed through the list which is then either screwed, or clipped, to the roof. You will need a tack remover or chisel and mallet for the rather fiddly business of removing the tacks. First

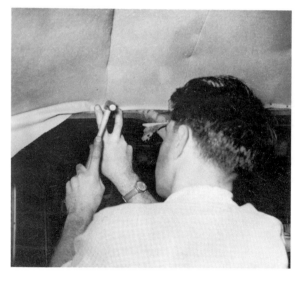

(*Both above*) Applying the securing rods to the lists in the head lining. Once the lining is in position it can be tacked round the edges

The finished product, and without a tack head in sight!

remove the double piping around the finishing line and beginning at the nearside front, remove all the tacks that you can see around the edge of the lining. When you have completed this part of the operation, the lining will only be held in position by the lists. If tacks are used to secure these, knock them out, beginning at the front of the car. Should metal roof bars be favoured, unscrew or unclip them as you go along, rolling them up in the cloth. Once you have reached the back of the car, the rear curtain, which is a separate piece of material, can be removed. To do this, take out the tacks around the rear window, then the side windows, the bottom finishing line and finally the top one.

With the lining out of the car, now is the time to deal with any rusting which may be revealed. treat with a rust preventing agent, such as Jenolite, and then paint with an anti-rust paint. Replace the flex of the interior light, if necessary, as the insulation is likely to be perished, and fit new tack rails if they are needed. Ideally, they should be made from mahogany and then varnished.

Now you will need some new material. Cars of up to around 1200cc capacity will require about three yards of 50in. wide cloth, while three and a half yards will probably be needed for larger vehicles. You will be able to tell exactly from the old lining. This material is also available from Edgware Motor Accessories. Then, using the old material as a pattern, mark out the new cloth with chalk, allowing 2in. for each list. There may be three or four of these, depending on the size of the car. Begin at the rear window end, allowing an additional 2in., then measure the distance to the first list or batten. Draw a chalk line and then measure an inch either side of it and draw two lines to sandwich the original one. You then have three lines in all. The cloth is then drawn together and machined along these two outside lines so that a loop is formed, which provides you with an inch deep tuck, which can either be tacked directly to the roof batten, when the time comes, or fitted with a metal bar, whichever method is favoured. Make the other lists in the same way. There are two important points to remember when carrying out this part of the operation. The machining should be done on the inside of the lining and the cloth should be laid so that the nap brushes to the front of the head lining, and towards the seats as far as the back curtain is concerned.

To replace the head lining, start at the back of the car. Find the centre of the first list, and tack it in position, then keeping the list straight, tack at two inch intervals. The machined line should be about 0.25in. below the batten. Then stretch tight, and tack the next one, working your way gradually down the car. If metal bars are used, then the job will obviously be that much easier, with these being positioned before the lining is fitted in the car. Once all this has been done, the sides can be tacked at inch intervals. The time has now come to fix the back curtain. Tack the cloth at the top, following the line of the heading, though turning the material inwards to present a neat finish, and tack between the head lining tacks. Do the top first, followed by the sides and edges, bottom, centre and corners. All that is now required is to cut out the rear window. Push the material against the edge of the window and tack it in position, then using a sharp knife, cut out the window space. All joints can be concealed using a double cord piping. Alternatively, you can disguise them with stiff card, covered with cloth, securing with panel pins. If draught excluder is fitted around the door surrounds, now is the time to secure it.

Carpets

If your car is comparatively modern, you may be able to obtain ready cut carpets for it, but if not you will have to make them, using the old ones as a basic pattern. Stiff brown paper, rather than the previous carpet, does an excellent job. Make sure that the pattern is face down on the back of the new carpet, otherwise you can end up with a mirror image of the intended shape. It is important to bind the edges of the carpet you intend using (unless it is a heavy pile rubber back variety). The traditional binding material was hide, which probably lasted longer than the pile! Your local trimmer may be able to do this for you, as a domestic sewing machine will not be up to the job. A good carpet fastener is the Veltex dot type. The fastener is secured to the underside of the carpet with three prongs which sprout from a metal ring, and are virtually invisible in a pile carpet. Its male opposite number is screwed to the floor.

It is essential, incidentally, to ensure that the car's floor is absolutely watertight. If it is not, water will get in and rot the carpet. A metal floor can be repaired by welding, while should floor boards be fitted, and they look in the least doubtful, then make new ones from marine ply, using the old boards as a pattern. Set them in Dum Dum, which is an excellent sealant, having the advantage of never setting completely solid, so that it 'gives' slightly when the body flexes.

Instruments

A complete, and matching set of instruments, all working and in good order make a satisfying and functional contribution to your car's interior. But because it does a lot of work, the speedometer will probably need overhauling. Most governor speedomers of the Vintage era can be overhauled by Thomas Richfield Ltd., of London W1, while Smiths Industries Ltd., of London NW2 also operate a renovation service for later instruments of their own manufacture. The former company can also make up new speedometer drives to a required length. Other instruments, including car clocks, can be reconditioned by John Marks of Vintage Restorations, of Tunbridge Wells, Kent. The following table may help you to sort out any speedometer shortcomings:

A typical Smiths speedometer of the vintage era. Black faced instruments were introduced in about 1929. Both types can be overhauled by Thomas Richfield Ltd of London W1

This speedometer for a post war MG was restored by the makers, Smiths Industries Ltd., of London NW2

A typical vintage dashboard. The driving compartment of a 1928 Austin 12

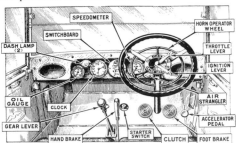

The instrument panel of a 1936 Austin 14. *Key* A, panel light switch; B, trip speedometer; C, eight day clock; D, inspection lamp points; E, ignition key; F, lighting switch; G, ignition warning lamp; H, oil gauge; I, fuel gauge; J, ammeter, K, starter switch

234

Symptom	Causes
No speed, or fixed speed registered, or tendency for pointer to go to 'Full Speed'. Mileometer working correctly	Clearly flexible drive is operating and instrument fault exists, though check drive for excessive lubrication
Neither speedometer needle or mileometer working	Probably broken drive. If not failure probably in gearbox take off
Speedometer working, but mileometer not	Instrument failure
Mileometer satisfactory, but speedometer needle wavers	Likely damaged flexible shaft. Check inner drive for kinks and irregularities and outer case for bad insulation
Inaccuracy in both speedometer and mileometer	Apart from the possibility of a defective instrument, the most likely failing is in the gearbox drive.
Noisy instrument	Faulty instruments or kinks in drive shaft.

If the flexible drive has a small black outer casing of about 0.25in. diameter, the inner drive may be removed by unscrewing the knurled union nut at the speedometer end. On the larger diameter cable, the drive is removed by unclipping the C washer from one end. To test the condition of the inner cable, lay the drive on a clean surface, such as a sheet of newspaper, and gently roll it between the thumb and forefinger. If any part of the drive lifts or kinks or any irregularities are felt, dispense with it. It is hopeless trying to straighten it! For the 'kink' is sufficient to cause needle flutter. Also check that the cable clamping clips have not distorted the outer casing. Lightly grease the inner cable, but on no account use oil as this can force its way into the instrument.

If your car is fitted with a Hobson telegauge, this can be overhauled by Classic Restorations of Broughton, Lincolnshire, while 'do-it-yourself' renovation kits can be obtained from the Complete Automobilist of Baston, Huntingdonshire.

Should your steering wheel be suffering from the rigours of old age, causing the plastic coating to crack and peel, then Exceloid Ltd., of Lichfield, Staffordshire can recover it for you.

Renovating interior woodwork

There is one further item that will respond to restoration in your own workshops and this is your car's interior woodwork. Many vintage cars, even some of the cheapest, initially used solid wood facias and although metal dashes soon gained popularity at the lower end of the market, the more expensive cars continued to use them, often faced with walnut veneers well into the post-war years.

So if you're faced with faded or stained wood you've got to recognise that, to do a good job, ideally it will have to be removed from the car. Also if you attempt the restoration of just one item it will stick out like a sore thumb. So you've got to remove the lot and this may prove to be rather more difficult that you might imagine, particularly the dashboard. The Mark II Jaguar dash, for instance, has no less than 25 pieces. If it really does look to be a difficult job, this might be an instance of leaving things as they are, carrying on the restoration in situ and just removing the door fillets which are usually rather easier to deal with. Prior to removing the woodwork first try and discover just why it might have suffered in a particular way. The most usual problem is water leaks, particularly around the windscreen or doors. The latter may be suffering from badly worn hinges and such a shortcoming will have to be rectified prior to the repairs to the woodwork being carried out.

When you come to remove the wood, take special care that you collect all the screws and special clips that may be associated with it. Also take great care that you've got precisely the right sized screwdriver for when you remove the screw, a slip with the wrong one will scratch the wood and give you more work. Once you've removed the various items, carefully examine them and check for splits or signs of the veneer lifting. In the former instance these should be carefully opened up, glue inserted and the wood damped but not so that it marks the surface. In the case of veneers that have lifted, repair them with glue and gently re-position by a warm but not hot iron.

235

Tudor Rees of Bristol specialises in the restoration of elderly valve radios for cars. This is an example of his restoration work

The 'office' of Bob Bingham's 1933/4 Wolseley Hornet Special

The plain but practical dashboard of a 1935 Morris Eight. Mike Finnigan's car again

Now on to the restoration proper. You can strip off the clear cellulose lacquer used on most woods with the sort of paint stripper you used for removing the car's paintwork. The exception will be more modern cars that had a polyurethane varnish. It's therefore important that you check with your car club, or the manufacturer if the make is still in production, because this type of finish demands its own special stripper. You might also find that the "grain" is in fact imitation added artificially on top of a cheap, soft wood. Carefully check the edges of the wood where the lacquer might have worn through. If you strip the lacquer off you'll take the colour and grain with it so be on the lookout for such deception.

Apply the stripper with a brush and you'll almost certainly find that you have to apply about two or three coats. Don't start scraping until you can see that the stripper has done its work otherwise you risk damaging the surface of the wood. Whatever you do, don't attack the veneer with too much vigour, it's not difficult to damage and this particularly applies to those sections that are angled on the wood. Once you've completed the stripping clean the wood with water to neutralise the stripper and then let it dry naturally. Don't skip this part of the operation for if there are any traces of stripper left in corners and crevices it will damage the new lacquer when it is applied.

With the wood completely dried, you can then proceed with the next stage of the operation which is rubbing down the veneer with $1\frac{1}{2}$ grade sand paper and methylated spirits making sure at the same time that you don't damage the edge of the veneer. Once completed, you can go over the wood with a fluff-free rag soaked in meths. You'll then have a better idea of the extent of the damage but if large areas of veneer have lifted you'd be probably well advised to leave the task to an expert. You can use a wood filler to deal with any holes that there might be present and obviously try and get the shade as close as possible to the original.

The next stage is to stain the wood and you should go for a spirit rather than water based wood stain as you'll probably find it easier to use. It should be applied with a linen pad and you should use a sufficient amount of stain to apply it in one session without having to stop. Apply single coats to each item and gradually build up the colour. In those areas where you've used a filler to fill holes you'll probably find that you need some extra stain so it doesn't look too light.

Then on goes the sanding sealer. It's here that you'll prove your dexterity with a spray gun as it has to be sprayed on as it dries too fast for application with a brush. You'll need at least six coats of this sealer and it should be applied at 10 minute intervals. A ratio of five parts of cellulose thinners to one of sealer should be fine. Make sure that you don't apply the sealer in sunlight and let it dry without any artificial warmth. Having left the surface for a day, very carefully rub down with 400 grade wet or dry paper and apply the minimum of pressure to the surface otherwise you'll rub right through, particularly around the edges. This part of the operation is vital because any imperfection will be exaggerated when the final coat of lacquer is applied.

When you consider that the filler has been sufficiently smoothed down you can apply the lacquer and this also has to be sprayed on though ensure that you don't do this in a warm atmosphere. Thin the lacquer to a ratio of around eight parts of thinners to one of lacquer. You'll need about six or seven coats, allowing about 10 minutes for each to dry. It's a matter of letting the lacquer dry for at least a day. Then carefully go over with wet or dry paper with soap and water. Ensure that you don't break through the lacquer on the edges: it's all too easy to do!

Next application should be *T Cut* which is more normally associated with cutting back paint on bodywork. Next use a liquid polish and finally go over the woodwork with a solid one. Prior to returning the woodwork to its place on the car, make a point of cleaning out the holes and recesses in the dashboard otherwise you'll find that the lacquer cracks when the screws are tightened. After the woodwork has been replaced, clean occasionally with a wax polish.

Suction operated windscreen wipers

It is important that the rubber tubing connecting the wiper to the source of the suction should be free from kinks. It is also a good idea to split the rubber with copper tubing when it has to turn a sharp corner. If the tubing is connected to the inlet side of the Autovac, so much the better, but if it is attached to the inlet manifold direct, keep an eye (and ear) open for leaks because it is far more susceptible to the rigours of petrol, oil and heat. If the wiper will not work, and the rubber tubing is intact, it may be due to dirt on the slide valve (which directs the suction to one side or the other) or oil gumming up the pistons. If gummed oil is the reason, the wiper will have to be taken apart and the pistons and the cylinder walls washed with paraffin to remove the dirt. Do not be tempted to pull the wiper apart without carefully studying the positions of the relative parts. A sketch might help. I speak from experience! Re-oil and then re-assemble. On the other hand the stoppage may simply be due to lack of oil, and you can inject some into the unit without dismantling it.

Notes on development

One of the consistent threads running through the development of interior trim is the use of leather as an upholstery material. It was, of course, a natural progression from its use in carriages to 'horseless carriages', being usually presented in diamondal or buttoned designs. The use of this type of pleating got over the recurring problem of trying to find large areas of unmarked hide, the most usual scars being inflicted by warble fly and barbed wire. Bedford Cord was another material inherited from the carriage trade. However, not every car built before the First World War was so upholstered. Artificial materials, such as Duretex and Rexine, were to be found on cheaper vehicles. Both these crop up on post-war cars, though leather was almost universally favoured. But up until 1927 hides were only available in five colours: brown, tan, red, green and blue. However, in that year, Connolly Brothers, who supplied practically the whole of the British Motor Industry with leather, introduced their Vaumol process which permitted a far greater range of colours. Today the company lists 7000 different shades!

The introduction by William Morris of the pressed steel body rendered the traditional ash frame obsolete, and although wood continued to be used to retain trim, it no longer served any structural purpose. It was the start of a long chain of events that led to the complete elimination of wood from car bodies.

Very few plastics are to be found in Vintage cars. The only exception is Bakelite which crops up on distributor caps, gear lever knobs and ash trays, the material having been invented by a brilliant Belgium chemist, Dr. L. H. Baekeland, back in 1907.

Instruments tended to be handsome affairs with nickel plated bezels, and silvery white dials with the mileometer readings appearing through small holes on the face. Smiths, who had been making instruments since 1904, dominated the instrument market, though in 1929 they dropped their attractive silver faced instruments for more sober black faced dials. At night, the faces of the dials were illuminated with a dash lamp mounted on the front of the wooden dashboard, and very easy they were to read as well!

Although leather continued to be used on nearly all cars up until the outbreak of the Second World War, it persisted into the post-war years, being finally ousted by PVC upholstery at the lower end of the market, and it was not long before the traditional cloth headlining gave way to a Rexine substitute. Although leather is still to be found on most expensive cars, the present day seat is most likely to be a polyester foam cushion with a PVC covering clipped to the frame. Perhaps the only reminders of the days when practically all car upholstery was leather are the imitation flute marks, created by a hot press process.

During the 'thirties, as wood gave way to steel dashboards, instruments became simpler on cheaper cars, the ammeter being one of the first to disappear (see Electrics Section). Also, by the end of the decade illumination from the rear of the dials was universally accepted. The post-war years saw an even greater simplification of instruments. The familiar oil pressure gauge which had been fitted to all but the cheapest of cars (the smaller Austins and Fords were two notable exceptions) disappeared to be replaced by a warning light. The water temperature gauge was another casualty. Such hand controls as the advance and retard lever finally disappeared in the post-war era, though its companion hand throttle still crops up in unlikely vehicles, such as the Fiat 126!

A good example of the preformed 'heat moulded' trim found in many late classics. Restoration of such items can be very difficult, replacement with new parts being a much more satisfactory approach

Restoration at its finest. Tom May's ex Ecurie Ecosse XK120 Jaguar. This car was raced by Sir James Scott-Douglas and has been completely restored, being re-sprayed in the original metallic Flag Blue finish

Alvis TC 21/100 drophead coupe, 2993 cc 1954-56. The model first appeared at the 1953 Motor Show, being powered by the six cylinder engine which first appeared in the TA 21 of 1950. Both were fast comfortable cars, and still are, providing they are regularly serviced and not driven at 90 mph plus for long periods. The TC 21/100 saloons (by Mulliner) are prone to bad rusting at the rear but fortunately the drophead coupe by Tickford (a 1954 car is illustrated) is made of aluminium, with the exception of the wings, which are steel

Chapter Nine

The right tools for the job

Motorists' workshops are of all sorts and sizes. Some of us can afford to have a shop finely equipped with machine tools, which usually means employing men to look after them; but most of us have to make the best of existing accommodation, get together our tools as we go along and learn to do everything for ourselves. . . . **The Motorist's Workshop (1920)**

When I purchased my Vintage car, I remember surveying my tool kit and finding that I was the proud possessor of a set of bicycle spanners and a rachet screwdriver which only turned one way; hardly the sort of tools with which to undertake a restoration! Since then I have built up a reasonable kit, but the thing about tools is that you can go on collecting them for ever. However, I will try and list the ones which can be regarded as being particularly important.

I put a socket set as being high on the list of priorities. It is only when you come to get one that you realise what a waste of time all those barred knuckles and damaged nuts were. A reasonably priced set should last you a lifetime and, of course, you can use them on your modern car as well. Next item on the agenda is ring spanners, a set really is essential when you are working in a confined space. You can tell the really strong ones by the thickness of the 'ring', the thinner it is the better. A decent set of open ended spanners are needed for light work, but you will find that they start to slip when you come to apply a lot of pressure. If you go to a reasonable tool shop, you will find that you do not have to buy spanners in sets if you do not want to. It is quite possible to purchase them individually, and so gradually build up a collection. And if you are stuck for a size, then the chances are that it is going to be a small one, so a set of what are still charmingly known as magneto spanners is a worthwhile buy. The size of spanner will obviously be dictated by the type of nuts and threads fitted to your car. The guidelines set down in Chapter Two should point you in the right direction, but if you are in any doubts about the sorts of hexagons used on your car, check with your spares registrar *before* splashing out on an expensive set of spanners. Of course, if you cannot afford a socket set, then the next best thing is a set of box spanners and a tommy bar. They can often be picked up quite cheaply at government surplus stores, such establishments also being a good source for 18mm plug spanners. Adjustable spanners are fine providing you do not want to use the nut again, because the slightly sloppy fit can damage the flats. Having said this, one of the most frequently used tools in my kit is the invaluable 'third hand'; the Mole wrench. You will also find that a pair of Spencer Wills artery forceps (which have the advantage of locking closed) can be extremely useful when you are working in confined areas, such as behind the dashboard. If you are embarking on an engine rebuild, then a torque wrench is a vital tool, and although somewhat on the expensive side, it will last indefinitely and can also be used on your modern car. A set of taps and dies is worth having, and in addition to their conventional use they also lend themselves for cleaning up dirty or rusted threads.

Files should not be forgotten. A flat file, with serrations on the edge, and about 10in. long, is always going to be useful, a 0.25in. diameter round one is ideal for opening out holes, while a

A clean bench and clearly laid out spanners contribute to the ideal workshop. Note that the vice is mounted directly over the supporting leg

When splitting a nut, position the chisel on the edge of the flat

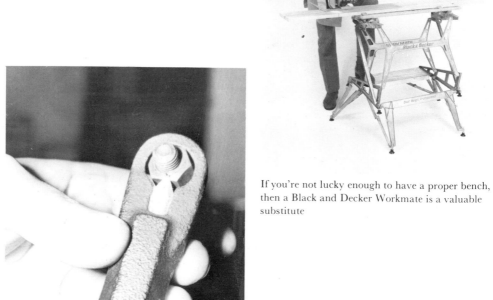

If you're not lucky enough to have a proper bench, then a Black and Decker Workmate is a valuable substitute

A nut cracker is another invaluable tool for dealing with stubborn nuts

A stud remover is another useful tool

triangular shaped file can be used for cutting grooves. Hammers are, of course, another essential, and try and get one with a ball pein end, as this is an essential tool if you have to do any rivetting. If you do decide to do some, make sure that the rivet is a good interference fit in the hole, and do not make the mistake of allowing too much of the rivet end to project proud of the metal surface. About 0.06in. is quite sufficient. Hammers fitted with composite heads often get more use than the conventional sort, being designed to minimise damage, so do not be without one of these. A nut cracker is another useful aid for removing stubborn nuts. If you have not got one, then use a cold chisel to split the nut, remembering to position the blade on the tangent of the flat, although you are going to undo it. A brass drift is another item that no restorer should be without. Then you will need a hacksaw, and it is worth getting large and small variants, though you will probably find that the latter one gets more use. A pad saw handle is another essential because it allows you to reach otherwise inaccessible places and is a good way of using up broken hacksaw blades.

Screwdrivers are obviously an essential item in any tool kit, but it is worth ferreting around in your local junk shop for old screwdrivers which are fitted with wooden oval handles. You will find that you will get a far better grip with this traditional shape than the more modern round plastic sort. A small electrician's screwdriver is another essential. On post-1945 cars, Phillips and later GKN Pozidriv heads will be encountered and it is important to use the correct screwdriver. The Pozidriv screwdriver, made by Stanley, can be identified by its blue handle. A pair of pliers is essential, and I have always have a pair of Bib wire strippers in my tool kit, together with an electric soldering iron for wiring jobs. And while in the electrical department, a battery charger is a worthwhile investment, particularly if you are trying to start a recalcitrant engine, which is a sure way of running down a battery. Again, a lead lamp is one of those simple items which will get plenty of use, but it is easy to overlook when equipping yourself with restoration aids.

Power tools are obviously marvellous time savers. An electric drill is an absolute 'must', for apart from being used to drill holes, it can be fitted with a variety of different attachments from a polishing mop to a wire brush and a grinding wheel. You also need a set of drills ranging in size from around 0.375 to 0.6in. These will be essential when you come to take on the business of drilling out broken off studs. To successfully carry out this operation, it is very important to first 'pop' the centre of the stud with a punch (another useful item). Then using a number of drills, progressively increasing in size, gradually drill out the stump applying pressure to either one side or the other if you have not managed to get your 'pop' mark absolutely central. If you do the job properly, the last drill should leave a sliver of metal, the idea being not to damage the thread. If you do, then you will have to tap out a new thread, fitting a stepped stud in place of the original.

You will find that a set of feeler gauges get plenty of use, together with that all-important aid: the micrometer. This is essential for measuring the engine wear and when checking crankshaft ovality, for instance. Make sure that you measure part of the journal which takes all the thrust which is the top and bottom (the 12 and 6 o'clock positions) comparing the readings taken on the

243

sides of the journal (9 and 3 o'clock, in both cases imagining you are looking at the journal end on). As micrometers are relatively cheap instruments, I think it is worth reflecting for a moment how to read them.

The most popular sort of micrometer is the external variety, movement of the spindle of all-British instruments being limited to one inch. They are available in a number of sizes, perhaps the most likely ones you are liable to encounter start at two and three inches, or less. For example, with a two to three inch type, and the reading is zero, the gap between the spindle and the anvil is already two inches so when you take your reading you add two inches to it.

On British micrometers a screw thread of 40 threads per inch is used, so one turn of the thimble advances the spindle 1/40th of an inch or 0.025in. The sleeve and the spindle provide the readings, the datum line on the sleeve, being marked in 0.025in. divisions, so four divisions represent 0.1in. Now we come to the thimble, for there are 25 divisions on the bevelled edge and at each turn the spindle moves 0.025in., and each division is therefore equivalent to 0.001in. So to read the setting shown in the drawing:

Check the number of tenths 3 × 0.1	= 0.300
The number of 0.025in. graduations 2 × 0.025	= 0.050
Thimble graduations which coincide with the datum line	= 0.012
	0.362 in.

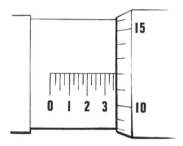

When you come to use the micrometer, use the rachet, if one is fitted, and this will ensure even tightening and give you consistent readings. If your micrometer is not fitted with a rachet, then turn the thimble slowly until resistance is felt. Remember to always hold the micrometer square to the work. An internal micrometer is designed for measuring bores, and unlike the external instrument spindle movement is limited 0.5in. the method of reading is, however, the same as the external micrometer.

All the tools that I have mentioned so far have the advantage of being portable, but we now move on to the more substantial consideration of workshop facilities. Obviously the focal point of the workshop is the bench and if you build one, the emphasis should be on sturdiness. Do not be tempted to use an old kitchen table as it will probably be the wrong height and will not be up to the job anyway. An engineer's vice is your next priority and remember to mount it over one of the legs, so when you have occasion to apply pressure, the bench can take it. It is a good idea to position a peg board above the bench and hang your spanners on it. Apart from being visually acceptable, it allows you to keep your tools clean, and you can instantly tell whether there is one missing. While on the subject of cleanliness, it is impossible to over estimate the importance of keeping the bench and its surrounding area as tidy and as presentable as possible. So often I have seen engines being rebuilt in filthy surrounding with the bench covered with dirty tools and oil stained rags. It is also a good idea to paint the workshop floor, so there is an incentive to keep it clean and dropped parts can be easily noticed.

Of course, no really well equipped workshop is complete without a lathe, the Myford ML7 with a 3½in. centre giving you a swing of about 7in. being a well proven model. This allows you to make plain bearings and bushes and such things as spigot bearings, trunnion blocks and clevis pins, stepped and conventional studs, on-centre drilling and much more. Milling and grinding machines are obviously desirable additions to any workshop, if you have the space and the financial resources.

The ideal workshop should have a suitably strong support from which a block and tackle can be hung for engine and gearbox removal. But if you have any doubts about the strength of the beams in your workshop, then fit one for the express purpose. It is not altogether unknown for a rickety garage to be demolished by the strains imposed by the removal of an engine!

If you have read this far and have not got a workshop, then I suggest that you invest in a Black and Decker Workmate. This portable work bench folds up to a handy size for transportation, is light and very strong and contains a built-in vice. For if you are having to carry out a restoration in a rented garage, then this portable bench has much to recommend it.

'Craftsmanship in a factory context', the bodyshop of a large British car company in the early 'twenties, which clearly indicates the amount of wood used in body construction. Note the workbench on the *left foreground* showing a good cross section of the hand tools used

Pressed steel body design at its best. A prototype *Traction Avant* Citroen pictured in 1934, the model remaining in production until 1957. The visual success of this mass produced Citroen was in part due to the use of pressed steel body panels and monocoque construction which freed the car's designers from the angular fashion of the day (inherited from the production saloon of the 'twenties, where the shape was conditioned by the internal ash frame work) and accentuated by a low centre of gravity, made possible by front wheel drive. The Citroen retains a sense of movement, even when stationary

Chapter Ten

The aesthetics of restoration

The engineers are our Hellenes, from them we receive our culture **Adolf Loos (1910)**

Everything you have read so far has a factual basis, but in this final chapter, I intend to stray from these safe, but shallow, waters and step into the more dangerous and faster flowing stream of opinion and talk about aesthetics. For aesthetic appreciation, or taste, represents an intensely personal viewpoint. This is, in itself, refreshing, for how boring it would be if we all liked the same wallpaper, carpets and three-piece suites. No, the trouble really starts when the products and ideas of one age are unsympathetically imposed on to those of another.

I think that even the most insensitive eye would recoil, for example, from painting a gallery of magnificent Tudor linen fold panelling with one of the present day vinyl paints, or fitting an easy-to-wipe plastic top to an elegant antique table. This is not to say that the paint and the plastic are not remarkable achievements in their own right, but each is a product of its age and when thrown into uneasy juxtaposition neither object benefits. For the panelling and table represents a commentary of the age in which they were built and applying 20th century outlooks and finishes is a distortion of that truth.

The same attitudes should apply with cars, though some qualifications are necessary in this context. With the business of restoration the foremost concern in most enthusiasts' minds is that the car should run effectively and reliably. The restoration process sweeps away the years of neglect, with the dynamo, Autovac or carburettor running as effectively as it did when the car was built. So far, so good, for at least in one context truth is upheld. But the finish of the component, what the eye sees, and *should* appreciate, is just as important. Unfortunately, all too often the pupil is dazzled by an excess of nickel or chrome, with humble items burnished with a frenzy usually reserved for an Army kit inspection. For in embracing these excesses, the over zealous restorer has turned his back on the age in which the car was built and substituted a garish latter-day gloss. Thus, truth is distorted.

Here, I am mainly concerned with Vintage cars, though the same issues still apply to later vehicles, to a lesser degree. This is because cars built in the 'twenties display a *natural variety* of materials. For there is iron, steel, aluminium, brass, bronze, leather, nickel and wood present to delight and interest the eye and it is just these contrasts that makes the underbonnet prospect of an old motorcar so interesting.

The other outstanding aesthetic quality of a Vintage car is its bodywork, and to qualify what I am saying a brief, though relevant diversion is necessary. In his book, *The Nature and Art of Workmanship* (Cambridge University Press), David Pye examines the aesthetic quality of design in our environment and explores the differences between the so-called hand-made and machine-made objects. But the particularly relevant part of his thesis, as far as elderly motor cars are concerned, lies in his definition of hand- and machine-made work; for he dubs them respectively, the Workmanship of Risk and the Workmanship of Certainty. In the case of articles produced by the Workmanship of Risk the finished product is wholly the result of the workman's deftness, visual skill and judgement. But when it comes to the Workmanship of Certainty, the manufacturing process is out of the control of the operative, the shape, sizing and contours being completely predetermined.

But this is not to say that the machine-made item cannot have an aesthetic quality. It simply means that greater emphasis has to be placed on good design because the minute imperfections, which are the hallmark of the Workmanship of Risk and which so delight the eye, are eliminated.

Now the largest single item on a Vintage motorcar which is an outstanding example of the Workmanship of Risk is the bodywork. For these coachbuilt hand-made bodies have an individuality and vitality which ensures that no two are alike. And if you want to prove the point for yourself, seek out an early example of a car fitted with pressed steel bodywork, which has simply aped the angular coachbuild design. The results are invariably flat, dull and lifeless because that vital element of risk has been removed. Comparison of a flower pot produced on a potter's wheel and one of the same design reproduced in plastic will produce the same response.

For the coachbuilt car inherited a functional *tradition* reaching back to the 18th century, and beyond. Add to this the essential integrity of design in the Vintage era in that slow cars look stately and pedestrian and sports car retain an *elan* which is forever the hallmark of high performance and you have the essential appeal of the Vintage motorcar. In other words, it was the engineer, not the salesman who had the last word, and is a reflection of the fact that in the early days of the motor industry, the man at the top was often responsible for the car's design.

By its very nature, craftsmanship in a factory context embodies a necessary degree of economy, both of time and effort. Naturally, the craftsman takes far longer than the machine, but the good worker has always aimed to produce the maximum effect with the minimum of effort. Lengthy and elaborate over restoration betrays this vital principle.

This, of course, leaves us with the vast majority of cars, the bodies of which are pressed steel and produced by the Workmanship of Certainty. To my mind the most successful application of this principle can be found in those vehicles that were designed specifically with the new process in mind, rather than copying a coachbuilt shape which drew its visual strength from the risk involved in making it. The 7CV *traction avant* Citroen of 1934 is an outstanding example of an inspired design being successfully produced in pressed steel.

All these factors should be considered when the restoration process is underway, and to paraphrase, I will end with these few points:

When you come to restore your car, aim to reproduce the state in which it left the factory.

Avoid the use of materials which were not current at the time.

Do not plate things that were not plated in the first place, or paint items that were originally left in their natural state, and vice versa.

By all means clean metal surfaces, but do not polish them unless you use your car on the race track.

If you carry out this advice, you may not win every Concours d'Elegance you enter, but you will, at least, be running a car which has retained its historical integrity. By contrast, the polished and plated vehicle will appear as incongruous as a chromium-plated penny in a handful of change. change.

THE END

Bibliography

Magazines and periodicals

Automobile Engineer
The Autocar (now *Autocar*)
Bulletin of the Vintage Sports-Car Club
Car Mechanics
Garage and Motor Agent
The Motor (now *Motor*)
Motor Trader
On Four Wheels
Practical Classics
Classic and Sportscar
Thoroughbred and Classic Cars
Veteran and Vintage Magazine

Books

The Austin Seven by R. J. Wyatt (Macdonald, 1968)
Automobile Design: Great Designers and their Work, edited by Ronald Barker and Anthony Harding (David and Charles, 1970)
Automobile Engineer's Reference Book, edited by E. Molloy and G. H. Lanchester (Newnes, 1956)
Automobile Electrical Equipment by A. P. Young and L. Griffiths (Iliffe, 1942 and 1950)
Automobile Refinishing by Keith Hammond (Robert Draper, 1972)
Automobile Steering, Braking and Suspension Overhaul by Staton Abbey (Pitman, 1960)
Automobile Transmission Servicing and Overhaul by Staton Abbey (Pitman, 1971)
Basic Bodywork and Painting (Petersen Publishing, 1975)
Bodies Beautiful by John McLellan (David and Charles, 1975)
Bodywork Maintenance and Repair including Interiors by Paul Browne (Autobooks, 1975)
British Solex Carburettors (Speedsport Motorbooks, 1976)
The Bullnose Morris by Lytton P. Jarman and Robin Barraclough (Macdonald, 1965)
Cars of the 1930s by Michael Sedgwick (Batsford, 1970)
The Complete Encyclopedia of Motor Cars edited by G. N. Georgano (Ebury Press, 1968)
The Designers by L. J. K. Setright (Weidenfeld and Nicholson, 1976)
Enjoy Servicing Your Car by Jack Hay and Joss Joselyn (Nelson, 1975)
Hepolite Service Manual (Hepworth and Grandage Ltd., 1966)
The History of the Vintage Sports Car Club by Peter Hull (Cassell, 1964)
How to Choose and Use Car Tools by John Humphries (Haynes, 1974)
Metals in the Service of Man by William Alexander and Arthur Street (Penguin Books, 1973)
The Motor Car by John Day (Collins, 1975)
Modern Motor Cars, edited by Arthur W. Judge – three volumes (Caxton, no date)

Motor Repair and Overhauling, edited by George T. Clark – three volumes (Newnes, no date)
Motor Car Refinishing by De Vilbiss (De Vilbiss, no date)
The Motor Guide to Makes and Models by David E. Culshaw (Temple Press, 1959)
The Motor Manual (Temple Press, 1954)
Motor Vehicle Technology by J. A. Dolan (Heinemann, 1971)
Motor Year Books, 1949 – 57 (Temple Press)
The Nature and Art of Workmanship by David Pye (Cambridge University Press, 1968)
Post War British Thoroughbreds by Bruce Hudson (G. T. Foulis, 1972)
Practical Automobile Engineering Illustrated (Odhams, 1945 and 1962)
The Restoration of Vintage and Thoroughbred Cars by Richard C. Wheatley and Brian Morgan (Batsford, 1960)
The Restoration of Vintage and Thoroughbred Motorcycles by Jeff Clew (Haynes/Foulis, 1976)
Rolls-Royce Enthusiasts' Club Technical Manual, 1972
The Rolls-Royce Motor Car by Anthony Bird and Ian Hallows (Batsford, 1972)
Sports Car Bodywork by B. W. Locke (Batsford, 1960)
The Spray Way of Painting (De Vilbiss, 1969)
The Story of Triumph Sports Cars by Graham Robson (Motor Racing Publications, 1973)
The Vintage Alvis by Peter Hull and Norman Johnson (Macdonald, 1967)
Vintage Cars by Cyril Posthumus (Hamlyn, 1974)

Appendix 1

Regulations governing lights, windscreens, washers, etc.

The following brief notes are intended as a guide to, rather than a definite statement of, certain provisions of government regulations which particularly concern Veteran, Vintage and Post-Vintage (but Pre-1951) vehicles, other than motorcycles. They were compiled by Peter Graham, MA,LL.B(Cantab), Barrister, who is a member of the Historic Vehicle Clubs Joint Committee and President of the Delage Section of the VSCC.

Preliminary

Almost all the regulations relating to lights are now to be found in the Road Vehicles Lighting Regulations 1971, but Regulation 38 of the Construction and Use Regulations 1973 also has particular significance. In essence, this provides that if you have at least one front or rear light on a vehicle then, even though it may be daylight, you must have all the lights and reflectors which, if it were dark, would be necessary to comply with the Lighting Regulations (but not apparently, a rear number plate illuminating light).

There are important exceptions to this rule because certain lights do not count as front or rear lights and do not bring the requirements of Regulation 38 into play:

(1)   stop lights and reversing lights do not count as rear lights and direction indicators do not count as front or rear lights;

(2)   lights which are painted over or masked so that they are 'not capable of being immediately used, or readily put to use' do not count; and

(3)   lights which are designed to be operated by electricity but which do not have any wiring do not count (but taking the bulb out is not enough).

Regulation 38 is, of course, of fundamental importance when submitting a vehicle for its annual test.

Lights at the front

1   Sidelights

During 'the hours of darkness', every motor vehicle on a road must carry two sidelights 'kept properly trimmed, lighted and in clean and efficient condition'. If the sidelights are lit electrically and do not also purport to be headlights, the wattage of each bulb must not exceed seven watts. 'Hours of darkness' means the time between half an hour after sunset and half an hour before sunrise. The light shown by a sidelight must be white, and the glass should be frosted or the light must be diffused in some other way.

2 Headlamps

Vehicles first used before January 1931 are exempt from the requirement of the Lighting Regulations to have double dipping headlights but if such vehicles do carry one or more headlights then at least one of them must be permanently dipped or capable of being dipped and the other or others must be capable of being either dipped or extinguished when the primary headlight is dipped. Any vehicle first used on or after 1st January 1931 must, at all times on roads (whether during the hours of darkness or not), carry either two headlamps fitted with a double dipping system or four headlamps, two on main beam and two on dipped beam.

So far as appearance of the headlamps on post-vintage cars is concerned:
(a) The lamps must be symmetrically located on either side of the centre line of the vehicle,
(b) they must be at the same height,
(c) they must have the same area and shape when illuminated,
(d) they must both emit the same colour of ligl.., which may be white or yellow, and
(e) there must be at least 35 centimetres between the inner edge of each light.
Note that there is, however, no minimum height Regulation for headlamps in the case of pre-1951 vehicles.

3 Use of headlamps at night

Any vehicle which is required to be fitted with double-dipping headlamps – which for our purposes means a post-vintage vehicle – must, while on a road, have at least the dipped beams illuminated during the hours of darkness unless:
(a) it is on a road with street lights at intervals of not more than 200 yards and the lights are lit, or
(b) it is foggy or snow is falling and the car has two illuminated fog lights.
For the purposes of sub-paragraph (b) above the two fog lights are lights which comply with precisely the same rules as are set out for headlamps in sub-paragraphs (a) to (e) of para. 2 above. The point is of course that fog lamps on *any* vehicle may be mounted at *any* height whereas the headlights on post-1951 cars must be at least two feet from the ground. There is of course no distinction for the purposes of this exception between a fog lamp and a spot lamp.

4 Use of lights in conditions of poor visibility

As a result of the Road Vehicles (Use of Lights during Daytime) Regulations 1975, most vehicles are required to show lights when on a road in daytime hours if 'poor visibility conditions' prevail. The requirements are:
(a) in the case of a vehicle which is required to be fitted with double-dipping headlamps (see paragraphs 2 and 3 above) at least dipped beams and, if they are in separate units, the sidelights must be illuminated;
(b) in the case of any other car which is in fact fitted with sidelights (whether electrically operated or not) the sidelights must be illuminated.

The Regulations define 'poor visibility conditions' in relation to a vehicle as 'such conditions adversely affecting visibility (whether consisting of, or including, fog, smoke, heavy rain or spray, snow, dense cloud, or any similar condition) as seriously reduces the ability of the driver (after the appropriate use by him of any windscreen wiper and washer) to see other vehicles or persons on the road, or the ability of other users of the road to see the vehicle'.

Reflectors and lights at the rear

1 Reflectors

Every vehicle on a road must, during the hours of darkness, carry two unobscured and efficient red reflectors marked either with the specification number of the British Standard, namely BS2515 or AU40 or with an 'approval mark' incorporating the roman numeral I or II. There are no exceptions in the case of pre-1951 vehicles.

There must be one reflector on each side of the longitudinal axis of the vehicle and each reflector must:

(a)   be not less than 16in. nearer to the centre line of the vehicle than the widest part of the vehicle;

(b)   be not less than 21in. from the reflector on the other side;

(c)   be not more than 30in. from the extreme rear of the vehicle;

(d)   be not more than 3ft. 6in., and not less than 15in., above the ground; and

(e)   be on the same level as the other reflector.

2   *Rear lights*

Every vehicle on a road must, during the hours of darkness, carry two lamps, each showing to the rear a red light visible from a reasonable distance. The lamps must 'be kept properly trimmed and in a clean and efficient condition'. Each rear light must have an illuminated area which, if circular, must be at least 2in. in diameter and, if not, must be at least of equivalent area and must be capable of containing a circle of 1in. diameter. If the lights are illuminated by electricity the bulb in each rear light must have a rated wattage of not less than 5 watts and the lights must be wired in parallel not in series. The Regulations also require that both rear lights must 'have the same appearance when illuminated, and the same illuminated area'.

The rules in paragraph 1 above relating to the position of reflectors apply also in relation to rear lights except that:

(1)   in rule (a) 24 in. is substituted for 18in., and

(2)   in rule (d) there is no minimum height.

It is also permissible to combine a rear light and a reflector in such a way that the glass of the rear light is a reflector. In this case it is sufficient for the combined unit to comply with the requirements as to rear lights when the light is lit and with the requirements as to reflectors when it is not.

By virtue of the Road Vehicles (Use of Lights during Daytime) Regulations 1975 referred to above, while any vehicle which is fitted with rear lights is on a road in daytime hours in 'poor visibility conditions', the rear lights must be illuminated.

3   *Number Plate light*

This cinderella of lights is required by Regulation 23(1) of the Road Vehicles (Registration and Licensing) Regulations 1964. There are no relevant exceptions for pre-1951 vehicles. Equally there are no specific requirements as to the manner in which the number plate is lit. Nevertheless if the vehicle was first registered *before* 1st October 1938 the number plate must be so illuminated as to 'render easily distinguishable every letter and figure' on the rear number plate. In the case of vehicles registered on or after that date the number plate must be illuminated so that, except in conditions of fog, every letter and figure is 'easily legible' in effect, from a distance of 60 feet. You may well feel that this is a distinction without much difference.

4   *Stop lights*

Vehicles first used on or after 1st January 1936 are required to be fitted with at least one stop light. A stop light fitted to a vehicle first used after 1935 must be at the rear of the vehicle and in the centre, or to the right of centre of the vehicle. The light from any stop light (whenever the vehicle was first used) must be 'diffused by means of frosted glass or other adequate means' and it must give a steady light. The light from a stop light fitted to a car first used after 1935 must be red, but stop lights on earlier vehicles may be amber. There is of course nothing to prevent the fitting of twin stop lights but note that the one on the nearside is *not* required by law so that, if one of the bulbs goes, you should retain or fit the good bulb in the offside stop light to remain within the law.

DIRECTION INDICATORS

Vehicles first used on or after 1st January 1936 are required to be fitted with direction indicators.

The old semaphore type indicators are adequate to comply with this requirement if they are 'in good and efficient working order' and are fitted not more than 6 feet behind the windscreen. When illuminated they must 'alter the outline of the vehicle to the extent of at least 6 in. measured horizontally'.

If new direction indicators have to be fitted it is, in practice, probably advisable to fit the flashing type of indicator. In the past many people have fitted this type of indicator to post-vintage vehicles by converting the sidelights and rear lights to double-filament bulbs. For such a conversion to comply with the requirements of the regulations the illuminated area of each indicator must not be less than $3\frac{1}{2}$ sq. in. (which, in the case of circular lights means a minimum diameter of just over 2in.). The colour of the indicators need not be amber on pre-1951 vehicles but can be white to the front and red to the rear. Make sure that you fit a serviceable modern flasher unit in order to ensure that the frequency of the flashes is within the required limits – 60 to 120 flashes per minute.

WINDSCREEN WIPERS AND WASHERS

1 *The Requirements*

Subject to the exceptions mentioned below, all vehicles must be fitted with:
(a)   efficient automatic windscreen wipers 'capable of cleaning the windscreen so that the driver has an adequate view of the road in front of the near and offsides of the vehicle in addition to an adequate view to the front of the vehicle', and
(b)   a windscreen washer 'capable of clearing, in conjunction with the windscreen wiper, the area of the windscreen swept by those wipers of mud or similar deposit'.

2 *The Exceptions*

First, let it be noted that there is no age exemption (for vehicle or driver). The fundamentally important exceptions are, however, that *neither* of the requirements apply if (1) the vehicle has no windscreen or (2) the vehicle is so constructed that the driver can 'obtain an adequate view to the front of the vehicle without looking through the windscreen by opening the windscreen or otherwise'. The last two words are a clear challenge to our ingenuity.

There must be one reflector on each side of the longitudinal axis of the vehicle and each reflector must:
(a)   be not less than 16in. nearer to the centre line of the vehicle than the widest part of the vehicle;
(b)   be not less than 21in. from the reflector on the other side;
(c)   be not more than 30in. from the extreme rear of the vehicle;
(d)   be not more than 3ft. 6in., and not less than 15in., above the ground; and
(e)   be on the same level as the other reflector.

2 *Rear lights*

Every vehicle on a road must, during the hours of darkness, carry two lamps, each showing to the rear a red light visible from a reasonable distance. The lamps must 'be kept properly trimmed and in a clean and efficient condition'. Each rear light must have an illuminated area which, if circular, must be at least 2in. in diameter and, if not, must be at least of equivalent area and must be capable of containing a circle of 1in. diameter. If the lights are illuminated by electricity the bulb in each rear light must have a rated wattage of not less than 5 watts and the lights must be wired in parallel not in series. The Regulations also require that both rear lights must 'have the same appearance when illuminated, and the same illuminated area'.

The rules in paragraph 1 above relating to the position of reflectors apply also in relation to rear lights except that:
(1)   in rule (a) 24 in. is substituted for 18in., and
(2)   in rule (d) there is no minimum height.

It is also permissible to combine a rear light and a reflector in such a way that the glass of the rear light is a reflector. In this case it is sufficient for the combined unit to comply with the

When it all seems worthwhile! There's nothing more pleasant than getting together with other enthusiasts for a natter about cars. *Above*, a gathering of post-war Morgans and *below*, a meeting of the Riley RM Club.

2   *The Exceptions*

First, let it be noted that there is no age exemption (for vehicle or driver). The fundamentally important exceptions are, however, that *neither* of the requirements apply if (1) the vehicle has no windscreen or (2) the vehicle is so constructed that the driver can "obtain an adequate view to the front of the vehicle without looking through the windscreen by opening the windscreen or otherwise'. The last two words are a clear challenge to our ingenuity.

Appendix 2

Vintage and classic car clubs

ABC Owners' Club (section of Bean CC). David Hales, 20 Langbourne Way, Claygate, Esher, Surrey KT10 0DZ. 0372 62046.

AC Owners' Club. Tudor House, Manor Road, Gt Bowden, Market Harborough, Leics.

Alfa Romeo Owners' Club. Michael Lindsay, 75/79 Regent Street, Cambridge CB2 1BE.

Alfa Romeo Section (VSCC Ltd). *Pre-1941 models only.* Mr. and Mrs. A. Cherrett, The Old Forge, Quarr, Gillingham, Dorset SP8 5PA. 07476 2756.

Alfa Romeo Montreal Owners' Register. R. Winwood, 20 East Street, Quarry Bank, West Midlands.

Alfa Romeo 2600/2000 Register. Roger Monk, New Walk Gates, 14/16 King Street, Leicester.

Alfa Romeo 1900 Register. Peter Marshall, Mariners, Courtlands Avenue, Esher, Surrey KT10 9HZ.

All Wheel Drive Club. PO Box 6, Fleet, Hants.

Allard Owners' Club. Miss P. Hulse, 1 Dalmeny Avenue, Tufnell Park, London N7 0LD. 01-607 3589.

Alta Register. G. Fleming, 16 Queen Elizabeth's Walk, Wallington, Surrey.

Alvis 12/50 Register, The. G.M. Tomlin, Holly Bank, Chancery Lane, Bollington, near Macclesfield, Cheshire SK10 5BJ. 0625 74196.

Alvis Owner Club. The Hill House, Rushock, Droitwich, Worcs. 056 283 309. Secretary: M.J. Cummins.

American Auto Club. Anne Thomas, 57 Turnley Road, Shard End, Birmingham B34 7DR.

American Auto Club, Pre '50. Luke Arnott, Pubs End, Drayton Parslow, Bucks MK17 0JG.

Amilcar Register. Flat 3, Buxton Old Road, Disley, Stockport, Cheshire SK12 2BB. Secretary: Roger Howard.

Amphicar Register. K. Gould, Park Lane, Ladburn Lane, Shilton, Oxford OX8 4AJ.

Armstrong Siddeley Owners' Club. 15 Plantation Drive, West End, South Cave, North Humberside HU15 2JD. Secretary: D. Robinson, Spares Manager: R.G. Allen, Conkwell Farm, Winsley, Bradford on Avon, Wilts BA15 2JG.

Aston Martin Owners' Club (AMOC Ltd). Jim Whyman, Burtons Lane, Chalfont St. Giles, Bucks HP8 4BL. 02404 4742.

(Austin) A40 Farina Club. Alan Barton, 5 Othello Close, Colchester, Essex CO4 3LB.

Austin A30-A35 Owners' Club. John Jewison, 42 Boswell Road, Doncaster DN4 7DD.

Austin 3 litre Club. R. Mossop, "Motorspeed", School Lane, North Mundham, Chichester, West Sussex.

Austin Cambridge/Westminster Car Club. *A40/A50/A60/A90/A105/A99/A110 and all derivatives.* T. Spearing, 2 Bloomfield Close, Timsbury, Bath BA3 1LP

Austin Counties Car Club. *8/10/12/16, A40, A70, A90 1939-54.* Philip Carpenter, 68 Upper Road, Plaistow, London E13 0DH.

Austin Seven Clubs Association, The. Robin Newman, 9 Glendower Street, Monmouth, Gwent NP5 3DG.

Austin Big 7 Register. R.E. Taylor, 101 Derby Road, Chellaston, Derby DE7 1SB.

750 Motor Club. Dave Braddley, 16 Woodstock Road, Witney, Oxon OX8 6DT. 0993 2285.

Pre-war Austin 7 Club. W.J. Tantum, 142 Curzon Street, Long Eaton, Nottingham.

Austin Eight Owners' Club. Duncan Clague, 15 Oriel Road, Tranmere, Birkenhead, Merseyside.

Austin Gypsy Register. Simon Frazier, Murray Cottage, Monxton, Andover, Hants.

Austin Ten Drivers' Club. Peter Woodend, 3 Eastcourt Drive, Widmen End, High Wycombe, Bucks.

Austin 3 Litre Club. Unit 10, Newcroft Industrial Estate, Tangmere, Chichester, West Sussex.

Vintage Austin Register. Frank Smith, The Butts House, Ashover, near Chesterfield, Derby. 0246 590295.

Austin Healey Club. Mrs. Carol Marks, 171 Coldharbour Road, Bristol BS6 7SX.

Autovia Car Club. Nigel Plant, 14 Sycamore Crescent, Barnton, Northwich, Cheshire.

Bean Car Club. Mrs. Wendy Cooksey, 32 Wellington Road, Wokingham, Berks.

Bentley Drivers' Club. Mrs. B.M. Fell, 16 Chearlsey Road, Long Crendon, Bucks.

Berkeley Enthusiasts' Club. M. Rounsville-Smith, 41 Gorsewood Road, St. John's, Woking, Surrey.

Berkeley Register. 44a London Road, Welwyn, Herts.

BMW Car Club (Great Britain) Ltd. A.W. Rippon, 7 The Crescent, Pattishall, Towcester, Northants NN12 8NA.

BMW Drivers' Club. Judy Stewart, PO Box 8, Dereham, Norfolk.

Bond Equipe Club. 320 Old London Road, Hastings, East Sussex. 0424 51277.

Bond Info. *For Minicars.* Steve Vagg, 320 Old London Road, Hastings, East Sussex TN35 5LR.

Borgward Drivers' Club. R.R.D. Richmond-Jones, 22 Warburton Road, Canford Heath, Poole, Dorset.

Bristol Owners Club. Tim Frost, Abbotswood, Belbins, Romsey, Hants SO5 8LF. 0794 513237. Telex: 477842.

British Automobile Racing Club Ltd. Thruxton Circuit, Andover, Hants. Weyhill 026 477 2607, 2696/7. Telex 47591.

British Racing Drivers' Club Ltd. Silverstone Circuit, Silverstone, Towcester, Northants, NN12 8TN. 0327 857271. Telex: 311164. Secretary: Pierre Aumonier.

British Salmson Owners' Club. General Secretary: A.E. Armitage, Silverdale, Broad Lane, Bracknell, Berks RG12 3BL.

British Two Stroke Club. W. Balsham, 10 Eynsford Road, Seven Kings, Ilford, Essex.

Brooklands Society, The. P. Dench, Reigate Lodge, 17 Chartwell, Reigate, Surrey.

Brough Superior Club. Peter Rhodes, 15 Barnfield, Bollington Cross, Cheshire.

BSA Front Wheel Drive Club. 13 Rosemary Crescent, Guildford, Surrey.

Buckler Car Register. John Orpin, 16 Bullstag Green, Hatfield, Herts.

Bugatti Owners' Club. Geoffrey Ward, Prescott Hill, Gotherington, Cheltenham, Glos GL52 4RD. 024267 3136.

Bullnose Morris Club. D.F. Williams, 123 Lakeside Close, Hough Green, Widnes, Cheshire WA8 8RQ. 051 424 6151.

Cambridge-Oxford Owners' Club. *Cambridges A40-A60, Oxfords 5/6, Wolseleys 15/60, 16/60, Riley-MG Farinas.* SAE: 10 Harewood Place, Upton Road, Slough, Berks.

Chevrolet Corvair Owners' Club. Peter Neale, 24 Macready House, Crawford Street, London W1.

Citroën Car Club. P.C. Brodie, 53 Norman Court, Nether Street, London N3 1QQ.

2CV (Citroën Deux Chevaux) Club of GB. Nigel Callaghan, 12 Leam Street, Royal Leamington Spa, Warks.

(Citroën) Traction Owners' Club. Mrs. M. Hodgekiss, 94 Oving Road, Chichester, West Sussex PO19 4EW.

Clan Owners' Club. Robert Russell, 77 Ashby Road, Woodville, BOT, Staffs. 0283 217361.

Classic Corvette Club (UK). Keith Beschi, 15 Lawrence Avenue, Letchworth, Herts.

Classic and Historic Motor Club. Mrs. T. Burridge, The Smithy, High Street, Ston Easton, Bath.

Classic Saloon Car Club, The. Peter Deffee, 7 Dunstable Road, Caddington, Luton, Beds LU1 4AL. 0582 31642.

Clyno Register. J.J. Salt, New Farm, Startley, Chippenham, Wilts. 0249 720271.

Connaught Register. Duncan Rabagliati, 4 Wood Road, Wimbledon, London SW20.

Cooper Car Club, The. R. Tolhurst, Innstones, Pye Corner, Ulcombe, Maidstone, Kent.

Crayford Convertible Car Club. Rory Cronin, 68 Manor Road, Worthing, West Sussex.

Crossley (Climax) Register. Bob Fleet, Langhurst, Swannells Wood, Studham, Dunstable, Beds.

DAF Owners' Club. S.K. Bidwell, 56 Ridgedale Road, Bolsover, Chesterfield, Derby.

Daimler and Lanchester Owners' Club Ltd (inc. some BSAs). John Ridley, Boxtree Cottage, Brightwalton Green, Newbury, Berks RG16 0BH. 048 82 563.

Dart/Valiant Slat 6 Club. D.R. Fenwick, 23 King Edward Road, Woodhall Spa, Lincs LN10 6RL.

Datsun Z Club. Penny Coken, Woodlands, Horsham Lane, Ewhurst, Surrey.

Davrian Owners' and Supporters' Club. Tregaron Road, Lampeter, Dyfed SA48 8LT. 0570 422390.

De Tomaso Drivers' Club. Philip Stebbings, 19 Westpark, Eaton Rise, London W5.

Delage section of VSCC. F.O. Annett, 43 The Highway, Sutton, Surrey.

Delahaye Club (GB). A.F. Harrison, Orchard Cottage, Lawford Lane, Rugby, Warwicks. 0788 813587.

Dellow Register. Douglas Temple Design Group, 4 Roumelia Lane, Bournemouth, Dorset.

Diva Register, The. 8 Wait End Road, Waterlooville, Hants PO7 7DD. 070 145 1485.

DKW Owners' Club. C.P. Nixon, Rose Cottage, Rodford, Westerleigh, Bristol.

Dutton Owners' Club. Philip Brice, 26a Roderick Avenue, Peacehaven, Newhaven BN9 8JJ.

Elva Owners' Club. R.A. Dunbar, 124 Marine Crescent, Goring-by-Sea, Worthing, West Sussex.

ERA Club. Guy Spollon, Arden Grange, Tanworth-in-Arden, Warks.

Facel Vega Owners' Club. 17 Crossways, Sutton, Surrey. SM2 5LD.

Fairthorpe Sports Car Club. *Incorporating Turner, Rochdale and Tornado Registers.* R.B.B. Gibbs, Rose Cottage, Hollington, Long Crendon, Bucks HP18 9EF. 0844 208418.

Ferrari Owners' Club. Godfrey Eaton, 10 Whittox Lane, Frome, Somerset BA11 1BY. 0373 2987.

Fiat Dino Register. Mr. Morris, 59 Sandown Park, Tunbridge Wells, Kent.

Fiat Motor Club (GB). Miss M.B. Berryman, 82 Addington Road, Reading, Berks RG1 5PX.

Fiat Osca Register. M. Elliott, 36 Maypole Drive, Chigwell, Essex.

Fiat Register, The. *Models to 1940.* A. Cameron, 7 Tudor Gardens, West Wickham, Kent. 01 777 4729.

Fifties Sports and Saloon Car Clubs. Mrs. Lee Moriarty, 33C Oldfield Lane South, Greenford, Middlesex. 01 575 5692.

Fire Service Preservation Group. Richard Smith, 25 Stanley Road, Teddington, Middx TW11 8TP.

Five Hundred Owners' Association. Barry Brant, 104 Lowbrook Lane, Tidbury Green, Solihull, West Midlands.

Ford AVO Owners' Club. Peter Williams, 67 Rolls Park Avenue, Chingford, London E4 9DG.

(Ford) RS Owners' Club. *RS1600, 1800, 1600i, 2000, Mexico, Twin Cam, RS Capri.* David Harris, 18 Hornbeams, Benfleet, Essex SS7 4NP.

259

(Ford) Capri 70 Owners' Club. Nigel Powell, 56 Cockshute Hill, Droitwich, Worcs.

Ford Classic 315 Owners' Club. John Cantwell, 118 Elgin Road, Seven Kings, Ilford, Essex. 01 599 6650.

Ford Consul Capri Club. *'61 to '64 Capris and Classics.* 53 Middle Street, Brockham, Betchworth, Surrey RH3 7JT. Answerphone: 9928 3850.

(Ford) Mark I Cortina Club. R.J. Raisey, 51 Studley Rise, Trowbridge, Wilts.

Ford Cortina 1600E Enthusiasts' Club. Peter Underwood, 54 Fairfield Drive, Dorking, Surrey.

Ford Cortina 1600E Owners' Club. Alan Clarke, 22 Stonehurst Road, Braunstone, Leics LE3 2QA.

Ford Mark I Consul, Zephyr, Zodiac Owners' Club. Dick Barry, 25 Charlwood Gardens, Burgess Hill, Sussex.

Ford Mark II Consul, Zephyr, Zodiac Owners' Club. Dave Debenham, 26 Burwash Road, Plumstead, London SE18.

Ford Escort 1300E Owners' Club. Vic Herman, 74 Nettlecombe, Crown Wood, Bracknell, Berks.

Ford Mark III Zephyr and Zodiac Club. 102 Alderney Gardens, Wickford, Essex.

Ford Sidevalve Owners' Club. D. Laxton, 4 Windsor Close, Wilbarston, Market Harborough, Leics LE16 8QT.

Ford 105E Owners' Club. John Colyer, Ambercot, Copperfield Drive, Leeds, Maidstone, Kent ME17 1SY.

Ford Model T Register of Great Britain. Alan J. Meakin, 14 Breck Farm Lane, Taverham, Norwich. 0603 867700.

Ford V8 Pilot Owners' Club. Trevor Millard, 31 School Road, Dagenham, Essex RM10 9QB.

Ford Y and C Model Register, The. 61 Gallows Hill Lane, Abbotts Langley, Herts WD5 0DD.

Frazer Nash section of VSCC. C.R. Newton, 8 Edge Hill Road, Four Oaks, Sutton Coldfield, West Midlands.

Frisky Register, The. John Meadows, 8 Ruston Way, Blythewood, Ascot, Berks.

Gentry Register, The. Nick Welch, 26 Derwent Road, High Lane, Stockport, Cheshire.

Gilbern Owners Club Ltd. Hillside House, Newmarket Road, Royston, Herts SG8 7LE. 0763 44602.

Ginetta Owners' Club. S. Greensword, 1 Cherry Gardens, Cobbs Fenn, Lambs Lane, Sible Hedingham, Halstead, Essex.

Glas Goggomobil Register. Alan Hitchcock, 56 Lechlade Road, Faringdon, Oxon. 0367 20125.

Gordon-Keeble Owners' Club. Ann Knott, Westminster Road, Brackley, Northants NN13 5EB. 0280 702311.

Healey Owners, Association of. Neil Mackay, 53 Parkside Gardens, Wollaton, Nottingham NG8 2PQ.

Heinkel/Trojan Owners' Enthusiasts Club. C. Main, 45 Falsgrave Crescent, Clifton, Yorks.

(Hillman) Imp Club, The. R. Knight, 71 Inglesham Road, Penhill, Swindon SN2 5DJ.

Hillman Register, The. *Pre 1940.* Clive Baker, 16 Parklands, Wotton-under-Edge, Glos.

Historic Commercial Vehicle Club. M. Banfield, Iden Grange, Cranbrook Road, Staplehurst, Kent.

Historic Sports Car Club. Brian Cocks, West Lodge, Norton, Wilts.

Honda S800 Sports Car Club. Clare Farrow, Rowan Wood, Southwell Road, Benfleet, Essex.

HRG Association. Wellhampton House, Upper Green Road, Shipbourne, Tonbridge, Kent.

Humber Register. H. Gregory, 176 London Road, St. Albans, Herts.

Post Vintage Humber Club. Stephen Lewis, 11 Boundary Road, Colliers Wood, London SW19.

Isetta Owners' Club. Membership Secretary, Hilary Hill, 61 Longeights, Northway Farm, Tewkesbury, Glos. GL20 8QZ.

Jaguar Driver's Club. Jaguar House, 18 Stuart Street, Luton, Beds LU1 2SL. 0582 419332.

Jensen Owners' Club. Charles Edward, 127/128 Brighton Road, Birmingham, West Midlands.

Jowett Car Club. Alan Merry, 29 St. Margaret Avenue, Deepcar, Sheffield.

(Jowett) Jupiters Owners' Auto Club. Steve Keil, 16 Empress Avenue, Woodford Green, Essex. 01 505 2215.

Karmann Ghia Owners' Club (GB). Andrew Holmes, 23 Kestrel Close, Downley, High Wycombe, Bucks.

Kit Kar Club of Great Britain. Ian Lockhart, 24 Calfcote Lane, Longridge, Preston, Lancs.

Kougar Owners' Club. Patrick Smith, 13 Main Street, Yaxley, Peterborough.

Lagonda Club. Mrs. V. May, 68 Savill Road, Lindfield, Haywards Heath, Sussex RH16 2NN. 0444 414674.

Lamborghini Owners' Club. Hanna Ashley, 44 Sussex Road, Haywards Heath, Sussex.

Land Rover Register, The. *1947-51.* Tony Hutchings, Bridge Cottage, 11 Tilmore Road, Petersfield, Hants.

Land-Rover Series One Club, The. *Series 1 to 1958.* David Bowyer, East Foldhay, Zeal Monachorum, Crediton, Devon.

Lancia Motor Club Ltd. Mrs. B.M. Rees, The Old Shire House, Aylton, Ledbury, Herefordshire HR8 2QE.

Lea Francis Owners' Club. R.B. Sawers, 2 St. Giles Avenue, South Mimms, Herts. EN6 3PZ. 0707 42214.

Light Car and Edwardian section of VSCC. Mrs. Sue Dowell, 233 Barking Road, London E6.

Lincoln-Zephyr Owners' Club. Colin Spong, 22 New North Road, Hainault, Ilford, Essex.

London Bus Preservation Group. T. Stubbington, Cobham Bus Museum, Redhill Road, Cobham, Surrey.

London Vintage Taxi Association. Keith White, 50 Southwood Avenue, Knaphill, Woking, Surrey.

Lotus Cortina Register. 47 Leslie Crescent, St. Michael's, Tenterden, Kent.

Lotus Drivers' Club. Jenny Barton, 2 Charlbury Mews, Sydenham, Leamington Spa, Warwicks. 0926 313514.

Club Elite. 1957-63. Miles Wilkins, The Coach House, The Street, Walberton, Arundel, West Sussex.

Club Lotus (and Lotus Register). Margaret Richards, PO Box 8, Dereham, Norfolk NR19 1TF. 0362 4459.

Historic Lotus Register. Victor Thomas, Badgerswood, School Road, Drayton, Norwich, Norfolk NR8 6EF. 0603 86764.

Marcos Club, The. Colin Feyerabend, 62 Culverley Road, Catford, London SE6.

Marendaz Special Car Register. John Shaw, 23 Vineries Close, Leckhampton, Cheltenham, Glos.

Maserati Club. Michael Miles, The Paddock, Old Salisbury Road, Abbotts Ann, Andover, Hants SP11 7NT. 026 471 312.

Club Matra. M. van den Berg, 1 Wells Road, Bickley, Bromley, Kent.

Mazda Owners' Club. Ray Smith, 23 Redwood Glade, Leighton Buzzard, Beds. 0525 376608/370920.

Mercedes-Benz Club. Mrs. Erika Gupwell, The Firs, Biscombe, Churchstanton, Taunton, Somerset TA3 7PZ. 082 360 385.

Messerschmitt Enthusiasts' Club. Sir John Knill, Canal Cottage, Bathampton, Bath BA2 6TW.

Messerschmitt Owners' Club. Mrs. M. Tilbury, 35 Rectory Road, Tiptree, Colchester, Essex.

Metropolitan Owners' Club. W.E. Dowsing, 4 Burnham Road, Knaphill, Woking, Surrey GU21 2AE.

Micro-Cars, Register of Unusual. Mrs. J. Hammond, 28 Durham Road, Sidcup, Kent.

Mini Cooper Club. Ray Holman, 9 Walesbeach, Furnace Green, Crawley, West Sussex.

Mini Owners' Club. Chris Cheal, 18 Mercia Close, Coton Green, Tamworth, Staffs.

Mini Marcos Owners' Club. Gavin Jones, 267 Holy Head Road, Coundon, Coventry.

Mini Seven Racing Club. Mrs. Heather Beckwith, 141 Walton Drive, Terriers, High Wycombe, Bucks.

MG Car Club, The. 67 Wide Bargate, Boston, Lincs PE21 6LE. 0205 64301.

261

MG Owners' Club. 2/4 Station Road, Swavesey, Cambs CB4 5QJ.

MG Y Type Register, The. J.G. Lawson, 12 Nithsdale Road, Liverpool, L15 5AX.

(MG) Octagon Car Club. *Pre-1955.* Harry Crutchley, 36 Queensville Avenue, Stafford. 0785 51014.

Monoposto Racing Club. Sean Ross, 10 Clandon Drive, Boyatt Wood, Eastleigh, Hants.

Morgan Sports Car Club. Barry Iles, 22 Montpelier Spa Road, Cheltenham, Glos. 0242 517412.

Morgan Three Wheeler Club. K. Robinson, Correction Forum, Middlewood, Poynton, Ches.

Morris Cowley and Oxford Club. *1954-59 and Isis.* D.J. Garrett, 28 Dermott Avenue, Comber, Co Down BT23 5JE.

Morris Minor Owners' Club. Jane Flanders, 127/129 Green Lane, Derby.

Morris Register. *Pre 1940.* Arthur Peeling, 28 Levita House, Chalton Street, London NW1.

Nimrod Register, The. Nigel Talbott, 24 Tything Way, Wincanton, Somerset.

NSU Owners' Club. Mrs. Rosemarie Crowley, 58 Tadorne Road, Tadworth, Surrey KT20 5TF. 9925 2412.

Opel Drivers' Club. Margaret Harwood, Borrow Hall Studios, Dumpling Green, Dereham, Norfolk.

Panhard et Levassor GB, Les Amis de. Denize Polley, 11 Arterial Avenue, Rainham, Essex.

Club Peugeot UK. Paul Davies, 91 Mill Road, Burgess Hill, Sussex.

Piper Club. Clive Davies, Pipers Oak, Lopham Road, East Harling, Norfolk.

Porsche Club Great Britain. 64 Raisins Hill, Pinner, Middx. 01-866 7110. Executive Director: Roy Gillham.

Railton Owners' Club. B. McKenzie, Fairmiles, Barnes Hall Road, Burncross, Sheffield S30 4RF. 0742 468357.

Raleigh Safety Seven and Early Reliant Owners' Club. Mick Sleap, 55 Beacontree Avenue, Walthamstow, London E17 4BU.

Rapier Register. Mr. and Mrs. D.C.H. Williams, Smithy, Tregynon, Newtown, Powys. Tel: Tregynon 396.

Reliant Owners' Club. Jim Riley, 23 Cowley Road, Rodley, Leics.

Reliant Rebel Register. T.A. Howe, Becketts, 7 Helville Heath, South Woodham, Ferrers, Essex.

Reliant Sabre, Scimitar Owners' Club. The Old Bakery, 1 Silver Street, Brixworth, Northants.

Renault Owners' Club. N.J. Patten, Silvermere, Krooner Road, Camberley, Surrey GU15 2QP.

Riley Motor Club Ltd. A.C. Farrar, The Gables, Hinksey Hill, Oxford OX1 5BH.

Riley Register. I. Thorpe, 26 Hillcrest Close, Tamworth, Staffs B79 8PA.

Riley RM Club. Margaret Goding, 3 Shepreth Road, Barrington, Cambridge.

Riley Elf and Wolseley Hornet Owner's Club. A. Penfold, 97 Highfield Road, Yeovil, Somerset.

Ro80 Club GB. Brian Taylor, 38 Yew Tree Drive, Oswaldtwistle, Lancs BB5 3AX. 0254 37187.

Rolls-Royce Enthusiasts' Club. Lt-Col E.B. Barrass, 6 Montacute Road, Tunbridge Wells, Kent TN2 5QP. 0892 26072.

Rover P4 Drivers' Guild. Colin Blowers, 32 Arundel Road, Luton, Beds.

P6 Rover Owners' Club. Dr. M.J. Beetham, 11 Coleshill Place, Bradwell Common, Milton Keynes, Bucks.

Rover Sports Register. Cliff Evans, 87 Herbert Jennings Avenue, Wrexham, Clywd.

Rover 3/3½ litre Club. J.P. Dickenson, 21 Hyde Park Corner, Leeds 6, West Yorks.

SAAB Owners' Club (GB). 49 Rogers Road, Tooting, London SW17 0EB.

Scamp Owners' Club. R.F. Cake, 25 Deanlane End, Rowlands Castle, Hants PO9 6EJ.

Scootacar Register. Stephen Boyd, Pamanste, 18 Holman Close, Aylsham, Norwich, Norfolk NR11 6DD.

Skoda Owners' Club. Ray White, 78 Montague Road, Leytonstone, London E11 3EN.

Simca Aronde Owners' Register. Bob Friendship, 4 Queen Anne's, High Street, Bideford, Devon.

Simca Owners' Register. Dick Husband, Green Farm, Bennett Road, Keresley, Coventry.

Singer Owners' Club. Martyn Wray, 52 Waverley Gardens, Stamford, Lincs.

Singer Car Owners, Association of. Barry Paine, 41 Folly Road, Wymondham, Norfolk. 0953 605411.

Spartan Owners' Club. Peter Scrutton, 28 Lamerton Road, Berkingside, Ilford, Essex.

Stag Owners' Club. K.M. Saggers, 37 Elmstead Avenue, Chislehurst, Kent BR7 6EF.

Standard Motor Club. 1 York Gate, Southgate, London N1.

Star, Starling, Stuart and Briton Register. D.E.A. Evans, 9 Compton Drive, Dudley, West Midlands.

Sunbeam Alpine Owners' Club. Brenda Harpham, 11 Aspin Gardens, Knaresborough, North Yorkshire.

Sunbeam-Talbot Alpine Register. Secretary: P.E. Shimmell, 183 Needlers End Lane, Balsall Common, West Midlands, 0676 33304.

Sunbeam, Talbot Darracq Register. H. Tennant, North Mill Farm, Membury, Axminster, Devon.

Sunbeam Rapier Owners' Club, Peter Meech, 12 Greenacres, Downton, Salisbury, SP5 3NG. 0725 21140.

Sunbeam Tiger Owners' Club. Ray Murray, 25A The Drive, Ilford, Essex. 01 518 0709.

Swift Register. John Harrison, 7 Oakfield Road, Ashtead, Surrey KT21 2RE. 03722 75340.

Tornado Register. Dave Malins, 48 St. Monicas Avenue, Luton, Beds. 0582 37641.

TR Register, The. 271 High Street, Berkhampstead, Herts. 044 27 5906.

TR Driver's Club. Gill Warr, The Lodge, The Drive, Ifod, West Sussex.

Trident Car Owners' Club. Mrs. Jill Morgan, Rose Cottage, 45 Newtown Road, Verwood, Dorset BH21 6E9.

Club Triumph Ltd. Malcolm Warren, 14 John Simpson Close, Wolston, Coventry CV8 3HX. 0203 544770.

Triumph Mayflower Club. G. Deagan, 36 Stephen Road, Tadley, Basingstoke, Hants.

Pre-1940 Triumph Owners' Club. A.G. Noble, 20 Station Road, Littlethorpe, Leics LE9 5HS.

Triumph Sports Six Club. Trudi Squibbs, 24 Prince Rupert Avenue, Desborough, Kettering, Northants.

Triumph Razor Edge Owners' Club. Stewart Langton, 25 Mawbys Lane, Appleby Magna, Burton-on-Trent, Staffs.

Triumph Roadster Club. R. Fitsall, 11 The Park, Carshalton, Surrey. 01 669 3965.

Triumh Sporting Owners' Club. G. Richard King, 71 Beech Road, Cale Green, Stockport, Cheshire. 061 480 6017.

Triumph Stag Owners Club. Miss S. Gee, 28 Waltham Way, Chingford, London E4 8HE.

Triumph 2000/2500/2.5 Register. Nick Barner, 29 The Lawns, Penn, High Wycombe, Bucks.

Trojan Owners' Club. Carl J.A. Tantum, Headley House, Chalet Hill, Bordon, Hants. 04203 3434.

Turner Register. Dave Scott, 21 Ellsworth Road, High Wycombe, Bucks, HP11 2TU.

TVR Car Club. John Bell, 1 Clyde Court, Clyde Close, Redhill, Surrey.

Unipower Owners' Club. Gerry Hulford, 8 Coppice Road, Horsham, Sussex.

United States Auto Club. 4910 West 16th Street, Speedway, Indiana 46224, USA. **317/247 5151.** *(Promoters of Indianapolis 500, etc).* Newsletter Editor: Dick Jordan, Statistician/Historian: Donald Davidson.

United States Army Vehicle Club. J.D. Markham, 58 Dunkirk Street, Droylsden, Manchester.

Vanden Plas Owners' Club. C. Dawe, 10 Playses Green, Hambridge, Langport, Somerset.

Vauxhall 30/98 Register. David Marsh, The Garden House, Middleton-by-Youlgreave, Nr. Bakewell, Derbyshire.

Vauxhall Droop Snoot Group. K. Spackman, 28 Chatham Street, Derby.

F (Vauxhall) Victor Owners' Club. Ronald Ruggins, 65 Huntingdon Close, Mitcham, Surrey.

Vauxhall Motorists' Club. Graham Levers, Woodlands, Woollards Road, Ash Vale, Aldershot, Hants GU12 5DR.

Vauxhall Owners' Club. Membership Secrtary, 19 South Road, Portishead, Bristol BS20 9DU.

Vauxhall PA Owners' Club. *Incorporating E, F, FB, PB, Series.* Simon Walker, 39 Kent Gardens, Ealing, London W13 8BU.

(Vauxhall) Viva HB Owners' Club and GT Register. Adrian Miller, 30 Wingfield Road, Norwich.

Veteran Car Club of Great Britain. Mrs. Joan Innes-Kerr, Jessamine House, 15 High Street, Ashwell, Herts. 046274 2818.

Vintage Sports Car Club. P.M.A. Hull, 121 Russell Road, Newbury, Berks RG14 5JX, 0635 44411, 0635 298323 (home).

VW Club. *Historic.* Graham Tansley, Poplar House, Station Road, Potter Heigham, Norfold NR29 5AD. 06927 363.

Volkswagen Split Window Club. Roger Beasley, 2 Wickenden Road, Sevenoaks, Kent.

VW Cabriolet Owners' Club. Derek Copas, 28 Woodlands Avenue, Worcester Park, Surrey.

Volvo Owners' Club. Mrs. Suzanne Groves, 90 Down Road, Merrow, Guildford, Surrey GU1 2PZ.

Vulcan Register (section of Bean Car Club). David Hales, 20 Langbourne Way, Claygate, Esher, Surrey KT10 0DZ. 0372 62046.

Wartburg Owners' Club. Mrs. Therese Mudie, Ella-More, Heather Drive, Sunningdale, Ascot, Berks.

Wolseley Hornet Special Club. R. Banks, Taliesin, Heath Road, Horsell, Woking, Surrey.

Wolseley 6/80 and Morris Oxford (MO) Club (Incorporating the Wolseley 4/50, Morris Six (MS) and related commercial vehicles.) John Billinger, 67 Fleetgate, Barton-on-Humber, North Lincs DN18 5QD. 0652 635138.

Wolseley Register. Secretary: David Allen, Glenville, Glynde Road, Bexleyheath, Kent DA7 4EU.

Appendix 3

Torque wrench settings for British and foreign cars 1932–1965

The following figures are the manufacturers' recommended settings.

Make	Model	Cyl. head lb–ft	Cyl. block lb–ft	Con-rods lb–ft	Main bearings lb–ft
ALVIS					
	1934/5 11.9 hp SB Firefly, 16.95 hp SF16, 16.95 hp TE Crested Eagle, 19.82 hp TD, TE Crested Eagle	26.2	—	26.2	front 135, inter 135, rear 65
	1935/6 19.82 hp SC, SD, Speed 20, TF, TG Crested Eagle, 16.95 hp SG Silver Eagle, 13.22 hp SA Firebird	26.2	—	43.2	front 135, inter 43.3, rear 65
	1936 25.63 hp SA 3½ litre, 31.48 hp SA 4.3 litre				
	1937/8/9 25.63 hp SB, SC, Speed 25 TA, TB, TC, TD Crested Eagle 25	26.2	—	43.3	65
	1938/9 31.48 hp SB, SC 4.3 litre				
	1937/8 19.82 hp TJ, TK Crested Eagle	26.2	—	43.3	front 135, inter 43.3, rear 65
	1937/8/9 16.95 hp TF Silver Crest, 19.82 TH Silver Crest				front 43.3, inter 43.3, rear 65
	1938/9 13.22 hp SB, SC, 12/70	26.2	—	43.3	
	1946/50 TA14				
	1950 TB14 2-seater sports				
	1950/1/2 TA21, 3 litre				
	1952/3 TB21 3 litre	31.2	—	43.3	43.3
	1953/4 TC21 3 litre				
	1954/5 TC21/100 3 litre				
	TD.21				
	TD.21 Series II	32	—	44	44
	TE.21				
ARMSTRONG SIDDELEY					
	1939/49 16 hp 1991 cc 2 litre Lancaster, York, Typhoon Saloons, Hurricane Coupe	30–40	—	18–26	30–40
	1950/51 18 hp 2309 cc 2.3 litre Lancaster, Typhoon, Hurricane, Whitley				
	1953/5 30 hp 3.4 litre Sapphire	60–65	—	30–35	60–65

Make	Model	Cyl. head lb – ft	Cyl. block lb – ft	Con-rods lb – ft	Main bearings lb – ft
	1956/7 20 hp 2290 cc ohv Sapphire		60		
	1959/60 3990 cc ohv Star Sapphire		70		

ASTON MARTIN

Make	Model	Cyl. head lb – ft	Cyl. block lb – ft	Con-rods lb – ft	Main bearings lb – ft
	1950/1 22.6 hp 2508 cc ohc, DB, Mk II 2.5 litre LBS }	55	—	45	—
	DB4 / DB4GT / DB4 Series 5 / DB4 Series 5 Vantage / DB5 }	60–65	—	52–55	85–90

AUSTIN

Make	Model	Cyl. head lb – ft	Cyl. block lb – ft	Con-rods lb – ft	Main bearings lb – ft
	1947/51 10.65 hp ohv A40 Devon, Dorset 4 cyl }	40	—	33–35	77–80
	1948/51 16 hp ohv A70 Hampshire, Hereford 4 cyl }	60	—	60	—
	1948/51 18.9 hp 2.7 litre A90 Atlantic 4 cyl	60	—	60	—
	1948/51 4 litre 28.8 hp ohv A125 Sheerline, A135 Princess, 6 cyl 4 litre Truck Loadstar, 6 cyl ohv }	60	—	60	—
	1952/5 8.3 hp 803 cc ohv A30 4 cyl	40	—	33–35	60–65
	1954/5 13.2 hp 1489 cc ohv A50 4 cyl	40	—	33–35	77–80
	1957/9 948 cc ohv A35 / 1959-on 948 cc ohv A40, Austin Healey Sprite / 1960 848 cc ohv Seven (Mini) }	40	—	35	60
	1956/57 2639.4 cc A95, A105, Westminster, Healey 100 six, 2.6 litre / 1959/60 2912 cc A99 Westminster 2.9 litre, 3 litre Princess, Healey 3000 2.9 litre }	75	33	50	75
	1957 1500 cc A55	40	—	35	70
	Mini	40	—	35	60
	Mini Cooper				60
	A55 Mark II				70
	A60				70
	A110	900 lb ins.	—	600 lb ins.	900 lb ins.
	A40 (1100 cc)	40	—	35	60

AUSTIN-HEALEY

Make	Model	Cyl. head lb – ft	Cyl. block lb – ft	Con-rods lb – ft	Main bearings lb – ft
	Sprite Mk II	40	—	35	60
	3000 Mk II	900 lb in.	—	600 lb in.	900 lb in.
	Sprite Mk III	40	—	35	60
	3000 Mk III	900 lb in.	—	600 lb in.	900 lb in.

BRISTOL

Make	Model	Cyl. head lb – ft	Cyl. block lb – ft	Con-rods lb – ft	Main bearings lb – ft
	407 / 408 }	65–70	—	40–45	85

CITROEN

Make	Model	Cyl. head lb – ft	Cyl. block lb – ft	Con-rods lb – ft	Main bearings lb – ft
	1935/9 15 hp 1911 cc Light 15, Big 15 / 1940/55 15 hp 1911 cc ohv 4 cyl }	36	—	22–29	50

Make / Model	Cyl. head lb – ft	Cyl. block lb – ft	Con-rods lb – ft	Main bearings lb – ft
22.6 hp 2866 cc ohv 6 cyl	36	—	22–29	87
1950/5 375 cc ohv 2 cv horizontally opp 2 cyl	18	—	—	32.5

DAIMLER

Model	Cyl. head lb – ft	Cyl. block lb – ft	Con-rods lb – ft	Main bearings lb – ft
1934/5 15 hp 2003 cc Model 15				
1946/51 10 hp 1287 cc ohv Ten LD10 (Lanchester)	26–41	—	14–21	43–67
1939/50 2½ litre DB18	26–41	—	26–41	65–80
1946/51 27 hp 4095 cc ohv DE27 4 litre / 36 hp 5460 cc ohv DE36 5.5 litre	43–67	—	26–41	65–80
8.6 litre CD6, CVD6, DI Diesel	65	—	70–90	65–80 (short) 90–100 (long)
1948/51 10.6 litre CD650, CD650H, CVD650 DI Diesel	65	—	70–90	90–100 (short) 160–200 (long)
1953/5 21 hp 2½ litre ohv Conquest and Century	45 waisted studs	—	30–35	50–57
1955 3468 cc 3½ litre ohv Regency	50 parallel studs			
1955 4½ litre Limousine	55	—	40–50	50–57
1964/5 2½ litre V8 Saloon	50–55	—	25–30	30–35
Majestic Major & Limousine	55–60	—	25–30	50–57
1961/2 'SP 250' Sports Car	40–45	—	25–30	25–30
DF 318 Majestic	40–45	—	30–35	50–57
DQ.450 Majestic Major & DR 450/1 Limousine	55–60	—	25–30	50–57
1963/4 SP.250 Sports Car	50–55	—	25–30	30–35
1962/3 2½ litre V8 Saloon	40–45	—	25–30	30–35

FORD

Model	Cyl. head lb – ft	Cyl. block lb – ft	Con-rods lb – ft	Main bearings lb – ft
1940/50 8 hp 933 cc sv Anglia				
1939/50 10 hp 1172 cc sv Prefect	35	—	cast 30 self lock 20–23	50
(Also 10 hp Export Anglia)				
1947/50 30 hp 3622 cc sv 3.6 litre V8 Pilot	Alloy Iron 60–65	—	45	70
1937/41 30 hp V8				
1951 15.5 hp 1508 cc ohv Consul 4 cyl				
23.5 hp 2262 cc ohv Zephyr 6 cyl	65–70	—	main 20–25 lock nut 2½–3	55–60
1954 10 hp 1172 cc SV New Anglia 4 cyl				
New Prefect 4 cyl				
1960 997 cc ohv Anglia 105E, Prefect 107E	65–70	—	20–25	55–60
1956/60 1703 cc ohv Consul Mk II 2553 cc Zephyr, Zodiac	65–70	—	20–25	55–60
Popular 107E				
Anglia 105E	65–70	—	20–25	55–60
Consul Classic and Consul Capri 1340 cc				
Consul 375				
Zephyr & Zodiac Mk II	65–70	—	20–25	55–60
Anglia Super				
Consul Cortina 1198 cc				
Consul 315 (Classic) Consul Capri 1498 cc	65–70	—	20–25	55–60
Zephyr 4 and 6, and Zodiac				

Make Model	Cyl. head lb–ft	Cyl. block lb–ft	Con-rods lb–ft	Main bearings lb–ft
Consul Capri GT	} 65–70	—	20–25	55–60
Consul Cortina (1500) and GT				
Lotus-Cortina	60	—	20–25	55–60
Consul Corsair and Corsair GT	65–70	—	20–25	55–60
HILLMAN				
1932/49 9.8 hp 1185 cc sv Minx Mk I, II and III				
1950/1 10.45 hp 1265 cc sv Minx Mk IV, V, VI, VII and VIII; Husky sv Mk VIII ohv	42	—	14–20	44–65
1959/60 15.5 hp 1494 cc ohv Minx, 1½ litre	41–43	—	17–21	50–60
HUMBER				
1949/50 1944 cc sv 2 litre Hawk Mk I, II and III	54	—	30–40	} rear 30–45
1951 16.25 hp 2267 cc Hawk Mk IV, V and VI	54	—	25–29	} others 45–65
1936/51 26.88 hp 4086 cc sv Super Snipe Mk I, II and III; Imperial Pullman Mk I, II and III	42	—	30–45	45–65
ohv Super Snipe Mk IV / ohv Pullman Mk IV	58	—	60–65	80
1959 25.5 hp 2651 cc ohv Super Snipe 2.6 litre	60–65	—	35–37	70–75
JAGUAR				
1938/49 14 hp 1776 cc 1.5 litre	92			
1937/50 20 hp 2664 cc 100 2½ litre Mk V	63 (waisted) / 92 (plain)	—		83
1938/51 25 hp 3485 cc 3½ litre ohv Mk V	63	—	Steel 38	83
1949/54 25.6 hp 3442 cc 3½ litre ohc XK 120 Mk VII	55	—	Alloy 29	
1955 25.6 hp 3442 cc 3½ litre ohc XK 140 Type M Mk VII	55	—		83
2.4 litre Mk II / 3.4 litre Mk II / 3.8 litre Mk II / S Type 3.4 and 3.8 litre / 4.2 litre Mk 10 / E Type	54	—	37	83
JENSEN				
541S	65	—	50	80
C-V8	70	—	45	85
JOWETT				
1945/53 8 hp 1005 cc SC 10 cwt Bradford Van	42	—	30	—
1947/53 13 hp 1486 cc 1½ litre ohv Javelin and Jupiter	42	75	33	—
LAGONDA				
Rapide	60–65	—	52–55	85–90

Make / Model	Cyl. head lb–ft	Cyl. block lb–ft	Con-rods lb–ft	Main bearings lb–ft
LEA-FRANCIS				
1945/51 13.95 hp 1767 cc ohv Fourteen	40	—	40	5/16–30 3/8–40
1950/1 17.9 hp 2496 cc ohv Eighteeen 2½ litre	50	—	50	70
LOTUS				
Elite Series 2	240–250 lb in.	—	220–230 lb in.	440–456 lb in.
Elan 1600	60	—	20–25	55–60
Elan S2	60	—	20–25	55–60
M.G.				
1940/55 11 hp 1250 cc Midget 1¼ litre Series TB, TC, TD, TF, Y and YB	42	—	27	62.5
1953/5 13.5 hp 1489 cc ohv Magnette, Series ZA	40–45	—	35	70
1954/9 13.2 hp 1489 cc ohv Magnette, Series ZA, ZB and M.G.A.	50	—	35	70
1958/9 14.03 hp 1588 cc 1.6 litre twin-cam MGA	70	—	35	70
Midget Mk I and II	40	—	35	60
MGA 1600 Mk II	50	—	35	70
Magnette Mk III and IV	40	—	35	70
1100	40	—	35	60
MGB	40	—	35	70
MGB (5 main bearing crankshaft)	45–50	—	40–45	70
MORGAN				
4/4 Series IV & V	65–70	—	20–25	55–60
Plus-4 and Plus-4 Plus	100–105	—	55–60	85–90
MORRIS				
1939/53 8 hp 918 cc sv Series E and Series MM, Minor	44	—	27	42
1953/5 8 hp 803 cc ohv Series II, Minor	40	—	33	40
1949/54 13.4 hp 1476 cc sv Oxford Series "MO"	46	—	33	75
1954/5 13.5 hp 1489 cc ohv Oxford Series II	40–45	—	35	70
1949–54 hp 2215 cc ohc Morris Six Series "MS"	42	—	33	75
1960 848 cc ohv Mini-Minor 1957/60 9.8 hp 948 cc Minor 1000	40	—	33	65
1955/6 10.65 hp 1200 cc ohv Cowley	40–45	—	35	70
1955/8 23.44 hp 2639-4 cc ohv Iris, LC5 2.6 litre	75	33	50	75
Mini Minor	40	—	35	60
Mini Cooper				60
Minor 1000				65
Oxford Series VI				70
1100				60

Make	Model	Cyl. head lb–ft	Cyl. block lb–ft	Con-rods lb–ft	Main bearings lb–ft
RILEY					
	1935/55 12 hp 1496 cc 1½ litre	45	—	35	{ centre 21 rear 65
	1935/55 16.07 hp 2443 cc ohv 2½ litre	75	—	38	75
	1958/60 13.2 hp 1489 cc ohv 1.5 4 sixty eight	40	—	35	70
	1957/60 23.44 hp 2639 cc ohv 2.6 litre	75	33	50	75
ROVER					
	1934/47 10.8 hp 1389 cc 10	40	—	30/40	80
	1934/47 11.9 hp 1496 cc 12				
	1939/47 14.9 hp 1901 cc 14				
	1937/47 16.9 hp 2147 cc 16				
	1948/9 11.98 hp 1595 cc 1½ litre P3 Type 60	45–50	—	40	80
	1948/9 15.81 hp 2103 cc 2.1 litre P3 Type 75				
	1950/1 15.81 hp 2103 cc 2.1 litre P4 Type 75	7/16″ 50 3/8″ 30	—	40	80
	1948/51 11.98 hp 1595 cc 1½ litre Land Rover	7/16″ 50 3/8″ 30	—	40	80
	1952/5 15.01 hp Land Rover 1997 cc 2 litre	7/16″ 50 3/8″ 30	—	40	80
	1952/4 15.81 hp 75 2103 cc 2.1 litre				
	1955 19.85 hp 75 2230 cc 2¼ litre				
	1954/5 15.01 hp 60 1997 cc 2 litre				
	1954/5 19.85 hp 90 2638 cc 2.6 litre				
	1958/9 15 hp 1997 cc 60	50 (7/16″ bolts) 33 (3/8″ bolts)		30	75
	1959/60 22.5 2995 cc 3 litre				
	1960 22.3 hp 2625 cc 100 2.6 litre				
	1960 20.4 hp 2286 cc ohv 80	75	—	35	85
	80 Mk IV	75	—	25 (formerly 35)	85
	100 Mk IV	3/8″ 30 7/16″ 50	—	30	65
	3 litre, Mk Ia and II	3/8″ 30 7/16″ 50	—	{ machined threads 30 rolled threads bolts 25	65 65
	95 Mk I	3/8″ 30 7/16″ 50	—	30	65
	110 Mk I	3/8″ 30 7/16″ 50	—	30	65
SINGER					
	1949/51 SM 1500 1½ litre	58–67	—	33–48	58–67
	1951 1497 cc Roadster Series 4 AD				
	1955 1500 cc ohc 1½ litre Hunter				

Make / Model	Cyl. head lb – ft	Cyl. block lb – ft	Con-rods lb – ft	Main bearings lb – ft
STANDARD				
1945/8 7.97 hp 1009 cc sv Flying Eight	35–38	—	35–38	90–100
1937/47 12 hp 1608 cc Flying Twelve	} 90–100	—	35–38	90–100
1937/47 14 hp 1776 cc Flying Fourteen				
1948/51 17.9 hp 2088 cc ohv 20S Vanguard	60–65	—	50–55	85–90
1954/5 8 hp 803 cc ohv	} 38–42	—	42–46	55–60
1954/5 10 hp 948 cc ohv				
1954/5 2092 cc 2.1 litre ohv Diesel	75–80	—	65–70	25–30
1958/9 14.3 hp 1670 cc ohv Ensign	} 60–65	—	50–55	85–90
1957/8 17.9 hp 2088 cc ohv 2.1 litre Vanguard Sportsman				
Vanguard VI	42–46	—	42–46	55–60
Ensign	60–65	—	50–55	85–90
SUNBEAM				
Alpine Series II	45 (Cold)	—	23–25	50–60
1961/62 Rapier Series IIIA	45 (Cold)	—	23–25	50–60
Alpine Series III	48 (Cold)	—	23–25	50–60
1962/63 Rapier Series IIIA	48 (Cold)	—	23–25	50–60
Alpine Series IV	48 (Cold)	—	24	55
Rapier Series IV	48 (Cold)	—	24	55
Tiger	68	—	22	65
SUNBEAM-TALBOT				
1939/June 1948 9.8 hp 1185 cc sv Ten	} 42	—	14–20	45–65
1948/50 9.8 hp 1185 cc ohv 80				
1939/48 14 hp 1944 cc sv 2 litre	54	—	35–40	rear 30–40 / others 45–65
1948/50 13.95 hp 1944 cc ohv 90 Mk I	} 54	—	alloy rod 25–29	rear 30–40 / others 45–65
1950/1 16.25 hp 2267 cc ohv 90 Mk II				
1954 16.25 hp 2267 cc ohv Mk III	54	—	25–29	rear 30–40 / others 45–65
1956/8 14.2 hp 1390 cc ohv Rapier	54	—	25–29	rear 30–40 / front and centre 45–65
1958/9 15.5 hp 1494 cc ohv Rapier II	} 41–43	—	17–21	50–60
1955/7 16.35 hp 2267 cc ohv Mark III Alpine				
TRIUMPH				
1950/1 9.9 hp 1247 cc sv 1¼ litre 1200 Mayflower	} 35–38	—	35–38	85–90
1946/8 14 hp 1776 cc ohv 1800 18T, 18TR	90–100	—	35–38	90–100
1949/51 17.9 hp 2088 cc ohv 2.1 litre Roadster Renown	} 60–65	—	50–55	85–90
1953/5 20 hp TR2 1991 cc ohv	100–105	—	55–60	85–90
VAUXHALL				
1939/48 12 hp 1442 cc Twelve-Four I				
1948/51 12 hp 1442 cc ohv 1½ litre Wyvern LIX	53–57	—	38–43	47–50
1951/2 1½ litre ohv EIX Long Stroke				

Leonard Reece and Company Ltd,
Beeches Avenue, Carshalton, Surrey

Thos Richfield and Son Ltd,
8 Broadstone Place, Baker Street, London
W1H 4AL

Schofield and Samson Ltd,
4 Roger Street, London WC1

Smiths Industries Ltd,
Motor Accessory Sales and Service Division,
50 Oxgate Lane, London NW2 7JB

T. Smith and Co. Ltd,
35 Clerkenwell Close, London EC1

TDC Components (Kingston) Ltd,
14a Clifton Road, Kingston-upon-Thames,
Surrey

Herbert Terry and Son Ltd,
Ipsley Street, Redditch, Worcestershire B98
7AH

F.W. Thornton and Son,
57 Wyle Cop, Shrewsbury, Shropshire

Thornton Heath Shot Blasting,
9 Lancing Road, Croydon, Surrey

Vintage Racing Cars (Northampton) Ltd,
Derby Road Garage, Derby Road,
Northampton, Northamptonshire

Vintage Restorations,
4 Whybourne Crest, Tunbridge Wells, Kent

James Walker and Co. Ltd,
Lion Works, Woking, Surrey GU22 8AP

Wilcot (Parent) Co. Ltd,
Alexandra Park, Fishponds, Bristol

Young's Motor Stores,
32 Tooting Bec Road, London SW17

Index

275